Other Books by David Rosenberg

A

———

LITERARY

———

BIBLE

A Literary

Bible

An Original Translation

by David Rosenberg

COUNTERPOINT

BERKELEY

Library of Congress Cataloging-in-Publication Data
Bible. O.T. English. Rosenberg. Selections. 2009.
A literary Bible / an original translation by David Rosenberg.
p. cm.
ISBN-13: 978-1-58243-514-5
ISBN-10: 1-58243-514-6
I. Rosenberg, David, 1943-   II. Title.
BS1091.B37 2009
220.5'209—dc22
2009025587

Cover design by Attebery Design
Interior design by David Bullen
Printed in the United States of America

COUNTERPOINT
2117 Fourth Street
Suite D
Berkeley, CA 94710

www.counterpointpress.com
Distributed by Publishers Group West

10 9 8 7 6 5 4 3 2 1

"BORN OF A LIONESS IS JUDAH."
Genesis

"AND THE LION WILL EAT STRAW WITH THE OX."
Isaiah

for Rhonda,
lioness of reading

CONTENTS

PART 3 *Writing: The Scrolls*

Epilogue: HOW THE BIBLE CAME ABOUT
Telling, Seeing, Writing:

Afterword: HOW THIS BOOK CAME ABOUT

PREFACE

It's a commonplace of interfaith and multicultural dialogues today that you never know your own so well until you sympathetically understand another's. I'd take it further: you never know your secular culture well enough until you've understood its counter-culture text of religion. For us, it comes down to the Bible, yet I've rarely found its literary depth adequately conveyed to the secular reader. There is plenty of discussion about what makes a Jew or a Christian, an atheist or an agnostic, but rarely are the arguments traced back to their historical origin in the writers of the Bible. Instead, we have the latest talking points about DNA and theology. For uncanny answers, we need to envision the aspirations, inspirations, and intellectual conflicts of the biblical writers—to see them within their ancient Hebraic culture (and for the early writers of the New Testament, within their Jewish and Judeo-Greek culture) well before religious tradition edited them into a sacred canon.

In the Epilogue (*How the Bible Came About*) and Afterword (*How This Book Came About*), I pose some of these answers. For readers absorbed in the literary world, and used to the absence of a beginning, middle, and end, it won't hurt to start with the Afterword. It briefly addresses where I come from as a writer who reads the Bible side by side with the crucial contemporary writers of our secular culture—American Ashbery or South American Bolaño, just for instance, or Michael Ondaatje and B.P. Nichol (simply to name two major Canadian authors). If you read these and other searching writers today, the prophetic question of where our culture is headed may concern you more than where it originated—but you'll still be anchored in the Bible, when time gained the prophetic dimension that is our bedrock. In the Afterword, I ask: "How does one become a serious writer within a culture that is lost in time such as ours, uncertain of a cosmic destiny, anchored in space on a ball of reason that may or may not be unmoored?"

For most readers, however, from the novice to the Bible scholar, the Epilogue will provide a guide and raison d'etre for this book. It may also inform you of why it's critical to grasp the failings in modern Bible translation—a type of failure that may reflect larger confusions in our secular culture.

The popular translations intend you to forget you are reading a translation; they substitute a conventional, novel-like narrative. But rather than a novel, which has recourse to three tenses, think of the great classic films (not "Bible movies"), which are limited to a complex present tense—just as was the most ancient biblical Hebrew, in its impression. Although more profound, the Hebrew Bible is full of action and voices, like an epic film. And to recreate this, a translation must become self-aware: it needs the translator's sensibility and experience, not simply a high-concept English style.

And yet, how not to awkwardly intrude on such a great complement of literary works as make up the core of the Hebrew Bible? I couldn't stop to address this question during many years of slow, absorbing work. But after more than thirty years of it now, I can suggest that only by writing through the changing stages of one's life do the centuries of original biblical composition resolve themselves into camera focus. Such transparency may allow us to read the origin of the Bible in the company of its original intended audience, as I suggest in a brief introduction to each book.

If you are encountering the Bible for the first time at the level of personal reading, it's my wish that *A Literary Bible* will open the gate to a longer journey of historical and cultural inquiry. Of course, you can read it deadpan, as if it will tell you whether you "approve" of God and his writers. But that would be like disapproving a great film, for instance Kubrick's *2001: A Space Odyssey*, while remaining ignorant of its director and its cultural history of the space program's impending first walk on the moon. As I've written in conclusion: "The better part of my own life as an author of books and texts has been a journey toward discovering a lost writer." If the Bible turns out to be a lost book in your life, so much the better for considering afresh today's secular canon of writers and works of art. Yet the Bible is a deeply complex text, and its primitive passages are set in a sophisticated writer's looking back, so it's the wrong material for literal-minded comedians and artists, who are prone to react before they think.

My translations, whether they render the Bible as strange or strangely familiar, engage the ancient texts in contemporary terms. I do not seek to embellish or alter the originals, but mainly to restore the original experience of reading them. To that end, I have provided an appendix that identifies chapter and verse, allowing you to compare my version with any other English translation. It should not be a question of which is the "better" translation; mine is incomplete, to say the least. Yet what we still have to learn about the Bible, and especially the Hebrew Bible, is why it remains a crucial foundation of Western culture.

A Literary

Bible

part 1

TELLING

the torah

Genesis is the literary and cultural foundation for the Hebrew Bible. Its human drama begins in the Garden of Eden, and from there until the birth of the first Jew, Abraham, the historical sources drawn upon include literatures already classical in Abraham's day, most prominently Sumerian. The history of Jewish ancestors proceeds to the end of Genesis, where some are living in Egypt and where Joseph has risen to the highest government office.

The cosmic theater of Genesis allows YHWH *(pronounced Yahweh in this primary source and mispronounced Jehovah in the King James translation) to interact with humans on a common stage, in person and through disguises, in disembodied speech and via angels.* YHWH, *in short, is always uncanny; and very often, so too are his human counterparts.*

Genesis contains two major literary sources—J from the ninth century BCE *in Jerusalem, and E from the eighth century* BCE *in Samaria—and the minor source, P from the sixth century* BCE *in Jerusalem. J and E narrate roughly the same stories and histories, and have been interwoven in later times, along with P and fragments of other sources. One of the latter, which tells of Abraham as a warrior, is designated X—although it appears to be a translation from Akkadian, the language that Abraham would have spoken, and written close to his lifetime. I have translated this passage in particular because it belies the sour grapes scholarship that postdates the writings of J and E to the seventh century* BCE, *thereby throwing their historical accuracy into question.*

But there is far more to the literary authenticity of J and E than scholarly analysis. Their styles, their archaisms and borrowings, their puns and wordplay, and their points of view are quite different. Scholars tend to avoid this and concentrate upon linguistic issues—upon the words designating God, for instance—and as a result, J and E are treated as if they are texts devoid of authorship.

If there were flesh and blood authors, however, then there must have been a living culture that is also being avoided. This Hebraic culture was lost to the first modern scholars of Germanic and Christian provenance (as well as to coy scholars today) who were happy to designate the whole culture as "primitive"—with the exception of divinely inspired authors who needed no more grounding description than would angels.

Modern biblical scholarship arose in European universities, yet in religion departments from Geneva to Oxford, Jews were prohibited. The professors of Bible were of Christian belief or education. The nineteenth-century German scholars who developed the Documentary theories known as Higher Biblical Criticism were charmed by their natural Christian superiority into primitive misunderstandings of the Hebrew. We cannot blame them, since they could only read through the filter of their primary source, the New Testament.

Yet even today, the dismissal of a writer by professors of religion is disheartening. "There are too many internal contradictions within the J complex of texts to support the idea that they were the work of one person," writes James Kugel, a conventional Harvard scholar with an unfortunately tin ear for authorship. If Kugel knew how to read a modern author, he might have recognized his misstep. Would he say of a powerful author like Freud: "How could one man have written such seemingly contradictory texts as Moses and Monotheism, Jokes and their Relation to the Unconscious, *and* The Ego and the Id? *Impossible! It must have been many men and even women lumped under the name 'Freud.'"*

When translating J, I nevertheless followed a conservative approach to the last hundred years of J scholarship. The general outline of her narrative can be easily tracked in the popular British translation by James Moffatt, published in 1922, where all suspected J texts are printed in italics. I address J as a living writer in greater detail, as well as the Hebraic culture in which she attained her scholarship, in my previous books appearing after The Book of J *(in particular,* Abraham: The First Historical Biography, The Book of David, *and* The Lost Book of Paradise*). And in the* The Book of J, coauthored with Harold Bloom, I began to describe the textuality of J's narrative, while both Bloom and I first addressed the likelihood of J being a woman.

What made J a great writer was the imaginative power that anchors every scene. Not a phrase, not a single word is not played upon—sometimes in the same sentence. A translation should require that every English word also be chosen with an ear to its tone and weight—and with a healthy skepticism toward simplification. As a poet of narrative, J can make any sentence of description or dialogue sound as if nothing had been described or said before.

In Hebrew, J's sentences, like lines of verse, are strung together in stanzas rather than paragraphs. Since the conventional biblical chapter divisions are arbitrary, made by later editors, I gave J a sequence that more naturally follows the breaks in her narrative. Whether she or her editors are responsible for discontinuities, we can only imagine.

J's stories are told or retold in scenes: as if the author were there when they were happening, as if she were a witness. The King James translation embodies the standard for English diction but substitutes much of J's ironic stance—the way she shades meaning—with a less modulated grandeur. Some later translations, especially recent ones, give up both grandeur and irony in one fell swoop of reduction.

The rhyme in J's narrative is shaded, an off-rhyming in Hebrew, primarily assonance and consonance. To parallel it in English requires an ear for ironic repetitions as well, since a greater range of variations on word roots is possible in Hebrew. A harmonics of repetition and a sophisticated sense of parallelism characterize J's writing.

When it comes to E, I've translated passages that most indicate his later origin and his Canaanite sources, especially the scenes concerning the near-sacrifice of Abraham's son, Isaac. J did not narrate dreams as a rule, but the E writer considered it more "modern" to do so. Thus, the story of Abraham and Isaac unfolds as a nightmare, both in style and substance, and with the sight of a natural ram caught in a thicket providing the moment of waking.

g e n e s i s [J]

Before a plant of the field was in earth, before a grain of the field sprouted—Yahweh had not spilled rain on the earth, nor was there man to work the land—yet from the day Yahweh made earth and sky, a mist from within would rise to moisten the surface. Yahweh shaped an earthling from clay of this earth, blew into its nostrils the wind of life. Now look: man becomes a creature of flesh.

⌖

Now Yahweh planted a garden in Eden, eastward, settled there the man he formed. From the land Yahweh grew all trees lovely to look upon, good to eat from; the tree of life was there in the garden, and the tree of knowing good and bad.

⌖

Out of Eden flows a river; it waters the garden, then outside, branches into four: one, Pishon, winds through the whole of Havila, land with gold—excellent gold, where the bdellium is, the lapis lazuli. The second, named Gihon, moves through the length of Cush; Tigris, the third, travels east of Asshur; and Euphrates is the fourth. Yahweh lifts the man, brings him to rest in the garden of Eden, to tend it and watch. "From all trees in the garden you are free to eat"—so Yahweh desires the man know—"but the tree of knowing good and bad you will not touch. Eat from it," said Yahweh, "and on that day death touches you."

⬚

"It is no good the man be alone," said Yahweh. "I will make a partner to stand beside him." So Yahweh shaped out of the soil all the creatures of the field and birds of the air, bringing them to the man to see how he would call them. Whatever the man called became the living creature's name. Soon all wild animals had names the man gave them, all birds of the air and creatures of the field, but the man did not find his partner among them. Now Yahweh put the man into a deep sleep; when he fell asleep, he took a rib, closed the flesh of his side again. Starting with the part taken out of the man, Yahweh shaped the rib into woman, returned her to the side of the man.

"This one is bone of my bone, flesh of my flesh," said the man. "Woman I call her, out of man she was parted." So a man parts from his mother and father, clings to his wife: they were one flesh.

And look: they are naked, man and woman, untouched by shame, not knowing it.

⬚

Now the snake was smoother-tongued than any wild creature that Yahweh made. "Did the God really mean," he said
to the woman, "you can't eat from any tree of the garden?"

"But the fruit of the trees we may," said the woman to the
snake. "Just the tree in the middle of the garden, the God
said. You can't eat from it, you can't touch—without death
touching you." "Death will not touch you," said the snake
to the woman. "The God knows on the day you eat from it
your eyes will fall open like gods, knowing good and bad."

Now the woman sees how good the tree looks to eat from,
how lovely to the eyes, lively to the mind. To its fruit she
reached; ate, gave to her man, there with her, and he ate.

And the eyes of both fall open, grasp knowledge of their
naked skin. They wound together fig leaves, made coverings for themselves.

⌖

Now they hear Yahweh's voice among the evening breezes,
walking in the garden; they hide from the face of Yahweh,
the man and his woman, among trees of the garden. "Where
are you?" Yahweh called to the man.

"I heard your voice in the garden," he answered. "I trembled,
I knew I was smooth-skinned, I hid."

"Who told you naked is what you are?" he asked. "Did you
touch the tree I desired you not eat?"

"The woman you gave to stand beside me—she gave me fruit of the tree, I ate."

※

"What is this you have done?" said Yahweh to the woman.

"The smooth-tongued snake gave me, I ate."

"Since you did this," said Yahweh to the snake, "you are bound apart from flocks, from any creature of the field, bound to the ground, crawling by your smooth belly: dirt you shall taste from first day to last. I make you enemy to woman, enmity bound between your seed and hers. As you strike his heel, he shall strike your head."

※

To the woman he said: "Pain increasing, groans that spread into groans: having children will be labor. To your man's body your belly will rise, for he will be eager above you."

To the man he said: "You bent to your woman's voice, eager to eat—from the tree of which you knew my desire: 'You will not eat from it.' Now: bitter be the soil to your taste; in labor you will bend to eat from it, each day you live.

"Thorns and thistles will bloom before you; you will grasp the bitter herbs the field gives you.

"As you sow the sweat of your face so you will reap your bread, till you return to earth—from it you were taken. Dust you are, to dust you return."

⋈

The man named his wife Hava: she would have all who live, smooth the way, mother.

Now Yahweh made clothes from skins of the wild animals for the man and woman, dressed them.

⋈

"Look," said Yahweh, "the earthling sees like one of us, knowing good and bad. And now he may blindly reach out his hand, grasp the tree of life as well, eat, and live forever."

Now Yahweh took him out of the Garden of Eden, to toil—in the soil from which he was taken.

The earthling was driven forward; now, settled there—east of Eden—the winged sphinxes and the waving sword, both sides flashing, to watch the way to the Tree of Life.

⋈

Now the man knew Hava, his wife, in the flesh; she conceived Cain: "I have created a man as Yahweh has," she said when he was born. She conceived again: Abel his brother was born. Abel, it turned out, was a watcher of sheep, Cain a tiller of soil.

⋈

The days turned into the past; one day, Cain brought an offering to Yahweh, from fruit of the earth. Abel also brought an offering, from the choicest of his flock, from its fat parts, and Yahweh was moved by Abel and his holocaust. Yet by Cain and his holocaust he was unmoved. This disturbed Cain deeply, his face fell.

"What so disturbs you?" said Yahweh to Cain. "Why wear a face so fallen? Look up: if you conceive good it is moving; if not good, sin is an open door, a demon crouching there. It will rise to you, though you be above it."

⌗

Cain was speaking to his brother Abel, and then it happened: out in the field, Cain turned to his brother, killing him.

Now Yahweh said to Cain: "Where is your brother, Abel?" "I didn't know it is I," he answered, "that am my brother's watchman."

⌗

"What have you done?" he said. "A voice—your brother's blood—cries to me from the earth. And so it be a curse: the soil is embittered to you. Your brother's blood sticks in its throat.

"You may work the ground but it won't yield to you, its strength held within. Homeless you will be on the land, blown in the wind."

"My sentence is stronger than my life," Cain said to Yahweh. "Look: today you drove me from the face of the earth—you turned your face from me. I return nowhere, homeless as the blowing wind. All who find me may kill me."

"By my word it will be known," said Yahweh, "any killer of Cain will be cut to the root—seven times deeper." Now Yahweh touched Cain with a mark: a warning not to kill him, to all who may find him.

Cain turned away from Yahweh's presence, settled in a windblown land, east of Eden.

⌧

Now Cain knew his wife in the flesh; she conceived, Hanoch was born. The days turned into the past: he has founded an ir—city—calling it by the name of his son, Hanoch.

Now Irad—a city lad—was born, to Hanoch; Irad fathered Mehuyael; Mehuyael fathered Methusael; and Methusael, Lamech.

⌧

Lamech rose up and married two wives for himself; one was named Adah, the second, Tzilah.

Adah bore Yaval, who became father to tent dwellers, watchers of flocks.

Yuval was his brother's name, father to musicians, masters of flute and lyre.

Tzilah also gave birth: Tuval-Cain, master of bronze and iron, to whom Naamah was sister.

"Hear my voice," sang Lamech to his wives, to Adah and Tzilah, "hear what's sung to Lamech's wives: A man I've killed if he wounded me; a boy too, for a blow—merely. If Cain's justice cuts seven deep—for Lamech, it reaches down seven and seventy."

⋈

Now Adam still knew his wife in the flesh; she bore a son, called him Seth—"God has settled another seed in me, reaching beyond Abel, whom Cain cut down"—which became his name. Now Seth grew to father a son, Enosh by name—"sweet mortal," he called him. And in that time began the fond calling by name of Yahweh.

⋈

Now look: from the earthling's first step man has spread over the face of the earth. He has fathered many daughters. The sons of heaven came down to look at the daughters of men, alive to their loveliness, knowing any they pleased for wives.

⋈

"My spirit will not watch man so long," Yahweh said. "He is mortal flesh." Now his days were numbered: to one hundred and twenty years.

⋈

Now the race of giants: they were in the land then, from the time the sons of heaven entered the rooms of the daughters of men. Hero figures were born to them, men and women of mythic fame.

⊠

Yahweh looked upon the human, saw him growing monstrous in the land—desire created only bad thoughts, spreading into all his acts. Now Yahweh's pain was hard, having watched the man spread in the land; it saddened his heart. "I will erase the earthlings I created across the face of earth," said Yahweh, "from human creature to wild beast, crawling creature to bird in the air—it chills me to have made them." But innocent Noah warmed Yahweh's heart.

⊠

"Come—you, your household," said Yahweh to Noah. "Enter the ark. It was you my eyes found upright in this generation, righteous before me.

"Gather in seven by seven—seven male and female mates—from each of the clean creatures; from the unclean creatures a male and female mate; also from the birds of the air, seven by seven, male and female: to spread life's seed over the whole face of earth.

"In another seven days rain spills on the land unceasing: forty days, forty nights. I will erase all that rose into living substance, spreading over the face of earth—all which I made."

Now Noah did it, all as Yahweh desired. Noah and his sons, his wife, the sons' wives—all came with him to the ark, facing the flood water.

Now look: the seven days and the flood water is on the land. Look: the rain would be on the land, forty days, forty nights.

Yahweh shut him in at the door.

⋈

So it was: forty days on the land, the flood; the water rose, the ark lifted up above the land.

The water overcame everything, overran the land; the ark made its way over a face of water.

Now the water was swelling fast, the earth was subdued: all the high mountains under the sky were covered.

Fifteen cubits higher grew the water, above the submerged mountains.

All living spirit on dry land—the wind of life in its nostrils—died. Erased: all that arose from the earth, earthlings from man to beast, creatures that crawl and creatures that fly. They ceased to exist, all but Noah, left alone in the ark with all his company.

⋈

Now it was held back, the rain from the sky. The water rolled back from over the land: so it had come and so it was going.

Now look: the window of the ark which Noah made opens, after forty days. He reaches out, lets go a dove—to see if the water slipped away from the land.

But the dove found nowhere to settle its feet, returning to him, to the ark, since water covered the face of the land. He reached out his hand, caught it, pulled it back to him, into the ark.

Another seven days passes: again the dove is sent away from the ark. Toward evening it comes back to him, the dove, but look: an olive twig dangles from its beak. So Noah knew that the water was slipping away from over the land.

Another seven days passes, again; once more he sends the dove. And now it didn't return to him, he didn't hold it again.

⊠

Noah rolled back the cover of the ark and looked: so, firm earth it was, facing him.

Now Noah built an altar to Yahweh, took from all the clean creatures, all the clean birds, offering them up: holocausts on the altar.

Now Yahweh smelled a soothing scent; in his heart, Yahweh was moved: "Never again will I judge the earth because of the earthling. Imagination bends his human heart to bad designs from the very start. Never again will I cut off all that lives, as I have done.

"Never again, for all the days on earth—sowing turning to reaping, cold turning hot, summer turning to winter, day turning into night—never ending."

⚹

And here they were: the sons of Noah leaving the ark, Shem, Ham, Yafat. It is Ham who is father to Canaan. From these three sons of Noah, man spread over the earth.

⚹

So it was: Noah, who tills the soil, is the first to plant a vineyard. Now he drank from the wine, now he was drunk, now he lay uncovered in the middle of his tent.

The one who fathered Canaan, Ham, enjoyed his father's nakedness: now he tells it to the two brothers outside.

But Shem and Yafat took a cloak, draped it over their shoulders, walked in backward, covered their naked father, faces averted: they never saw their father naked.

Roused from his wine, Noah learned what happened, what his youngest son made of him. "A bitter curse on Canaan," he said. "A servant to his brothers' servants.

"A blessing on Yahweh, Shem's God," he said. "But Canaan—his servant.

"God will fatten Yafat, make him welcome in Shem's tents. But Canaan—his servant."

Now listen: all the earth uses one tongue, one and the same words. Watch: they journey from the east, arrive at a valley in the land of Sumer, settle there.

"We can bring ourselves together," they said, "like stone on stone, use brick for stone: bake it until hard." For mortar they heated bitumen.

"If we bring ourselves together," they said, "we can build a city and tower, its top touching the sky—to arrive at fame. Without a name we're unbound, scattered over the face of the earth."

Yahweh came down to watch the city and tower the sons of man were bound to build. "They are one people, with the same tongue," said Yahweh. "They conceive this between them, and it leads up until no boundary exists to what they will touch. Between us, let's descend, baffle their tongue until each is scatter-brain to his friend."

From there Yahweh scattered them over the whole face of earth; the city there came unbound.

That is why they named the place Bavel: their tongues were baffled there by Yahweh. Scattered by Yahweh from there, they arrived at the ends of the earth.

✕

"Bring yourself out of your birthplace," Yahweh said to Abram, "out of your father's house, your homeland—to a land I will bring you to see. I will make of you greatness, a nation and a blessing; of your name, fame—bliss brought out of you.

"One who blesses you I will bless; curse those who curse you; bring all families of earth to see themselves blessed in you."

Now Abram comes out, follows Yahweh's words to him. Lot went out with him.

⊠

Abram crossed into the land, as far as the sanctuary of Shechem, the oak of Moreh; he found the Canaanites in the land, back then. Now Yahweh revealed himself to Abram: "I will give this land to your seed." He built an altar there: to Yahweh who appeared to him.

He rose, came to the hills east of Beth El, pitched his tent there—Beth El to the west, Ai to the east. It was there, building an altar to Yahweh, he called on him by name, Yahweh. Yet Abram kept on, journeyed down toward the Negev.

Now look: a famine grips the land. Abram went down further, toward Egypt, to live—starvation ruled the land.

At the point of entering Egypt, listen: "To look upon," he said to his wife, Sarai, "you are as lovely a woman as I have known. Imagine the Egyptians when they see you—'That one is his wife/ Now I am killed; you, kept alive.'

"Say you are sister to—and for—me, for my good and on your behalf. As my flesh lives, it is because of you and with you."

So it was: Abram crosses into Egypt; the Egyptians see the woman, how lovely. Pharaoh's officers see her, praise her to Pharaoh. Now the woman is taken away, into Pharaoh's palace.

On her behalf, it was good for Abram. Look: he had sheep and cattle, donkeys and asses, servants and maids, and camels. But Yahweh struck Pharaoh with disease as if with lightning—his whole house stricken—on behalf of Sarai, Abram's wife.

⋈

Now Pharaoh called for Abram: "On whose behalf have you done this to me? Why not tell me this is your wife? Why say, 'This is my sister'—I would of course take her in, for my wife. Yet now, look: a wife that's yours—take her out of here, for life."

Pharaoh hurried his men to take him out of the country— with his wife and his whole household.

Now Abram rose up from Egypt—wife, household, and Lot with him—up toward the Negev. He was surrounded with livestock, slowed with silver and gold.

His journey took him from the Negev to Beth El, to arrive at the very place he pitched his tent in the beginning, between Beth El and Ai. Here was the calling: the first altar made, he called the name Yahweh.

Lot who traveled with Abram—he too was surrounded by many sheep, cattle, tents. Now look: argument breaks out between Abram's shepherds and Lot's—this was when the Canaanites were settled on the land, along with the Perizzites, back then. "Please, hold off this quarreling between us, between our shepherds," Abram said to Lot. "We are men who hold each other as brothers. You may let go of me and face the whole country, open before us. Please yourself, make your own way: left, and I'll go right; south, I'll go northward."

Now Lot lifted his gaze, drank in the whole Jordan valley—how moist the land was everywhere (this was before Yahweh destroyed Sodom and Gomorrah)—like Yahweh's own garden, like Egypt—gazing as far as Zoar.

Lot chose all the Jordan valley for himself; he set out toward the east—and so a man let go of his brother. Abram settled in Canaan's land; Lot in the cities of the valley, his tents set beside Sodom.

✠

Now the people of Sodom had gone bad, parading contempt in Yahweh's eyes.

"Open your eyes, and may it please you look around you," said Yahweh to Abram after Lot had parted, "from the place you are standing to the north, then down to the Negev, to the sea and back, westward. The whole land you see I will give you: to your seed for all time.

"I have planted that seed, made it true as the dust—like each grain of dust no man could ever count. Rise, walk around on this land—open and broad—it is to you I will give it."

Abram folded his tents, moved on; he settled by the oaks of Mamre, beside Hebron, built there an altar to Yahweh.

⋈

These things had passed when Yahweh's word came to Abram in a vision passing before him: "Have no fear Abram, I am your shield and reward, a shield that prospers."

"Lord Yahweh," said Abram, "what good is prospering when I walk toward my death without children, my inheritance passed to a son of Damascus, Eliezer, accountant of my house. Look at me," Abram continued, "you have given me no seed; and look, a son not mine—though under my roof—inherits my household."

Now hear Yahweh's word that passed before him: "Not this one for your heir—only what passes between your legs may inherit from you." He drew him outside: "Look well, please, at heaven; count the stars—if you can count them. So will be your seed"—and so it was said to him. He trusted Yahweh, and it was accounted to him as strength.

"I am Yahweh, who drew you out from Ur, of the Chaldeans," he said to him, "to give you this land as heir."

"Lord Yahweh," he said, "how may I show it is mine to possess?"

"Bring me a heifer of three," he said to him, "a she-goat and ram, three-year-olds also, a turtledove and a fledgling dove." All these he brought, cut down the middle, placed each one's half opposite the other; the birds he left unparted.

And the vultures descended on the carcasses, but Abram scared them off. Now look: as the sun goes down, a deep sleep falls over Abram—a covering darkness thrown over him: underneath he is plunged in fear.

"Know this within," he said to Abram, "your seed will be strangers in a land not theirs; slavery will be their state—plunged in it for four hundred years. Yet the nation which enslaves them will also know judgment.

"After, they will come out prosperous, surrounded with it.

"You will come to your forefathers peacefully, when good and old be settled in your grave. They will be a fourth generation before they return: that long will Amorite contempt build, until the glass is full."

So it was: the sun gone, darkness reigns. Now look: a smoking kiln and its blazing torch pass between the parted bodies.

It was that day Yahweh cut a covenant with Abram: "I gave this land to your seed, from the river of Egypt to the great river, Euphrates—of the Kenite, the Kenizzite, the Kadmonite; of the Hittite, the Perizzite, the Rephaim; of the Amorite, the Canaanite, the Girgashite, the Jebusite."

⚌

Now Sarai, his wife, had no children with Abram; she had an Egyptian maid, Hagar her name. "See how it is," Sarai is saying to Abram, "Yahweh has held me back from having children. Please go into my maid now; maybe a child will come out of it." Abram grasped Sarai's words; his wife Sarai had taken in Hagar the Egyptian, her maid (it was ten years since Abram had settled in the land of Canaan), and hands her to Abram to go into as a wife.

Now he came into Hagar so that she conceived; she saw that she was pregnant and looked down at her mistress with contempt in her eyes. "I have been hurt on behalf of you," said Sarai to Abram. "I gave my maid into your grasp and now, seeing that she's pregnant, she looks down at me—may we know Yahweh's judgment between you and me."

"See how it is: your maid is in your hands," said Abram to Sarai. "Do as you see best." Now Sarai punished her; she fled beneath her eyes.

⊠

Yahweh's angel found her by a watering hole: a spring in the desert on the track to Shur. "Hagar, maid of Sarai," he called, "from where have you come, where are you going?"

"I am escaping," she said, "the cold eyes of my lady, Sarai." "Go back to your lady," Yahweh's angel said to her, "hand yourself back to her desire."

Now Yahweh's angel said to her: "Your seed I will sow beyond a man's eyes to count." "Look," said Yahweh's angel again, "you have been made pregnant. You will give birth to a boy: Ishmael, you will name him. Yahweh heard your *punishment*: you will hear a *male*.

"Impudent, he will be stubborn as wild donkeys, his guard up against everyone and theirs raised against him. The tents of his rebellion will rise before the eyes of his brothers."

Yahweh had spoken to her and the name she called him was "You are the all-seeing God," having exclaimed, "You are the God I lived to see—and lived after seeing." That is why the hole was called "Well of Living Sight"—you can see it right here, between Kadesh and Bered.

⊠

Now Yahweh was seen by Abram among the oaks of Mamre; he was napping by his tent opening in the midday heat.

He opened his eyes: three men were standing out there, plain as day. From the opening in the tent he rushed toward them, bent prostrate to the ground.

"My Lord," he said, "if your heart be warmed, please don't pass your servant, in front of his eyes. Take some water, please, for washing your feet; rest a moment under the tree. I will bring a piece of bread to give your hearts strength. Let your journey wait; let your passing warm your servant—to serve you."

"You may," they said, "make what you've said true."

⌘

Abram rushed toward the tent, to Sarai. "Hurry, three measures of our richest flour, to roll into our finest rolls."

From there to the cattle he runs, chooses a tender calf—the best—gives it to the servant boy, who hurries to make it ready.

Now Abram gathers curds, milk, and the tender meat he had prepared, sets it down for them under the tree, stands near, overseeing: they ate.

⌘

"Your wife—where is Sarai?" they asked of him. "Look, she is here," he said, "in the tent."

"I will appear again to you—in the time a life ripens and appears. Count on it and see: a son for Sarai, your wife." Sarai was listening by the tent opening—it was right behind them.

But Sarai and Abram were old, many days were behind them; for Sarai the periods of women ceased to exist. So within her Sarai's sides split: "Now that I'm used to groaning, I'm to groan with pleasure? My lord is also shriveled."

"Why is Sarai laughing," asked Yahweh of Abram, "when she says, 'Now I can count on giving birth, when I'm elderly?' Is a thing too surprising for Yahweh? In the time a life ripens and appears I will appear to you—and to Sarai, a son."

Sarai hid her feeling: "No, I wasn't laughing"—she had been scared. "No," he said now, "your sides split, count on it."

※

The figures rose, starting down toward Sodom; from there they could see its upturned face. Abram walks with them, showing the way.

"Do I hide from Abram," said Yahweh within, "what I will do? Abram will emerge a great nation, populous, until all nations of the earth see themselves blessed in him. I have known him within; he will fill his children, his household, with desire to follow Yahweh's way. Tolerance and justice will emerge— to allow what Yahweh says to be fulfilled."

Now Yahweh says: "The noise from Sodom and Gomorrah grows; as their contempt grows heavy, it rises. It weighs on me to go down, to see what contempt this disturbance signifies. If brought down to find offense, I will pull them down. If not, I will be pleased to know."

So the figures, leaving there, descend toward Sodom. Now Abram stands aside, facing Yahweh.

⌗

Abram drew close. "Will you wipe away the innocent beside those with contempt? What if there are fifty sincere men inside the city, will you also wipe the place away? Can you not hold back for the fifty innocent within it?

"Heaven forbid you bring this thing to light, to erase the innocent with the contemptuous—as if sincerity and contempt were the same thing. Can it be— heaven forbid— you, judge of all the earth, will not bring justice?"

"If I find fifty innocent inside the city," said Yahweh, "I will hold back from the whole place on their behalf."

"Listen please," said Abram, pressing further, "I have imagined I may speak to Yahweh—I, mere dust and ashes. What if we have less than fifty sincere, five less—for these five will you wipe away an entire city?"

"I will not pull down," said Yahweh, "if I find forty-five there."

Yet he found more to say. "Consider," he pressed on, "you find forty there." And he said, "On behalf of these forty I will not act."

"Please, do not lose patience my lord," he continued, "if I speak further. Consider thirty are found there." And he said, "I will not act if I find thirty there."

"Listen please," said Abram, pressing further. "I have imagined I may speak to Yahweh—I, made of mere dust and ashes. Consider twenty are found there." "I will not pull down," he said, "on behalf of these twenty."

"Please, do not lose patience my lord," he continued, "if I speak further—for the last time. Consider ten are found there." And he said, "I will not pull down on behalf of these ten."

Now Yahweh, having finished speaking to Abram, went on. Abram turned back, toward his place.

⊠

In the evening two angels arrived in Sodom. Lot was sitting in the courtyard of Sodom's gate. As he saw—then recognized—them, Lot rose, then bent prostrate, face to the ground. "Please hear me, my lords," he said, and stop at the house of this humble servant. Stay the night, wash your feet, rise refreshed, then go on—the road will wait."

"No," they said, "we will lie by the broad road."

Then he begs them, until they stop, to go with him to his house. Now he makes them a feast, complete with fresh-baked matzah and drink: they ate.

Yet before they had fallen asleep, the townsfolk—Sodomites—press round the house, from boys to gray-beards, the whole population from as far as the outskirts. "Where are the people who visited you tonight?" they call to Lot. "Bring them out for us," they ask. "We want to know their intimate ways."

Now Lot came to the door, closing it behind him. "Brothers, please don't act by showing contempt. Listen, I have two daughters who have not known a man intimately. Let me bring these out for you: handle them as you please. Only leave the visitors untouched, bring no hand to them: I have brought them under my roof's wing."

"Get out of the way," one said. "He comes here to share our shelter and already he hands down the law. Now you will know more than them, a touch of our contempt." They pressed against the man, against Lot, were ready to break down the door.

But from within a hand stretched out, brought Lot toward those visitors in the house. Now they shut him in. They blinded them with light: the people at the door, boys as well as graybeards. They would grope for the door handle vainly.

The visitors with Lot said: "Are there others of yours—a son-in-law, sons, daughters—anywhere in the city, to be gathered from this place? The offense has risen to Yahweh's ear. Yahweh sends us—to bring down this loud violence."

Lot hurries to speak to his sons-in-law—those his daughters prepared to marry. "Pack up now, leave this place," Lot said. "Yahweh is prepared to overturn the city." Now watch: the sons-in-law see only—in him—a joke on them.

Now the sun began to rise; the angels pressed Lot on. "Get up," they said, "gather your wife, your two daughters that are left—or be gathered into the crush of citizens—in this city's sin." He wavered; the figures grasped his arm, his wife's, the hands of his two daughters—it was Yahweh reaching out to him. They brought him out, stopping only outside the city.

So it was: while being brought out, one said to them, "Pity your lot—run, don't look back, don't stop until the end of the valley. Escape to the mountain—or be crushed."

"My lord," Lot said to them, "please not so. Listen to me: if this servant has warmed your heart, evoked your tender pity—you have kept me alive—then see: I cannot survive in the mountains, where the hand of contempt brands me. Look instead at this town within my chosen lot, small enough to overlook. Let me fly there, please, it is small, insignificant—and so will I be there."

"Hear," he answered, "I pity your lot again, will not over-turn this city you speak for. Hurry, run—I will do nothing until you're there." And this is how one came to call this city Smallah.

The sun rose above the earth as Lot came to Smallah.

Now Yahweh spilled on Sodom and Gomorrah a volcanic rain: fire from Yahweh, from the sky. These cities he over-turned, with the whole valley, all the citizens in the cities and plants in the earth.

Behind him, Lot's wife stopped to look back—and crystal-lized into a statue of salt.

Abram arose that morning, hurried to the place he had last faced Yahweh, had stood there with him. Looking out over the upturned faces of Sodom and Gomorrah, over the whole face of the valley, he saw—so it was—a black incense over the earth climbing like smoke from a kiln.

⊠

But Lot went out from Smallah, toward the mountains, his two daughters with him—he grew afraid to stay in Smal-lah, settled in a cave alone with his daughters.

"Father is getting old," the firstborn said to the youngest. "There are no men left on earth to enter us—to follow the way of the earth."

"We'll pour drink for our father; with wine we will lie with him—life will follow from our father's seed."

On that night their wine poured out for their father. The eldest now comes, lies with her father; he recalls no sense of her lying there, nor when she rises.

Now listen: "I lay last night with my father," said the eldest to the youngest. "Follow me. We will have him drunk with wine tonight again, so you may have from him. At his side, we will give life to our father's seed."

The wine flows on this night also, for their father. The youngest rises, to lie with him; he senses nothing of having her, nor her rising.

So Lot's two daughters became pregnant by their father. The eldest gave birth to a son named Moab— "from father"—the father of the Moabites we see today. A son was born as well to the youngest, whom she called Ben Ami—"son of my kin"—the father down through today's sons of Ammon.

⚎

Now Yahweh conceived for Sarai what he had said.

Sarai became pregnant and, the time ripe, gave birth: a son appearing from Sarai, for Abram in his ripe old age.

"Now who would conceive of Abram having children at Sarai's breast? But I gave birth to a son—not to wisdom—for his old age."

⊠

These things had passed when Abram would hear: "Listen carefully, Milcah too gave birth to children, for your brother, Nachor. Uz, the eldest; then Buz his brother, and Kemuel, father of Aram; then Che-sed, Hazo, Pildash, Jidlaph, Bethuel. Bethuel fathered Rebecca—but these eight were mothered by Milcah for Nachor, Abram's brother. His second wife also gave birth: Reumah mothered Tebah, Gaham, Tahash, and Maacah."

⊠

Now Abram was very old, his better days—thoroughly blessed by Yahweh—behind him.

"Please put your hand under my thigh," said Abram to the senior servant, head of all under his roof. "Swear for me, by Yahweh, God of sky and earth, that you will choose no wife for my son from Canaanite daughters, though I'm settled among them. Instead, visit my homeland, my birthplace, bring out a wife for Isaac, my son."

"What if the woman won't come, following me back to this land?" the servant asked him. "Do I then bring out your son—from here, back to the land you left behind?"

"Watch yourself," Abram said to him. "Don't turn to returning, especially my son. Yahweh, God in the skies, who took me out of my father's house, my homeland, who spoke to me, giving his word—'I will give this land to your seed'—will place his angel by your side, until you choose a wife from there, for my son. If she won't follow, won't be beside you, be cleansed of this vow—so long as my son doesn't settle there."

Now the servant places his hand under Abram's thigh—the lord to whom he vows in this matter. Ten camels he chooses, from among his master's camels.

He departs with precious goods in hand, his lord's; he comes out as far as the city of Haran, in Mesopotamia. He has the camels kneel outside the city by the well, toward evening, the time the women come to carry water.

"Yahweh," he said, "my lord Abram's God, let it happen please, today in my presence. Show tenderness for my lord, Abram. Look, I've placed myself by the watering place, the city's daughters are coming to draw from it. Allow that the young woman I am drawn to—to whom I will say, 'Please, lower your jug so I can drink'—will say, 'Drink, and let me water your camels also.' Let her prove the one unveiled for Isaac's servant, and for your servant Isaac. Through her may I see the tenderness you show to my lord."

Now before he had finished speaking, look: Rebecca appeared out of the city, child of Bethuel—a son to Milcah, the wife of Nachor, Abram's brother—and on her shoulder the jug. The young woman was lovely as an apparition, as fresh, one no man had known, and she went down to the well.

Now she fills her jug; as she ascends the servant runs toward her. "A sip, please," he says, "a little water from your jug." "Drink, my lord," she says, lowering her jug down quickly to her hands, letting him drink.

Allowing him all he could drink, she said, "For your camels I will pour too, until they've drunk enough." Quickly she turned over her jug, into the trough, then hurried back to the well to draw up more, watering all his camels.

〰

The man stood staring but silent, not to disturb the outcome: has Yahweh proved his journey fertile?

Look: as the camels finish drinking, the man takes a nose ring of gold—a half shekel its weight—and two bracelets for her arms, ten gold coins their weight.

"Whose daughter are you?"—he has spoken. "Please say— and of your father's house, tell: is there room for us to stop?"

"I am Bethuel's daughter," she said to him. "He is the son of Milcah, whom she had with Nachor." She continued, "There is straw and yes, there is feed, more than enough, and there's room to stay over."

Now the man was awed, fell prostrate to Yahweh. "Bless Yahweh, my lord Abram's God, who has not held back tenderness nor hidden his trust from my lord. And I—Yahweh ushered my feet to my lord's family."

The young woman hurries, tells those in her mother's house.

※

Rebecca had a brother, Laban his name. Laban rushes outside to the man, toward the well. He had seen the nose ring, the bracelets on his sister's wrists. And "So the man spoke to me," he heard his sister say—after hearing all her words. He approached the man and so it was: he was still standing by the camels, beside the well.

"Come, Yahweh's blessed," he said. "You are standing outside, yet I've already made room in the house and a place for the camels." Now the man draws near the house; the camels are unloaded, straw and feed provided for them, and water for washing feet—his, and the feet of the men who accompanied him. Yet when meat was placed in front of him, he said, "I won't open my mouth to eat until the words I bring are out." "Speak out," came the response.

"A servant of Abram am I," he began. "Yahweh has blessed my master, enriched him, given him sheep and cattle, silver and gold, servants and maids, camels and donkeys. My lord's wife, Sarai, gave birth to a son for him—in her old age—and he made him heir to all he has.

"He made me swear by these words: 'Do not choose a wife for my son from Canaanite daughters,' he said. 'I am settled in their land; instead, to my father's house journey, to my family, to choose a wife for my son.'

"'Yet what if the woman won't follow me?' I questioned. 'Yahweh,' he answered me, 'who has walked beside me, will send his angel with you. Your way will be smoothed, you will find my son a wife, among family, among my father's relations.

"'You will be cleansed from your vow only then— when you approach my family; if they won't give you, you are cleansed of it.'

"Today I came to the well, said, 'Yahweh, my lord Abram's God, if you are smoothing the way I walk, look: I've placed myself beside the well of water—let it happen the young woman comes out for water, so I may utter, "Let me drink, please, a little water from your jug." "Not only you," she will say, "but your camels will drink also"—let her be the woman Yahweh unveils for my lord's son.'

"I hadn't finished voicing these words to myself before— look—Rebecca comes out, jug on her shoulder, goes down toward the well, draws—and I say, 'Please, a sip.' Quickly she lowers the jug down from herself—'Drink,' she says, 'I will water your camels too.' I drank, along with the camels.

"'Whose daughter are you?' I asked—the words leaping out on their own. 'The daughter of Bethuel, son of Nachor—whom Milcah gave birth to,' she would say. I set the ring in her nostril, the bracelets on her wrists.

"I knelt, prostrated myself to Yahweh. 'I bless Yahweh, God of my lord Abram, who guided me in the true path, to the daughter of my lord's brother, to choose her for his son.' So, if you will generously act, genuinely on my lord's side, tell me; if not, speak also: I will turn to the right hand or to the left."

Then Laban and Bethuel answered: "This thing has unfolded from Yahweh," they said. "We could not say anything against it, bad or good. See: Rebecca is there beside you, provided; bring her out for a wife to your lord's son, just as Yahweh spoke."

⊠

So it was: as he heard their words, Abram's servant knelt face down, prostrate to Yahweh.

Now the servant draws out gold and silver jewelry, garments, gifts for Rebecca; and for her brother and her mother, precious objects.

They ate, drank—he and the men with him—and stayed over. Rising in the morning, he asked, "Send me back to my master."

"Let a virgin prepare. Even a few days, no more than ten," the brother and the mother answered. "Then she will come."

"Don't hold me back," he said to them. "Now that Yahweh has smoothed my path, let me follow it to my lord."

"We'll bring the young woman," they said, "and have it from her own lips." Calling Rebecca, they asked her, "Will you leave beside this man?" "I'll go," she said.

Now they go out with their sister, Rebecca and her maids, see her off with Abram's servant and his men.

So it was they blessed Rebecca: "Our sister," they said, "may you mother thousands and thousands, until your descendants inherit the gate their enemy goes out."

⌗

Now Rebecca was ready, along with her maids; she mounted the camels, followed the man—the servant who chose her, who is departing.

Now Isaac was coming home by way of the well known as "Well of Living Sight," since he had settled in that area of the desert. Out in a field in contemplation as evening approached, Isaac opened his eyes, looked up—and there were the camels, approaching.

Rebecca gazed out and Isaac was there. She leaned over on the camel, asking the servant, "Who is the man, that one walking in the field toward us?" "That is my lord," said the servant. She reached for the veil, covered herself.

The servant told Isaac the story of what he had done, the things that happened.

Isaac brings her inside his mother Sarai's tent; he chooses Rebecca, she becomes his wife; he loves her, is consoled when his mother passes away.

So Abram passed down all he had to Isaac. To his sons by concubines, Abram gave gifts, sent them away eastward— while he was still alive—away from his son Isaac, to the country in the East.

Now look: after Abram's passing, his son Isaac is blessed by God. So Isaac settled near Beer Lahai Roi (Well of Living Sight).

❊

Now Isaac appeals to Yahweh on behalf of his wife: she is childless. Yahweh responds, Rebecca becomes pregnant.

The children are struggling inside her; "Is this what I prayed for?" she said, questioning Yahweh.

"Two nations," Yahweh said to her, "are inside you—two peoples already at odds in your belly. One country grows stronger on the strength of the other; youth grows senior over age."

Her time for giving birth grown ripe, look: twins are in her belly. The first comes out ruddy, hairy all over as a coat, so they named him Esau, ruffian.

Then his brother comes out, his hand latching onto Esau's heel, like a figure J. He named him Jacob, heel-clutcher; Isaac was sixty when she gave birth to them.

When the youths are grown, look: Esau is a man with knowledge of the hunt, the outdoors; Jacob is quiet, keeping to the tents. Isaac loved Esau, whose game tasted sumptuous in his mouth. But Rebecca loved Jacob.

One day Jacob was cooking a stew of beans; Esau came back from the fields exhausted. "Please, pour me some mouthfuls from that reddish stuff," Esau asked Jacob. "I can barely speak." That's why he was called "Red," Edom.

"Sell me your birthright," said Jacob, "right now."

"Look, I'm fit to die," Esau said. "So what use is this blessing to me now?" "Vow it this very day," said Jacob. He swore to Jacob, selling his birthright to him.

So Jacob gave Esau bread, a stew of beans; he ate, he drank, got up and left—a blessing slighted by Esau.

✕

Now look: starvation grips the land—not the earlier famine in Abram's day, but again. Isaac journeys to Abimelech, Philistine king, to Gerar.

Yahweh appears to him: "Do not go down toward Egypt, stay on the land I envision for you.

"Reside in this land: I will be with you, bless you; it is to you, your seed, I will give all these lands. I will bring you to see the blessing I vowed to your father, Abram. I will make your seed numerous as stars, I will give your descendants all these lands; all the nations of earth will see themselves blessed in your future.

"For so it was: Abram heard my voice, kept watch by my word, my desire, by my laws, my way."

※

So Isaac remained in Gerar. The men around asked about his wife. "She is my sister," he said, afraid to say "my wife"—"What if the men here kill me over Rebecca?"—for what a vision she was.

Now see: he had been there for some time when Abimelech, the Philistine king, was looking out the window: there is Isaac fondling Rebecca, his wife. Abimelech called to Isaac, "It's plain as day she's your wife—how did you dare say, 'She is my sister.'"

"Because I thought, 'What if I'm killed for her?'" Isaac answered him.

"What drama have you brought us?" said Abimelech. "What if one man had acted in a moment, slept with your wife. You would have brought us guilt."

Now Abimelech proclaimed for all: "One who touches this man and his wife has felt his own death."

⋈

Isaac sowed seed in that land. Now look: he reaps a hundredfold, that same year; Yahweh was his blessing.

The man grows prosperous, success sprouts from success, blossoms into wealth.

Look: flocks of sheep, herds of cattle, throngs of servants. Philistine envy also bloomed. The wells dug by his father's servants, in Abram's day, were blocked by the Philistines, filled in with dirt.

"Go out from our people," said Abimelech to Isaac. "You have sprung up too strong for us."

Isaac went away from there, set up camp in the Gerar valley, took root there.

Isaac dug again for water, by the wells unearthed in his father's day, those covered by the Philistines after Abram's death. He called them names like those his father used.

While digging in the valley, Isaac's servants discovered a well with virgin water.

But the Gerar shepherds argued with those of Isaac: "The water is ours." So he named the well Opos, "they opposed." Yet another well, another argument over it—he named it Striving.

Moving on from there, he dug another well; they didn't struggle over this one, so he named it Reho-vot, or Open. "Now that Yahweh has opened a broad road for us, we can take root in the land."

From there he went up to Beersheba. Yahweh appeared to him on that night: "I am Abram's God, your father's. Have no fear, I am in back of you. I will bless you, further your seed, on behalf of Abram, my servant."

He built an altar and there called Yahweh by name. He pitched his tent, began to dig—Isaac's servants dug it—a well there.

Now Abimelech goes out to him from Gerar, along with Ahuzzath, his adviser, and Phichol, his army chief. "Why have you come to me?" Isaac asked them. "You let anger come between us, pushed me out from among you."

"We see how Yahweh is with you, viewed it and reviewed the vow between us—please, let's remake it personally between us, a covenant cut with you. If you turned against us . . . Yet we haven't touched you, and just as we acted— only for the best, turning you away in peace—now turn us to saying, 'Yahweh be blessed wherever you be.'"

He made them a feast; they ate, they drank.

When they awoke in the morning they swore as a man to his brother. Isaac walks with them as they turned to go, sent off in peace.

Now listen: on that same day, Isaac's servants approach with news about the well they are digging: "We have found water," they said. He called it Sworn-oath—"Sheb-oath"—which is why the city is named the Well of Sheba—Beersheba—to this day.

⌗

Now see: Isaac is old, his sight a dim blur, as he calls his older son, Esau. "Son of mine," he began. "Here I am. As you can see," he said, "I am old enough that any new day may be my deathday.

"Listen, please gather your weapons—your quiver, your bow. Go out in the field to gather game for me, then prepare the dish I love. Serve it to me: I will eat so that my flesh may bless you before death comes."

Rebecca listened as Isaac spoke to Esau, his son. Now Esau leaves for the fields to hunt, gathering game to serve.

"Listen," said Rebecca to Jacob, her son, "I heard your father speak to your brother Esau. 'Serve me game, serve me a sumptuous dish, so I may eat and bless you in the presence of Yahweh, in the face of my death.'

"You must go—see that my words guide you, dear son of mine—go out to the herd. Choose two perfect kids for me, and I will cook the delicacy he loves from them. Serve it to your father; he will eat so that he may bless you, before dying."

"But wait," said Jacob to his mother, Rebecca. "My brother Esau is hairy and I—my skin is bare. I would be in his eyes an impostor, should he touch me. I would be serving myself a curse, not a blessing."

"My son, any curse would be mine," his mother said to him. "My voice guides you—only follow, choose them for me."

He goes out, chooses, hands them to his mother. Now his mother cooks the dish, sumptuous as his father loves it. Rebecca chooses some of her older son Esau's clothes, those in the house ready for washing, gathers them for Jacob, her younger son. With the skins from the goats she gloves his hands, covers the bare nape of his neck. She put the dish, along with the bread she baked, into her son Jacob's hands.

He comes to his father, saying, "Father," and then, "Here I am." "Which one are you, my son?" "I am Esau, your first-born," Jacob said to his father. "I followed your words to me. Get up, please, sit now and eat from my hunt, so your flesh may bless me."

"Can it be you've found it this fast, my son?" asked Isaac. "Because Yahweh your God put it into my hands," he said.

Now Isaac asked Jacob, "Please, come near, so I may touch you, my son, and know for sure that you are my son Esau."

So Jacob approached his father Isaac, who embraced him: "The voice is Jacob's voice, yet the hands are the hands of Esau."

So it was: he did not know him—his hands were the hands of Esau, his brother, hairy. He is prepared to bless him yet he asks, "Is it you, my son Esau?" "It is I," he says.

"Put it near me," he said. "I will eat my son's game so my flesh may bless you." He serves it; he eats. He serves him wine; he drinks. "Come near, my son," his father Isaac said to him. "Please kiss me."

He approaches, kisses him. Now he smells the scent of his clothes and he blesses him. "So it is: the smell of my son is the smell of a summer field blessed by Yahweh. May God grant you sky's water, earth's milk—an overflow of grain, flowing wine. May countries cater to you; and people, be anxious to please. May you seem a lord to your brothers: your mother's sons look up to you. May your haters become hated; those who bless you, blessed."

So it was: Isaac finishes the blessing of Jacob, and in the moment Jacob is gone from facing his father Isaac—in comes Esau, his brother, back from his hunt.

Now he too prepares the delicacy, bringing the dish to his father. "May my father get up, to eat of his son's game, and so his flesh bless me."

"Who are you?" his father Isaac asked him. "It is I, your son," he said, "your firstborn, Esau."

Isaac shuddered; heavy trembling overcame him as he spoke: "Who then was he, who hunted game, who served me? I ate it all before you came, I blessed him—and blessed he must remain."

As Esau heard his father's words he moaned; bitter sobbing shook him as he spoke: "Bless me—me too, my father." He could only answer, "Your brother came as an impostor to clutch your blessing."

"Was he named Jacob, heel-clutcher," he groaned, "that he might jaywalk behind me, twice? My birthright and now look: he clutches my blessing. Can it be," he mouthed, "that you have no blessing for me?"

Isaac looked down. "Look hard, a master I've given you," he uttered to Esau. "His brothers I've given for his servants; I've backed him with grain and wine. Is there anything I would have held back?—for you, my son, what's left me to do?"

Of his father, Esau asked, "The one blessing is all you have, father? Bless me too," his voice tearfully burst, "my father."

⋈

Now Isaac looked up. "Look all around you, the creations of earth must serve you as walls, heaven's dew as a roof. You will live by your sword, use it to serve your brother. But if held back, you will use it to cut his yoke from your neck."

Yet Esau held a grudge against Jacob for the blessing his father bestowed. His feelings found words: "It's not so many days to my father's mourning time. Then my brother's day will come, when I can kill Jacob."

Rebecca was informed of these words of her eldest son Esau. She sent for Jacob her younger son, calling out for him. "Pay attention: your brother Esau is reconciled only to the aim of killing you. It is again time your mother's voice be your guide. Hurry, escape as you are, to my brother Laban in Haran. Stay over with him, as long as it takes your brother's feelings to lose their aim. When they go away, turn from what you've done to him—then I'll send for you to return from there. Could I ever be reconciled to losing you both in one day?"

Now Jacob comes out from Beersheba, journeys toward Haran. Encountering the spot, he stays over there: it is already sunset. So it was: Yahweh stood beside him.

"I am Yahweh, your grandfather Abram's God, Isaac's God," he said. "The ground you camp upon belongs to you: I bestow it on your seed. Like grains of dust on the ground your seed will be; you will burst out toward the sea and toward the east, northward and toward the Negev. All families of earth will see themselves blessed in you, in your descendants.

"Now look: I am beside you, to watch you wherever you go, to see you return to this soil. I will not abandon you before I have made these words deed—on your behalf."

In the morning Jacob said: "It must be Yahweh stands by this spot, only I didn't know it."

Beth El, a place of God, is what Jacob called the spot— although the city there was named Luz in the past.

⋈

Now Jacob broke camp, walking toward the eastern people's land.

He gazes out and there it is: a well in the field. Look: three herds of sheep lie there, around the well that waters them. The stone is huge over the mouth of the well.

When all the herds are gathered there, together the shepherds roll the stone from over the well's mouth, water the sheep, then lay the stone back in place, over the mouth of the well.

Now Jacob speaks to them: "From where do you come, my friends?" "We are from Haran," they answer.

"Do you know Laban, Nachor's son?" he asked. "We know him," they said. "Is he well?" he continued. "Well," they answered. "Turn and see: his daughter Rachel is coming with the flock."

"Yet observe," he responded, "it is still midday, long before time to gather in livestock. Why do you not water the flock, then go back to graze?"

"That can't be done," they said. "Only when all the shepherds are gathered can the stone be rolled away from the mouth of the well, to water the sheep."

As he continues speaking with them, Rachel approaches with her father's flock: she is a shepherd.

So it was: when Jacob saw Rachel, daughter to Laban—his mother's brother—he went to the stone and rolled it off the well's mouth. Then he watered his uncle Laban's flock.

Now Jacob kisses Rachel, bestows a deep sigh, weeps. He is her father's brother, Jacob tells Rachel, and Rebecca's son. Rachel runs to her father, telling him.

So it was: Laban knew the news of Jacob, his sister's son, and ran out to him, hugging him. Now Laban kissed Jacob, bringing him to his house, and he was told all Jacob knew.

"Of my bone and flesh you are," Laban said to him, "undoubtedly."

✄

He stayed on with him until the end of the month. "Just because you are my nephew you are at my service for nothing?" Laban said to Jacob. "Tell me, what can I pay you?"

Two daughters had Laban, the older named Leah, the younger's name, Rachel. The eyes of Leah were exquisite but Rachel was finely formed, a vision to grasp.

Jacob fell in love with Rachel, and he answered: "I will stay in a seven-year service—for Rachel, your youngest daughter."

"Better I give her to you," said Laban, "than give her away to another man. Stay on with me."

So Jacob would work for Rachel the seven years; they seemed in his eyes a few days, in the grasp of his love for her.

To Laban, Jacob now said: "Now let me enter my wife's arms; my service has been filled, so that we may fulfill each other."

Then Laban gathered all the people of the place for a feast with wine. But that night it was the daughter Leah who was brought in fulfillment; he grasped her body. For a maid to his daughter Laban had given Zilpah.

Now look: it is morning, it is revealed; she is Leah. "With what practice have you filled my arms?" Jacob asked Laban. "You undoubtedly know I stayed with you to work for Rachel. Why did you disarm me with empty words?"

⋈

"In our region it's not the custom to give away the younger one before the firstborn," said Laban. "Finish the bridal week for this one; then we can give you the other also, in return for her seven-year service."

This Jacob did, finishing the week for this one. Then Laban gave his daughter Rachel to him as a wife. For a maid to his daughter he had given Bilhah.

So he entered as well Rachel; he was in love with Rachel, instead of Leah. He worked with him seven more years, starting again.

⋈

Now Yahweh paid attention to the neglected Leah; he opened her womb, while Rachel remained unfruitful. Leah conceived, would have a son she named Reuben: "Yahweh has rued my emptiness," she said. "Now my husband will bend over me."

Again she conceived; having a son, she said: "As Yahweh heard my sigh—manless—he has given me this one also"—whom she named Simon.

And again she was pregnant, giving birth to a son. "Never," she said this time, "will my husband leave, for I've given him three sons." So she called him Levi.

Fruitful once more, a son was born and she said: "For this jewel I laud Yahweh." Judah was his name, the finish to her having of children.

⚹

Now the time of the wheat harvest found Reuben out in the field; there he unearthed a mandrake, carrying him home for his mother, Leah. "May I, please," Rachel said to Leah, "employ your son's mandrake?"

"Is it just a small thing that you have already employed my husband?" Leah answered. "You would also carry off my boy's manikin?"

"To be fair," said Rachel, "you may employ him tonight, in trade for your son's mandrake."

Now Jacob was coming in from the field in the evening as Leah went out toward him: "You must come into me," she was saying, "because I have employed you in outlay of my son's mandrake." On that night, he came to lie with her.

And she profited, bearing another son.

⊠

"May this son *enjoy safety* from Yahweh," said Rachel. So it was: Rachel had Joseph. Then Jacob turned to Laban: "Let me go to my birthplace, return to my family.

"Bestow my wives and children, for whom I worked with you, so I may leave. You know my service has brought good fortune to you."

"Please, if there is warmth in your heart, stay with me," said Laban. "I've seen the work of Yahweh in your service, as he blessed me with you. Fix your own wage for me," he continued, "and I'll pay it."

"You know the service my work performs for you, the fortunes of your livestock under me. That little you had before has built up, to encircle you with Yahweh's blessing—so it appears from where I stand. When comes the time to build a family—to serve myself?"

⊠

Jacob was ready to leave; settling sons and wives on his camels, he drove off with his livestock, surrounded by all his goods (the good he had carried out in Padan-aram)— on his way to Isaac, his father in the land of Canaan.

Laban was off to his sheepshearing when Rachel carried off the hearth idols her father kept. She and Jacob made off while Laban's attention was elsewhere; Jacob drove away beneath Laban's eyes, not to disturb his thoughts.

As Laban headlong caught up with Jacob: "What are you doing, making off with my daughters like prizes of war? Why did you just walk away—to walk all over my trust? Why not call my attention? I could have sent you off with music, harps and drums. You did not even call me to kiss my daughters and grandchildren—it's as if you walked all over appearance in your going. But even if you walked out—out of your own desire to go home again—why steal my gods?"

"I was worried," Jacob said to Laban. "I thought, 'Who knows what next: he may steal his daughters back from me.' But if someone is found with your gods—take his life. See for yourself, here among relatives: if I have taken something, take it for yourself." Jacob did not know that Rachel had stolen them.

Now Laban enters Jacob's tent, then Leah's, then into the two maids' tents—but he finds nothing. Leaving Leah, he enters Rachel's tent.

But Rachel had gathered up the idols, stowed them under the saddle cushions—now she sits upon them while Laban searches through the tent, finding nothing.

"Let it not inflame my lord if I do not appear beside you," she said to her father, "but I am in the way of women: my period is with me." Though he searches he does not find the idols.

Now Jacob has become inflamed by Laban's headlong pursuit, moves on.

⋈

On the way, Jacob was informed: "Your brother Esau is coming to meet you—along with four hundred men." A shudder went through Jacob, a deep unease. He began to divide his people into two camps, along with the cattle, sheep, camels. "If Esau arrives at one camp and attacks it, the other camp flees.

"Watch over me, please"—he asked Yahweh—"if the hand of Esau, my brother, overreaches its boundary—to destroy me, mother along with child."

He waited there that night, gathered whatever was at hand as a gift for Esau, his brother. Then he sent the gift ahead, as he waited there in the camp.

He rose in the night and led his wives, their maids, and his children to the river Jaboc. He sent them over with all he possessed.

⋈

That night Jacob waited alone. There some man struggled with him, even until daybreak. It was clear he could not overcome Jacob, so he broke his thigh at the hip. Jacob's thigh was limp as he struggled with him.

"Let me go, day is breaking," he said. "I won't let go of you," said the other, "until I have your blessing."

Now he asked him: "What is your name?" "Jacob," he said. "Not anymore Jacob, heel-clutcher, will be said in your name; instead, Israel, God-clutcher, because you have held on among gods unnamed as well as men, and you have overcome."

Now Jacob asked the question: "Please, what is your name?" "Why is it just this—my name—you must ask?" he answered. Instead, he blessed him there.

The name of that place Jacob called Deiface: I've seen God face to face, yet my flesh holds on.

Now the sun rose over him as he passed through the place called Deifus; he was limping on his hip.

⋈

Now Jacob looked out afar and there he was: Esau was coming, four hundred men with him. He divided the children among their mothers: Leah, Rachel, the maids. The maids and their children were placed first, Leah and her children behind them; Rachel and Joseph were in back. Then Jacob went out ahead, fell prostrate sevenfold— before Esau came running toward him.

And Esau fell on his neck—with kisses, embraces, weeping. Then he looked around, seeing the women and children. "Whose are these?" he asked. "The children," Jacob answered, "with whom God has blessed your servant."

The maids with their children bowed; Leah and her children approached afterward, bowing also. Finally Joseph and Rachel came and bowed. "But why have these come forward—and the whole camp you sent ahead?" Jacob answered: "To melt your heart, my master."

"I am rich enough, my brother. What is yours—should be."

"—Please don't," Jacob appealed. "If I may warm your heart, accept my gift. What came from my hand allows me to see your face—as if God's face had turned toward me, in peace.

"Accept my gift please, as it came to you. Embraced by God—now I have everything." Since he urged it, Esau took it.

"Let's travel on together, beside each other," said Esau.

Jacob responded: "My lord knows the children are delicate. The calves and kids as well: I must take account of them. If they're driven all day, the flock might end up destroyed.

"Let my lord go on ahead, please, while your servant makes his way at the pace of his charges—and in stride with the legs of his children. Eventually I will reach my master in Seir."

"Let me appoint to you some of the men with me," said Esau.

"But why? The warmth of my lord's heart is enough."

So Esau returned that day toward Seir. But Jacob traveled to Succot, building himself shelter. For his flocks he made succahs; after those sheds they called the place Succot.

⋈

Now Dinah went out—she was Leah's daughter by Jacob—to see some girlfriends in the country. It was then Shechem saw her—he was son to Hamor, the local governor—and seized her. Lying with her, her guard was broken.

But she had touched his heart: he had fallen in love, his reserve broken by tenderness for the young woman.

Jacob heard how he had fallen upon his daughter Dinah. Because his sons were out herding the cattle, Jacob restrained himself until they came in.

Yet Jacob's sons heard it out in the field; they came home hurt and angry the man had stained Israel's honor. To just lie with a daughter of Jacob—a desire never to be acted upon.

But Shechem said to her father and brothers, "Open your hearts, whatever you ask of me is yours. Set the dowry as high as you wish and I will give whatever you say; you need just give the girl in marriage."

The young man had no reservation about anything they might ask, because he had fallen in love with Jacob's daughter—and in his own family, he was held in the highest honor. "I will say to them," he said, "'Look: the land is broad enough to embrace them.'"

⌗

Now two of Jacob's sons, Simon and Levi, Dinah's brothers, buckled their swords and entered the city unsuspected.

So Hamor and his son, Shechem, died by the edge of the sword—as they seized Dinah from Shechem's house, slipped back out.

⌗

"You have stained me for the population," Jacob said to Simon and Levi, "and stirred up a scent to reach the Canaanites and Perizzites. There are few of us; they'll gather to destroy me, extinguish my whole household."

But they answered: "Should he just seize our sister as a whore?"

⌗

Now Joseph was a shepherd's helper to his brothers; he was still a boy among the sons of Bilhah and Zilpah, his father's wives. And Joseph was a little tattletale, straight to their father. For Israel loved him above all his children: the child of his old age.

A many-colored coat was made for Joseph. His brothers grasped that it was him their father loved most; they hated him, could not speak warmly to him.

☒

Joseph dreamed and told this dream to his brothers, so that their anger toward him only grew. He had begged them to listen. "So it was," he had begun, "we were binding bundles in the field when, to my surprise, my bundle lifted itself up, was standing upright. And then it happened your bundles got up, encircled mine, and fell prostrate before it."

Yet another dream followed which Joseph could not contain. "So it was," he concluded, "that the sun, the moon, eleven stars—all were prostrate before me."

"What kind of dream is that?" his father teased him, when Joseph told him as well. "Are we going to crawl before you, fall prostrate at your feet—myself, your mother, all your brothers?" On account of his telling of dreams, his brothers hated him more.

☒

Now his brothers were pasturing their father's flock near Shechem when Israel said to Joseph: "I'm worried about your brothers when they pasture near Shechem. If you're prepared, I'll send you to them." "I'm ready," he replied.

"Then go, and please inform me about your brothers: are they safe, are the flocks secure? Bring me your news." He sent him from near Hebron.

When he came near Shechem, a man found him wandering in the fields. "Whom are you looking for?" asked the man. "I'm searching for my brothers," he said. "Could you tell me where they're pasturing?"

"Not here. 'Dothan,' I heard them say."

⊠

As Joseph approached Dothan: "Look, here comes our master of dreams," the brothers said among themselves. "Now is a time to kill him, then throw him down an abandoned well. 'A mad animal has eaten him,' we will say. We will see what becomes of his dreams."

Now look: as Joseph greets his brothers they grasp his coat from off his back—the many-colored coat he is wearing. They seize him and put him down the well. It is an abandoned well, with no water in it.

Some Midianites are camping nearby. They are merchants who discover Joseph and draw him up from the well. For twenty pieces of silver, they sell him to Ishmaelites from Gilead when their caravan comes by—camels loaded with gum, balm, ladanum—on the way down to Egypt.

⚵

68

―――

PART I

―――

TELLING

―――

Genesis

Now with Joseph's coat in hand they killed a small goat, then dipped it in the blood.

The many-colored coat was conveyed to their father. Then they followed: "We found this coat. Can you tell if it's your son's?"

He grasped it. "My son's coat. Eaten by a wild animal. Torn limb from limb—Joseph!"

Jacob tore his shirt, covered his male parts with sackcloth, mourned his son a very long time.

All his sons and daughters gathered to console him, but he fought against consolation: "I will follow my son in grief, straight down to Sheol." So his father spoke, fighting his tears.

⚵

Now look: soon afterward Judah moves south from his brothers, down to the neighborhood of an Adul-lamite named Hirah. There a Canaanite named Shuah has a daughter and she catches Judah's eye. He asks her to be his wife, enters into her arms. Pregnant, she gives birth to a son he names Er.

Pregnant again, she bears a son whom she names Onan. She continues to conceive, this time a son she names Shelah; they are at Chezib when he is born.

Now Judah asks for a wife for Er, his firstborn; her name, Tamar. It happens Er turns corrupt before Yahweh's eyes; Yahweh hastens his death.

"Enter the arms of your brother's wife," Judah says to Onan. "Be a good brother-in-law: bear the seed for your brother." But Onan conceives the seed will not count as his. So it is: whenever he enters the arms of his brother's wife, he spills it to the ground—to keep his seed from counting for his brother.

But in Yahweh's eyes this conception was corrupt; he too was brought to his death.

"Settle as a widow in your father's house," says Judah to Tamar, his daughter-in-law. "Stay there while Shelah, my son, grows up." He thinks: "Heaven forbid death touch him too, like his brothers." So Tamar goes to live in her father's house.

⌧

A long time later Judah's wife died, Shuah's daughter. Consoled after mourning, Judah rose to join his sheepshearers in Timnath, along with Hirah, his Adullamite friend.

Now Tamar was informed: "Your father-in-law has arisen, goes to Timnath for sheepshearing."

She lays aside her widow's clothes, veils herself; cloaked in disguise, she lingers openly by the crossroads on the way to Timnath. She recognized that while Shelah had now grown up, she was engaged—yet not offered marriage to him.

Now Judah sees her, imagines she is a whore: her face is concealed.

He stepped off the road toward her. "Entertain me," he said, "in your arms. I wish to enter there." He did not recognize his daughter-in-law. "What will you pay me," she replied, "if I take you in?"

"I will pick out a kid from the flock by myself," he said.

"Only if you leave me security," she replied, "until you send it."

"What can I give you for security?" he asked.

"Your seal and ring, and the stick in your hand," she answered. So he gives them to her, then enters her arms, and by him she becomes pregnant.

She gets up, goes away, unwraps the veil and cloak around her; once again, she dresses in her widow's clothes.

⋈

When Judah sent the choice kid—by the hand of his friend, the Adullamite—to recover the security (those things in the woman's hand), she was not to be found.

"Where can I find your ritual prostitute?" he inquired of the local people. "The one standing openly by the cross-roads on the highway."

"No holy lady ever stood there."

Returning to Judah, he said: "I could not find her. And more than that, the local people reported, 'No holy lady ever stood there.'"

"Let her take those things," replied Judah. "Heaven forbid we are taken for fools here. They have seen the kid; though you couldn't find her, I sent it."

⋈

So it was: about three months pass when Judah was abruptly informed. "Your daughter-in-law Tamar has played the whore and now look: she is pregnant by prostitution."

"Take her away," judged Judah, "to be set afire."

When they came for her she would send a message to her father-in-law: "By the man whose things these are, am I pregnant. Please look at them; recognize whose seal, whose ring, whose stick they are."

Judah recognized his own. "She is a truer judge than I: I failed to marry her to Shelah, my son." Yet he would linger from entering her arms again.

⸾

So it was: the time for giving birth arrived. Now look: twins are within her.

And it happened, as she labored, one put out a hand—the midwife grabbed it, wrapped scarlet thread around it: "This one came out first." Yet look: he draws in his hand, and then, instead, out comes his brother. "With what power he crosses boundaries," was said, and so Peretz was he called.

Scarlet around his hand, the brother came out after, to be named after the red: Zerah, bright one.

Joseph had been taken down to Egypt, where an Egyptian bought him from Ishmaelites—out of the hands of those who brought him down. So it was: Yahweh attended Joseph. And so it happened that Joseph grew prosperous.

Now look: he is in the house of his Egyptian lord. His lord could see that Yahweh attended Joseph, in whose hands everything that he tended, matured. Joseph warmed his heart; he appointed him personal attendant, head of his household. All that he had was put into his hand.

So it was: Yahweh blessed the Egyptian's house on behalf of Joseph, from the time he became head over the household and all the holdings. So it happens: Yahweh's blessing covers all that he holds, in the house, in the field.

With everything committed to Joseph's hands, the Egyptian restrains his concern about almost anything—except the bread he ate.

⨯

Now look: Joseph is a finely formed man, a handsome vision. It happened that his master's wife, a good time later, beckoning Joseph with her eyes, whispered, "Recline by me."

He abruptly declines. "Look, my lord counts on me," he says to the lord's wife, "to handle the house. He has left everything in my hands, stands no watch over me. I am not restrained from anything but yourself, since you are his wife. How could I commit this height of offense—and show contempt for the gods?"

So it was: she would appeal to Joseph day after day, yet he declined her desire that he lie with her, attend her.

On one of these days, as he enters the house to work, he passes no servants, finds none in the room. Now she grasps hold of his coat: "Recline by me." But he abandons the coat in her hand, flees, runs outside.

As she stood there, empty coat in her hand, seeing he had run away, she screamed for the servants: "See how he has brought us a Hebrew man to handle us. He entered the room to lie with me. But I started to scream, and look: he realized I would not restrain myself and ran outside, left his coat in my hands."

Now the coat lay beside her until Joseph's master came home. These were her words to him: "That Hebrew servant— the one you brought us to fondle me—tried to enter me. Listen well: I raised my voice, I screamed—and he left his coat beside me when he ran outside."

Now look: as his lord hears his wife's words—"This is the way I was handled by your servant"—his anger bursts its bounds.

Joseph's lord took hold of him, threw him into prison—the place where high prisoners of the king were held.

See: he lies there in prison. Yet Yahweh attended Joseph, tendered care, putting warmth for him in the prison keeper's heart.

Now the prison keeper put his faith in Joseph's hands: of all the prison inmates and all that went on there, he was the head. Not a fault could the prison keeper find in all that was in his hands—because Yahweh attended him; all that he touched, Yahweh matured.

One morning Pharaoh awoke disturbed. He sent for all of Egypt's magicians, called together all its wise men to tell them his dream. Yet none could interpret it for him.

Now the head waiter to Pharaoh speaks up: "This day has brought back to me a past offense. Pharaoh once was angry with his servants; I was put under guard in the officers' prison—me, as well as the head baker.

"We had a dream on the same night, he and I—each with our own personal details. With us was a Hebrew boy, servant to the head guard; we told him and he interpreted our dreams for us. He interpreted each dream in a personal way.

"All happened just as he interpreted. So it was: I was sent back to my position and he—he was sent hanging."

Now Pharaoh ordered Joseph sent out; he was brought abruptly up from the prison depths. He shaves, changes his clothes, comes to Pharaoh.

"I have dreamed a dream," said Pharaoh to Joseph, "that there is no one to interpret. Yet I heard it said of you, that on hearing a dream your interpretation solves it."

Pharaoh continued: "In my dream I found myself standing on the bank of the river. Now look: abruptly up from the river come seven cows in beautiful health—delicious to gaze at. They were grazing in the reeds.

"Now I find seven other cows come up after them, emaciated and misshapen, their flesh stretched thinner than anything I've seen—in all Egypt never such repulsive ones.

"These emaciated and repulsive cows ate up the first seven cows, the hearty ones. Yet when they were fully digested inside them, you could not believe they had entered their bodies: they still looked emaciated as at first. I recoiled and was awake.

"I told this to the magicians, but none could say anything of any good to me."

Now Joseph answers Pharaoh: "The seven good cows are as seven years; the seven emaciated, repulsive cows that came up after them are as seven years. What the gods intend is made known to Pharaoh.

"Now see: seven fertile years approach, overflowing all of Egypt's land. But seven years of famine will come up after them, until the overflowing in Egypt is forgotten, the land swallowed by famine. Even the word for overflowing will be swallowed up by the famine that follows—heavy will it lie on the land.

"So that now Pharaoh must pick a man shrewd and wise— to put in charge, over Egyptian land. Let all kinds of food be gathered from these seven good years when they come; let grain be piled up, to be held in Pharaoh's hands: food to be protected for the cities."

"As a god has made you know all this," said Pharaoh to Joseph, "there is no man like you for intellect or wisdom. You shall be in charge of my house. By your word all my people shall be fed. Only on my throne will I rule over you. I am Pharaoh, yet without your protection no man shall raise his fist or boot in all of Egypt."

Pharaoh gave Joseph the name Zaphenath-paneah. For a wife he gave him Asenath, daughter of Poti-phera, the Priest of On.

Now Joseph rose in charge; he went out over the land of Egypt.

⊠

The seven years of famine, of which Joseph had spoken, started. Now look: all lands are gripped by famine, yet in Egypt there is bread.

When all the land of Egypt grows hungry too, the people cry to Pharaoh for bread. "Go to Joseph," said Pharaoh to all Egypt. "As he directs you, follow."

The face of the earth was covered with the famine. Now Joseph opens all that has been held, rations it to the Egyptians—as the famine continued growing stronger in the land of Egypt.

Now they come to Egypt from all over the earth, to buy rations from Joseph. The whole world is in the grip of the famine.

⊠

Jacob understood there was sustenance in Egypt. "Why do you stand around and stare?" he said to his sons.

So the brothers of Joseph—ten of them—went down into Egypt to buy rations. But Benjamin, Joseph's other brother—Jacob would not send him. "Heaven forbid disaster touch him," he thought.

⊠

Now Joseph was the governor in the land, in charge of selling rations to all peoples. When the brothers arrived, they fell prostrate at his feet, faces to the ground.

Joseph recognized his brothers, but they did not know him. He veiled his heart from them like a stranger. The dream returned to Joseph—the one he had dreamed about them.

At a night lodging on the way, as they return, one opens his bag to feed his ass. There, in the mouth of his sack, look: his money sits there.

"My money returns," he said to his brothers. "Look: it's in my bag." Their hearts sank.

⌘

The famine in the land had grown bitter.

So it was: the food brought out from Egypt had all been eaten. "Return on our behalf," their father said. "Buy us what rations we may."

"The man in charge warned us to watch ourselves," said Judah. "'Do not look upon my face,' he warned, 'unless your brother is with you.'

"If you are prepared to send our brother with us, we will go down to secure food for you. But if you won't send him we will not go—the man warned us not to see his face without our brother."

"Why did you make it bitter for me," Israel asked, "by telling the man you had another brother?"

"The man had many questions," they said, "about us, about our family; such as 'Is your father still alive?' and 'Do you have another brother?' We told him what he wanted to know. How could we have known ourselves he would warn, 'Bring your brother down here'?"

"This son will not go down with you," said Jacob. "Just he remains—his other brother is dead. If disaster were to touch him on the way, you would bend my head white with grief—straight down to Sheol."

Now Judah says to his father, Israel: "Let the boy leave with me. Let us go now; better to live than die—for all of us, even the youngest.

"Let me stand for security: you may request him out of my hands, and if I don't return him to stand before you, my life stands in contempt instead. And—if we stand around any longer, we could already have returned a second time."

"If it must be," said Israel their father, "at least do this: pack an assortment of our fruit delicacies in your jars, take it down for a present to the man—with a little balm, some honey, gum, and ladanum, a few pistachios and almonds.

"And for every silver piece in your hands take a second; take in hand as well those which returned in the mouths of your bags—perhaps they were there by mistake.

"As for your brother, take him and go; return to that man."
Now the men gather up the presents, doubling the silver
they carry in hand, with Benjamin as well, and leave, down
to Egypt; they would stand before Joseph again.

⌗

Now as Joseph observes Benjamin coming with them, he
speaks to the head of his house: "Usher the men home and
prepare a freshly slaughtered animal; these men will dine
with me this afternoon."

That man followed Joseph's words; he escorted the men
into Joseph's house.

But the men were alarmed. On being brought into Joseph's
house, they imagined "it has to do with the money finding
its way back into our bags: we are being summoned here so
it may recoil against us and they seize us for slaves, along
with our asses."

As they approach the head of Joseph's house, they speak to
him at the entrance: "Patience, kind sir. We came down the
first time simply to buy food.

"But a surprise awaited us when we came to our night's
lodging. We open our bags and look: each man's silver is at
the top of his bag—all of it, exactly. Now we bring it back
in our own hands.

"We came down again with more money too, bringing it all by hand to buy food. We never knew by whom our money was put back in our bags."

"But you are welcome; there's nothing to cause alarm," he replied. Ushering them into the house, the man had the water brought for washing feet; he provided feed as well for the asses.

Now they unpack their gifts for Joseph, being told he would arrive at noon—to dine with them.

⊠

When Joseph comes home, they take their presents in hand, enter the house, fall prostrate to the ground before him.

Now he asks about conditions at home: "Is your father doing well, the old man you mentioned? Does he remain healthy?"

"Our father, your humble servant, is safe, still strong." They fall prostrate as a sign of humility.

He gazed out and there was Benjamin, his brother—his own mother's son. "So that is your little brother, the one you spoke about?"

Joseph turns abruptly aside, his heart bursting with tenderness for his brother—he rushes to his room, to cry.

Then he washed his face, came back, restrained his feelings. "Serve the bread," he said.

⨳

They were served separately from him, and from the Egyptians eating with him. They ate by themselves, because Egyptians could not bear to eat a meal with Hebrews (that would be an outrage in Egypt).

First, the brothers were ushered to their seats as he directed, in order of age, from the firstborn down to the youngest—and the men stared at one another in amazement.

Joseph ordered additional courses sent to them from his own table but made Benjamin's ration five times larger than the others. They drank until they were merrily drunk around him.

⨳

Now Joseph takes aside the head of his house: "Fill up the men's bags with food, all they can hold. And with my interpreting cup—this silver cup—settle it in the mouth of the youngest's bag." All was done to the letter of Joseph's words.

Watch: the sun rises, the men are seen off, followed by their donkeys. They are out of the city, though not by far, when Joseph turns to his man: "Now go, catch up with them; when you do, say: 'Why pay back bad for good? See: isn't this the one?—the interpreting cup from which my lord would drink and then divine? Your acts speak badly of you.'"

Now he approaches them with these very words. "But sir," they answered, "why do you speak such words to us? Heaven forbid your servants would act on such words. Recall the money we found in our bags: we came back from Canaan with it. Why would we now steal silver or gold out of your master's hands? Find it among any of your servants and that one dies—while the rest of us will become your lord's slaves."

"Just as your words say," he answered. "Yet only the one who has it will be my servant. The rest go free." So quickly each man lowered his bag to the ground, and each opened it.

Now he searches, beginning with the oldest, until he reaches the youngest—and there it is, in Benjamin's bag. Now they tear at their clothes. Then each one returned his bag over his donkey, returning to the city.

Judah and his brothers approach Joseph's house; he is still there, and they fall before him—prostrate on the ground.

"What act is this you have dreamt up? Can it be you didn't know that a man like me practices interpretation?"

"What can we say to my lord?" says Judah. "What words can we find to speak our innocence? Lord, your slaves stand before you: all of us, not just he with the interpreting cup in his hands."

"Heaven forbid it," he interjects. "Such acts are beyond me. Just the one holding the interpreting cup—this one alone will be my slave. But you: go with clear conscience, up to your father."

Judah drew nearer: "Dear lord, allow a word from your servant to his master's ear. Hold your anger from burning your servant—you are like Pharaoh for us.

"'Have you a father, or a brother?' my lord asked his servants. 'We have a father, an old man,' we answered, 'with a boy of his old age, whose brother is dead. He alone survives his mother, and his father loves him.'

"Now," continued Judah, "please allow your servant to be held in place of the boy—a slave to my lord—so the boy can go up with his brothers. How could I go to my father and the boy not with me—heaven forbid I see the horror that will grip my father."

Now Joseph could hold himself back no longer. "Leave me alone with them," he called out. No witness stood by him when he revealed himself to his brothers.

He burst into sobs—even the Egyptians could hear, even Pharaoh's court heard of it.

"I am Joseph," his brothers were hearing. "Is my father still alive?" No word returned from their lips, stunned into silence.

⚊

"Now listen: your eyes can see—even Benjamin's eyes understand—it is from a brother's mouth I speak to you.

"And you will tell my father," he continued, "of my great honor in Egypt, all that you have seen. Hurry, bring my father down to me." Then he fell on the shoulder of Benjamin, his brother, weeping; and Benjamin wept, upon his neck.

⌗

Judah was sent ahead to Joseph, to arrange Israel's way to the Goshen district.

Joseph harnesses his chariot, goes up to meet Israel in Goshen. He rushes to his father as soon as he sees him, falls on his neck, weeping—a torrent of tears falling on his shoulder.

"I can die at last," Israel says to Joseph, "because I have seen your face, still so full of life."

"I will approach Pharaoh"—Joseph was speaking in the presence of his father's household and his brothers. "I will say to Pharaoh, 'My brothers and my father's house from the land of Canaan have made their way to me. The men are shepherds; they have made their way with sheep and cattle—in fact, all they have surrounds them.'

"Now listen: Pharaoh may call you over, ask, 'What is your livelihood?' 'We make our way with livestock,' you will say. 'Your servants have grown up among sheep—as our fathers before us.' That is the proper way to settle in the land of Goshen; in Egypt proper, a shepherd is a horror."

So it was: many years went past—Jacob was properly settled in Egypt—when Joseph would hear, "Listen: your father is sick." He took his two boys with him, Manasseh and Ephraim.

Now Jacob heard—"Hear: Joseph your son comes to you." Israel gathered his strength, rose up in his bed. Gazing at Joseph's boys, Israel exclaimed, "But whose are these?" "My sons." "Gather them by me, so I may bless them."

Now Israel's eyes were blurry with age, he could barely see; as he felt them in his arms, he kissed them, hugged them close. "I never dreamt to see your face, and now look: sweet faces of your seed."

Ephraim was by Joseph's right hand and he directed him to Israel's left side; Manasseh, by his left hand, he directed toward his father's right.

Yet Israel stretched out his right hand, settled it on Ephraim's head—but he was the younger—while his left hand reached over to Manasseh's head—his arms crossing direction, since the firstborn's right was Manasseh's.

Joseph gazed thunderstruck, seized his father's right hand, to reclaim it from Ephraim's head. "It can't be so, my father," he was exclaiming. "Your right hand belongs on the firstborn's head." But his father held back: "I know, my son, I know."

Now look: it was his father's face to which Joseph fell prostrate, sobbing over him, kissing him. Then Joseph directed his servants—the physicians among them—to embalm his father. Israel is embalmed; the physicians do it.

It took them forty days to complete; that is the way of the embalmed. And for seventy days, Egypt mourned over him.

Now these mourning days pass and Joseph speaks to Pharaoh's court. "If I touch your heart, please deliver this to Pharaoh's ear on my behalf: 'My father asked my vow with these words: "Look, I will die soon. Bury me in the grave I dug for myself, in the land of Canaan." Please let me go, to bury my father up there, and then return.'"

Then Pharaoh answered: "Go up to deliver your father, as he delivered the vow to you."

Now Joseph ascended to bury his father; going up with him were all the ministers of Pharaoh, the senior princes of his palace, and all the heads of Egypt.

And all of Joseph's household as well, his brothers' and father's households too. Their babies, their sheep, their cattle—just these were left behind in the land of Goshen.

Chariots and horsemen accompany them. Now look: a huge party is going up.

They arrive at Goren ha-Atad, beyond the Jordan, where they stop for lamentation—a huge lament goes up, the chants heavy with emotion. The mourning service he makes for his father lasted seven days.

As the inhabitants of the land, Canaanites, hear the lamentation at Goren ha-Atad, they are stunned: "What a heavy lamentation for the Egyptians." That is why they named it then Mourning-Egypt, though it is beyond the Jordan.

So Joseph returned to Egypt—he, his brothers, and all those who went up to bury his father—once he had delivered his father to his grave.

genesis [E]

These are the days when the four kings—Amraphel of Sumer, Arioch of Ellasar, Chederlaomer of Elam, and Tidal of Goiim—went to war with the five: King Bera of Sodom, Birsha of Gomorrah, Shinab of Admah, Shemeber of Zeboiim, and the king of Bela, *or Zoar as it now is called.* These last joined together in the Valley of Siddim, *or the Dead Sea.* Twelve years they had served Chederlaomer, but in the thirteenth they turned away. In the next year, Chederlaomer and his allied kings returned and conquered the Rephaim in Ashteroth-karnaim, and then the Zuzim in Ham, the Emim in Shaveh-kiriathaim, and the Horites in the hills of Seir, near El-paran, which borders the wilderness. After that, they turned around to En-mishpat, *now Kadesh,* overpowering the region of the Amalekites, including the Amorites who inhabited Hazazon-tamar. At that point, the kings of Sodom, Gomorrah, Admah, Zeboiim, and Bela, *which has become Zoar,* who had joined together in the Valley of Siddim, were attacked there, five kings taken on by the four, Chederlaomer of Elam, Tidal of Goiim, Amraphel of Sumer, and Arioch of Ellasar.

One bitumen pit after another—that was the Valley of Siddim. They dove into them as they ran—the kings of Sodom and Gomorrah hiding there, the others escaping into the hills. The conquerors took all the goods of Sodom and Gomorrah, and all their food, and left. Also captured was Lot, Abraham's nephew, who had been living in Sodom; they took him and all that he owned.

An escapee brought the news to Abraham the Hebrew at the terebinths of Mamre the Amorite, who was related to the allies of Abraham, Eshkol and Aner. When Abraham heard that Lot his relative had been captured, he gathered his men—all those serving or born into his household, numbering 318—and pursued the captors as far as Dan. He positioned all his men around the others at night, overcame them, and stayed on their heels as far as Hobah, north of Damascus. All the goods were recovered, along with his relative Lot and all that he owned, including the women and others.

As Abraham came back from defeating Chedorlaomer and his allied kings, the king of Sodom came out to the Valley of Shaveh, known as the King's Valley, to receive him. There too Melchizedek, king of Shalem, came out with bread and wine. As priest of El-Elyon, he blessed him, saying "Honored is Abraham by El-Elyon, creator of heaven and earth. Honored is El-Elyon, who brought your enemies to you." So Abraham allotted to him a tenth of everything.

Then the king of Sodom said to him, "Give the people to me and you take the goods." Abraham demurred. "I have promised Yahweh, El Elyon, creator of heaven and earth, that not even one thread or a sandal strap would I take of what belongs to you, saving you from ever saying, 'I made Abraham rich.' For me, nothing but what my men used up, but for the allies who joined me, Aner, Eshkol, and Mamre, a fair portion."

[translated by E from the Akkadian of X]

⬡

From there Abraham moved to the Negev
stopping between Kadesh and Shur
settling in Gerar.

"She is my sister," he said
of Sarah his wife.
When Abimelech, king of Gerar, heard

he took her. And God came too
that night in a dream
saying, "Death is the price
for taking a man's wife."

Abimelech had not touched her
when he asked, "My Lord, will you kill
a man who is innocent?
I heard 'She is my sister'
from him. And from her, 'He
is my brother.'

"My heart was innocent
my hands clean
when this happened."

And God answered in the dream:
"Because I knew it was innocently done
I held you back from touching her
from committing contempt.

"Now return the wife to the man
and live
for he is a man who speaks up:
he can plead your cause.

"Or else die, if you hold on to her.
You and all who are attached to you."

✴

Avimelech summoned his servants next morning
retelling the conversation in the night
until the men were overcome with fear.

Abraham was called and heard this plea:
"Why did you do this to us?
How did I move you
to settle upon me
and my kingdom
this charge of contempt?
How have I handled you
that you would touch me with contempt?

"What did you foresee
happening
to cause this thing?"

"I said to myself," Abraham began,
"'There is no fear of God here;
they'll kill me
to have my wife.'

"But she is also my sister
my father's daughter
yet not my mother's
and she became my wife.

"When heaven ordained I wander
far from my father's house
I said, 'Be my loyal wife
in whatever strange place we settle;
tell them this about me:
"He is my brother."'"

Avimelech took sheep and oxen
male and female servants
gave them to Abraham
and restored Sarah to him.

"Here, my land is yours to settle on,"
Avimelech said to Abraham,
"anyplace your eye prefers."

To Sarah he said,
"Here, a thousand pieces of silver
for your brother
enough to cover the eyes
of everyone attached to you
to what has happened,
proof of innocence."

Abraham pleaded his cause to God
and Avimelech was restored
along with his wife
and his female servants:
children could now be born.

For God had closed the womb of everyone
attached to Avimelech
as in a protective dream—
for Sarah, wife of Abraham.

⋈

The child grew
was weaned
and on that day a great feast
was made by Abraham
but Sarah saw the son of Hagar the Egyptian
the one carried by her for Abraham
laughing with her own son, Isaac
and she turned in protest to her husband

"Send away that servant and her son.
No son of hers can divide with Isaac
his inheritance." In Abraham's eyes
this was wrenching:
it was his son too.

Then God in the night said this:
"Do not be torn between boy and servant;
listen to Sarah's voice;
it is Isaac that continues your name.
But the servant's son too
will father a great nation
being your child."

Next morning, Abraham
got together bread and water
for Hagar, fixing a skin of water
to her back, sending her and the child away.
She wandered in the desert near Beer-sheva
Until the skin was dry, then sheltered
The child beneath a bush.

She walked away, far as an arrow flies and sat opposite,
weeping, saying to herself, "Let me not hear the child die"
and closed her eyes.

When God heard Ishmael's wail
his angel called to Hagar from heaven:
"What pains you, Hagar?

There is nothing to fear. God has heard
the child's cry, clear as day.
Arise, take the boy in your arms
soothe him, he will become
a great nation."

Then God opened her eyes:
a well of water was visible
before her. She walked over
filled the skin with water
let the boy drink.

God was with the boy
as he grew up
making the desert his home.
It was in Paran and he grew
skilled with arrow and bow.
It was his mother who got a wife
for him, from the land
of Egypt.

⬚

And some time later
after these things had happened
God tested Abraham
speaking to him
"Abraham"
"I am listening," he answered.

And God said
please take your son
whom you love
dear as an only son
that is, Isaac
and go out to the land of Moriah

There you will make of him a burnt offering
on a mountain of which I will tell you
when you approach

And Abraham rose early in the morning
saddled his donkey
took two of his young workers
to go with him and his son, Isaac
having already split the wood
for the burnt offering
and he started out for the place
of which God had spoken
to him

It was on the third day
Abraham looked out in the distance
and there, afar, was the place
and Abraham turned to his young men
you will wait here by yourselves
with the donkey
while the youth and I go on ahead
to worship and then
we will return here to you

Abraham took the wood for the burnt offering
laying it upon Isaac, his son
and in his own hands he took the flint
and the knife
then the two walked on together

At last Isaac spoke to his father, Abraham
"Father"
"I am listening, my son"
We have the flint and the wood
to make the fire, but where is the lamb
for a burnt offering?

Abraham answered
God will reveal his lamb, my son
for the burnt offering
and the two walked on together

And they approached the place
of which God had spoken
there Abraham prepared an altar
set the wood upon it
then bound his son, Isaac
and laid him there, on the altar
lying upon the wood

Abraham reached out
with his hand, taking
the knife, to slaughter
his son

But a voice was calling to him
an angel of the Lord, calling
from out of heaven
Abraham, Abraham
I am listening, he answered

Do not lay your hand upon the youth
you will not do anything to him
for now I know yours is an integrity
dedicated to God
not holding back your son
your dear one, from me

Then Abraham looked around and there
behind him
its horns tangled up in a thicket
a ram had appeared

And Abraham went over to it
carrying the ram to the wood
for a burnt offering
instead of his son

The name of that place
was given by Abraham, meaning
"The Lord reveals"
and today we still say
"The mountain of the Lord
is revelation"

The Lord's angel spoke again
calling to Abraham from heaven
By myself I have sworn
says the Lord
as by yourself you have acted—
have not held back even your son
dear to you as an only one—
and for this thing you are immeasurably blessed
and your seed multiplied
immeasurable as the stars in the sky
and as the grains of sand by the sea

For this thing you have done
your descendants will walk freely
through the gates of their enemy
and all the nations of the earth
will feel themselves blessed
one day, knowing
that your descendants thrive
living among them—
for it was you who listened
and heard my voice

So Abraham returned to his young men
they turned and started out together
for Beersheba
and Abraham stayed there, in Beersheba.

Exodus begins after a hiatus of four hundred years since the death of Joseph. The Egyptian Pharoah, who "no longer remembers Joseph," also disparages his Jewish descendants, having found them consigned to Goshen, an impoverished province, and having assigned them to slave labor. Yet these Hebrews are still to be feared, and against a historical background of unrest, Moses is born.

Less of J's narrative has survived in Exodus, compared with Genesis, and I have rendered it starkly. What remains held the authority of factual history for the biblical editors of a few centuries later. [Meanwhile, the fact that many biblical scholars today doubt the historical events of Exodus has less to do with the text and more to do with the modern disciplines of archaeology and reactionary linguistics, which turn up no unimpeachable stones or plausible evidence. And yet, whether the report is of 600,000 fleeing Israelites being improbable due to the prevailing landscape and size of oases, or the time and place of journey being improbable due to the area of settlement required for the large population, what remains most astounding is how close the events and conflicts come to rendering the complex ring of truth. J was foremost a historian, and even when it comes to portraying the cosmic drama at Mount Sinai, the details bear the veracity of original sources.

It appears that the great drama of Moses' life and leadership is nevertheless subordinate to God's presence. Thus the image of Moses as merely "God's secretary" has mistakenly taken hold. Moses has complained that he's slow of speech, that he can't handle the prophet's role. But in Exodus we hear God speaking to Moses with great irony, telling him that he, Moses, will play the god and Aaron will play the prophet. We don't really need to hear Moses' reply, because there can be no doubt that he understood and embraced such irony. He will use it himself when he speaks to Pharaoh as well as his own people.

Jewish tradition provided the figure of Moses as leader-writer. Along with David and Solomon, who are author-figures for other biblical books, he embodies the kind of hero we don't have in Western history: a national leader who is also a great poet. In post-biblical Jewish culture, bereft of a nation (until our time), the model of a leader-figure in itself was difficult to imagine, especially one who is a potent artist. Yet in the twentieth century we've seen great poets of the Hebrew language, and a lament by Bialik, a mythic story by Agnon, or a sonnet-psalm by Leah Goldberg is comprehensible beside the biblical canon. And that is how the voice of J crystallized for me: it was not until I read the modern Hebrew poets that I could imagine the biblical authors as living men and women.

Jewish biblical commentary is deep and imaginative because it does require an author. In fact, it requires quite a leap to imagine an author like Moses, one who could have written the entire Torah. By contrast, much biblical scholarship can rarely imagine an author of a fragment, and when it does it is unable to imagine him or her as human rather than as a voice of historical accretions.

In Jewish tradition still under the spell of superstition, the taboo against spelling even the word "God" is a sign of love and fear— an awesome tenderness felt for the Creator-father, at its best; at its worst, rote fear. Post-biblical Jewish writers long ago turned to the realm of imaginative commentary—midrash and aggadah—where they might again recreate scenes and conversations with God, as the Bible's writers had.

The mind of Moses is what we most often confront, and it is interpreted in some episodes more than others, often in the form of dialogue and speeches. This is how a writer reveals character today, and it was no different in the time of Moses, who himself described the presence of God on Mount Sinai in vivid, visual terms—as well as in "remembered" dialogue with the Creator. We now know that later Hebraic writers in Jerusalem were doing much of the writing; nevertheless, they did not get in the way of the crucial image of Moses as writer. It allowed them to continue revealing how he thought—or more precisely, how his memory was alternately seared by events and worked to interpret them.

> *Mount Sinai was wrapped in smoke. Yahweh had come down in fire, the smoke climbing skyward like smoke from a kiln. The mountain, enveloped, greatly trembled.*
>
> *[Ex. 19:16]*

This is a visual record, and the description continues as the mountain trembles, the thunder grows louder, and Moses was called to come up. Now, it is not hard to imagine that some months or years later, Moses wrote down these experiences. However, he might as well have been writing at the very moment when the Creator said: "I am YHWH your God who brought you out of the land of Egypt . . . You shall have no gods except me." [Ex. 20:1] It renders the words indelible, including the words of the Ten Commandments that Moses brought down from the mountain. However, if Moses wrote this experience down some years later, while writing the Torah, we must trust the accuracy of his memory.

Yet what we can now discern actually happened, is that the Hebraic writer more than two centuries later in Jerusalem wrote this down, based upon the earlier written or oral sources. And even these earlier sources must have had an authentic authorship to be so trusted by the writers in Jerusalem.

Nevertheless, today we have found that the description of violent atmospheric events on Mount Sinai is somewhat similar to those written down by writers and poets in other ancient cultures and in earlier centuries. So we may assume that these are poetic images of a writer, even in the Torah—but with a crucial difference. Because we have a writer at the scene—Moses as at least a figure of a writer— we can understand that these powerful images are used consciously to evoke God's presence. For even the most literal-minded reader is not thinking about whether these are natural manifestations, whether it be a volcano or some other upheaval. Unlike the pagan gods, YHWH, *especially as represented in dialogue with Moses, was wholly independent of nature; the image we are presented is purely a poetic sign that his presence has been felt. Not seen, that is; not made visible, but rendered in the same poetic idiom that earlier civilizations had used in a more literal manner—since their gods were, in fact, present or directly represented in nature.*

Now, for the first time in history, we've become conscious that the Hebraic writers in Jerusalem were deeply educated, no less than the Moses educated at the royal Egyptian school. They were able to transform mythic beliefs that depended upon gods inhabiting nature, and change them utterly, in order to convey that the transcendence of YHWH *nevertheless remained in touch with the history of civilization as it unfolded over time. Of course, we don't expect the recently freed Israelites in the wilderness to have studied Ugaritic (a Canaanite literary language that even Moses might not have known, but that contains some similar poetic images to what is found in the Torah). And certainly the Israelites would not have recognized the experience of their journey as a literary projection. They were witnesses, not writers, and what was important to them was not description but the words that came down through Moses from Mount Sinai.*

exodus

Now Joseph had died, and all his brothers, and all that generation.

⋈

A new king arose over Egypt, not knowing Joseph. "Look, the people of Israel are growing too large for us," he said to his people. "Listen, let's deal shrewdly with this, before they grow further. Or else, in a war, they may join those who hate us, or rise up from the land." They organized cadres to control them, harness their labor; yet, enslaved, as they were punished they grew, bursting their borders.

⋈

Proclaiming a law to his people, Pharaoh said, "All boys of Israel born, throw them into the Nile—the girls will live alone."

⋈

A man from the family of Levi rose up and married a Levite woman. She conceived, bore a son, and seeing that he was beautiful, kept him in hiding three months. But this couldn't continue; the woman rose, searched out a crib of papyrus; then tarred it with bitumen, with pitch; then she put the child in, placed it in the reeds by the Nile.

⊠

A daughter of Pharaoh descended to bathe in the river, her maidservants walking along the bank; she saw the crib among the reeds, sent her servant to bring it up. Opening it, she saw the child—"Listen, he is crying"—a youth bringing pity.

⊠

The child grew; he was a son to the princess: she gave him the name Moses.

⊠

Those times passed and Moses grew up; now, he goes out among his brothers, sees them suffering. An Egyptian had beaten dead a Hebrew, one of his brothers—he saw it. Turning around, he looked each way; seeing no officers, he struck—the Egyptian fell, the body hidden in the sand.

⊠

Pharaoh heard of it, this deed; he was ready to kill Moses. But Moses escaped from Pharaoh's power, settling in Midian. He camped by a well.

⊠

Now a priest of Midian had seven daughters, and they came to lift water, fill the basins for their father's sheep. Shepherds arrived, began to drive them away, but Moses stood up for the women; he watered their flock. "What brought you home so soon today?" asked their father, Reuel. "An Egyptian man," they answered, "intervened for us with the shepherds. He also lifted water for us and watered the flock." "Where is he?" asked the father. "Why did you just leave the man? Go call him to eat with us." Moses was pleased to stay on with this man, who gave him Zipporah his daughter. She gave birth to a son, whom he named Gershom, after saying, "A stranger I have been in a foreign land." Now during these many passing years, the king of Egypt died.

✕✕

Now Moses shepherded the flock of his father-in-law, priest of Midian, guiding it beyond the border of the desert— coming upon the mountain of God. There Yahweh's angel appeared to him as fire in a thorn bush. He looked closely: there a bush blazed with fire, yet the bush was not burnt away. "I must stop, come closer to this luminous thing," Moses thought, "to see why the bush is not eaten away." Yahweh saw that he approached, called to him from within the bush: "Moses, Moses." "I am listening," Moses answered. "You must not advance," he said. "Take the shoes from your feet. The place you are standing borders the holy."

✕✕

"I saw," spoke Yahweh, "I beheld the burden my people held—in Egypt. I come down to lift them out of Egypt's hand, to carry them to a broad, open land."

⌖

"They won't believe me," Moses said, "they won't even listen to my voice—'Yahweh doesn't appear to you' will jump to their lips." Yahweh asked, "What is that in your hand?" "My stick," he answered. "Throw it to the ground." He threw it down: a snake was on the ground. Startled, Moses turned around. "Put out your hand," Yahweh said to Moses, "grasp it by the tail." He reached out, took hold: in his fist, a stick.

⌖

"Please," Yahweh spoke further, "put your hand within, to your breast." He put his hand within, and when he brought it out: a hand leprous as snow. "Return your hand to your breast," he said. He put his hand within, and when he brought it out again it was his flesh returned.

⌖

"Please, my lord," Moses said to Yahweh, "I am not a man of words; neither was I yesterday or the day before. And since you first spoke to your servant I remain heavy-tongued— my mouth strains for words." "Who put the mouth in man?" Yahweh answered him. "Who makes him dumb? And who makes the deaf—or the seeing and the blind? Wasn't it I, Yahweh? Now go; I guide your mouth, teach you what you will say."

⁂

"Go again to Egypt"—Yahweh spoke to Moses in Midian—
"they've died, all those who would have your life." Moses
took his wife and sons, saddled the donkeys, returned to
the land of Egypt.

⁂

On the way, at a night lodging, Yahweh met him—and was
ready to kill him. Zipporah took a flinty stone, cutting her
son's foreskin; touched it between Moses' legs: "Because
you are my blood bridegroom." He withdrew from him. "A
blood bridegroom," she said, "marked by this circumcision."

⁂

Moses met with Aaron, went to gather all the elders of
Israel.

⁂

Later, coming to Pharaoh, Moses said, "Yahweh, God of
Israel, declares: 'Send me my people, to feast me in the desert.'" "Who is Yahweh?" Pharaoh replied. "To whom should
I listen and send out Israel? I haven't known Yahweh, nor
would I let go Israel."

He said: "The God of the Hebrews appeared to me. We
would go, please, three days into the desert, sacrifice to Yahweh our God—or else he wound us by disease, or send the
sword."

"The slave-workers' presence is pressing everywhere," Pharaoh said, "—and you would have them rest from labor." Pharaoh directed his officers that same day, and their policemen: "No more straw to make brick, as yesterday and the day before. Let them go—to collect their own straw. The quota of bricks stays the same; we won't relax the weight on those lax shoulders—or leave them time to groan, 'We must go sacrifice to our God.' Pile more work on them; let them groan with labor, not with slippery words."

Coming to the people, the officers and their policemen said, "Pharaoh declares: 'I won't give you straw. You may go out—for straw—wherever you find it, but you may not lose one minute of production.'" Through all the land of Egypt the people spread, searching out stubble for straw. The policemen pressed them: "Each day's quota as before, as a day when there was straw." The policemen who were Israelites—appointed by Pharaoh's officers—were beaten: "Why haven't you finished your baking of bricks, as yesterday, and filled your quota as the day before?" The Israelite policemen came to Pharaoh: "How could you do this to your slave-workers?" they groaned. "No straw is given to your slaves, yet the officers say, 'Make bricks.' Then the workers are beaten, yet it's your own people's fault."

"Idlers," he said, "you want to relax, that's why you idly groan, 'Let us go sacrifice to Yahweh.' Go to your work, instead; straw will not be given—but you will give back the full quota of bricks."

They saw their sad situation, the Israelite policemen having to say: "Each day's quota as before, not a minute's less." Leaving Pharaoh, they met Moses, waiting for them on the way. "May Yahweh see you and judge: you have given a stench to us, we are stained in the eyes of Pharaoh and his officers; you have given them a sword to kill us."

Returning to Yahweh, Moses said, "My lord, for what have you brought your people into this sad situation? For what have you sent me? Since I've spoken to Pharaoh in your name there are only sad consequences for the people. What of your uplifting? You haven't begun to lift out your people."

⊠

"Now you will see what I do for Pharaoh," Yahweh answered Moses. "With his strong hand he will send them out."

⊠

"Pharaoh's heart is rigid," Yahweh said to Moses, "he resists sending the people; but you will go to him. Wait, and meet him by the way: it is the morning he goes down to the riverbank. 'Yahweh, God of the Hebrews, sent me'—you will say this to him—'"Send me my people, to serve me in the desert. Until now you have not really heard—Yahweh speaks so—but in this it will be revealed to you: I am Yahweh. The fish in the Nile will die, the river will be a stench: it will be impossible for Egypt to drink from the Nile."'"

Moses did as Yahweh desired. The Nile fish died; the stench from the river prevented Egypt from drinking there.

But Pharaoh turned away, going into his palace, unmoved in his heart even to this. But now Egypt had to dig for water elsewhere, prevented from drinking the Nile. Seven full days passed after Yahweh struck the Nile; then Yahweh spoke to Moses. "You will come to Pharaoh and say, 'Yahweh speaks so: "Send me my people, to serve me. If you resist letting go, look: I strike down all your borders with frogs. The Nile will be pregnant with frogs; they will go out, out into your palace, your bedroom, onto your bed and into your servants' house and all the houses of your people, into your ovens and dough pans. The frogs will go upon you, upon your people, upon all your officers."'"

After the frogs came up, covering Egypt, Pharaoh called Moses: "Mediate with Yahweh—remove the frogs from me, my people—and I will send out your people: they will sacrifice to Yahweh." "You will be praised over me—" Moses answered Pharaoh— "When?" "Tomorrow." "—According to your word, then, not mine: so you will know there is nothing like Yahweh our God. The frogs will move back from you, from your officers, from your people—back to the Nile."

Then Moses left Pharaoh's presence; he mediated with Yahweh about the frogs put even in Pharaoh's lap. Yahweh performed according to Moses' word: the frogs died in the houses, the gardens, the fields. They were piled in bushelsful until the land was full of the stench. Pharaoh had breathing room again; now his heart swelled with indifference, dismissed Moses.

⊠

"Wake early, present yourself to Pharaoh," Yahweh said to Moses, "it is the morning he goes down to the riverbank. 'Yahweh, God of the Hebrews, sent me'—you will say this to him—'"Send me my people, to serve me. If you refuse to let my people go, I will let go—upon you, upon your servants, upon your people, upon your houses—flies. The houses of Egypt will be full, their floors will be one with the land: hidden under flies. That day I will distinguish the borders of Goshen—the land my people squat upon— to be untouched by flies, so you may know I am Yahweh, here on earth. I will put borders between your people and mine—by tomorrow this marking will be plain."'"

Now, Yahweh did so: powerful droves of flies entered Pharaoh's palace, his officers' houses; through all the land of Egypt land was ruined under the flies. Now, Pharaoh called for Moses: "Go sacrifice to your god, but in our country—"

⊠

"—and intervene on my behalf." "Listen," Moses said, "I leave your presence to represent you with Yahweh; the flies will be removed—from Pharaoh, his officers, his people— tomorrow; but Pharaoh must not play with us, not letting go: the people wait to give sacrifice to Yahweh."

Leaving Pharaoh, Moses returned to Yahweh's presence; and he performed according to Moses' word: the flies were removed—not one remained. But Pharaoh's heart stiffened this time also; the people were not sent out.

⊠

Now Yahweh said to Moses, "Approach Pharaoh and say, 'Yahweh—God of the Hebrews—speaks so: "Send my people out, to serve me. Resist letting go—tighten your grasp again—and listen: Yahweh's hand will grasp your cattle in the field, your horses, donkeys, camels, oxen, sheep—a hard thing, a stiff plague. Yahweh will mark out boundaries around the flocks of Israel, distinguish them from the flocks of Egypt, and among the Israelites not one thing will die."'"

Now Yahweh set the time: "Tomorrow Yahweh makes his word deed in the land." The next day: Egyptian cattle died, yet not one cow of the Israelites. Pharaoh sent out for word—"Listen, not even one cow of Israel died." Still, his heart was hard: he resisted sending out the people.

⊠

Now Yahweh said to Moses, "Wake early, present yourself to Pharaoh. 'Yahweh, God of the Hebrews, speaks so'—you will say this to him—'"Send me my people, to serve me."'"

⊠

"—Again you play with my people, resist sending them. Listen: tomorrow at this time a hard hailstorm falls, as has never been in Egypt, not from the day of its founding. Send out your word: the cattle, all that belongs to you in the field, all man and beast not in houses—if not brought into your house they will die as the hail falls." Among Pharaoh's men, those in awe of Yahweh's word chased their slaves and cattle inside; those who didn't take Yahweh to heart left their slaves and cattle in the field.

Now Yahweh let go thunder and hail, lightning touched the ground, hail fell on the land of Egypt: a hard hail, unknown since Egypt became a nation, striking through- out Egypt, cutting down everything in the field, from man to beast—plants, bushes were knocked over by the hail, trees shattered. Only in Goshen did the hail not fall, where the Israelites were.

Pharaoh sent for Moses: "This time I've offended; Yahweh is just, while I, my people—are guilty. Pray to Yahweh: it is more than enough, this god's thunder and hail; I will send you out—there is no longer need to hold you." Now Moses said to him, "As I leave the city, I'll spread my arms to Yahweh: the thunder will stop, hail will not exist—you will know the earth is Yahweh's. Yet you and your officers will not hold to awe in the face of God, Yahweh—this I can see."

⌖

Now Moses left Pharaoh's presence, left the city, opened his arms to Yahweh: thunder and hail faded away, rain was no longer spilling to earth. When Pharaoh saw the rain, hail, and thunder had stopped, he offended further, his heart stiffened even more— he and his subjects.

⁂

"We will enter Pharaoh's presence," Yahweh said to Moses. Moses entered: "Yahweh, God of the Hebrews, speaks so: 'How long will you hold a hard mask to my face? Send out my people, to serve me. If you resist sending my people, listen: tomorrow I will bring locusts across your borders, to blanket the land's surface until you won't be able to see it, to devour the living remnant that survived the hail— even the trees, that blossom for you in the field: eaten away. Your palace will be filled and the houses of your subjects—all the houses of Egypt overrun as no one has ever seen, not your fathers or fathers' fathers, not in a day they existed, or any until now'"—and Moses turned away, left Pharaoh's presence.

"How long will this man be our pitfall?" said Pharaoh's officers to him. "Send the men out to serve Yahweh their god—before we find out that Egypt is lost."

Moses was brought back to Pharaoh: "Go, serve Yahweh your god. But who—who are the ones going?" "We all go," Moses said, "including our young and our old, sons and daughters, sheep and cattle. It is a feast to Yahweh for all of us." "May Yahweh be with you," Pharaoh said, "—and with your little ones—were I to let you go together. No, schemes are written on your faces. You may go now—just you men, please—to serve Yahweh, since that is your request." And he was swept out of Pharaoh's presence.

⚅

All that day and night Yahweh drove a desert wind through the land: now it was morning, the desert wind had brought the locusts. Now the locust ascended over Egypt, obliterating all borders, a heavy blanket, no one had ever seen locusts that thick before—or ever will. The ground was smothered in darkness; the locust ate all vegetation and fruit that survived the hail. Nothing green was left on tree or bush in all Egypt. Now Pharaoh anxiously called Moses back: "I've offended Yahweh, your god and you. Please, overlook a first offense—intervene with Yahweh, your god, to roll back this death from over me."

Moses left Pharaoh, intervened with Yahweh. And Yahweh rolled back a strong sea wind, which lifted the locusts and swept them into the Reed Sea: not one locust remained within Egypt's borders.

⚅

Again Pharaoh summoned Moses: "Go now, serve Yahweh—only your cattle and sheep need wait behind for you. Even your children will go with you."

"You will also give us offerings—and a free hand with our sacrificial needs," Moses answered, "so we can prepare them for Yahweh our God. Not a hoof of ours may stay: we don't yet know what is required of us."

⊠

"Go as you are, with nothing," Pharaoh said to Moses. "Now leave my presence—but watch yourself. Don't let me see your face one more time; if I do, on that day you will die."

"Well said. I will not see your face another time," Moses answered—

⊠

"—as Yahweh," he said, "speaks so: 'In the middle of the night I will appear in the midst of Egypt. And he will die—each first-one in Egypt, from the son of the Pharaoh who sits on the throne, to the son of the slave maid sitting behind the millstone—to every beast firstling. There will be a great screaming throughout Egypt—as never before, nor ever to be. Yet not one dog shall snarl to all the children of Israel—not at a man and not even at his beast. Here you will know how Yahweh marks boundaries between Egypt and Israel.' All your subjects will lower themselves, bowing: 'Go: you—and the whole of your people in your footsteps.' And then I shall leave." Now he left Pharaoh's presence burning with anger.

⊠

Moses called together the elders of Israel: "Choose sheep for your families, and slaughter them for the Pesach offering. You will dip a bunch of marjoram into the blood now in the basin, and brush the lintel and the two doorposts, so they are marked from the blood in the basin. You will not go out again—not even one man—through the opening of your house, until morning. Yahweh will pass through, striking Egypt; when the blood on the lintel and doorposts is seen, Yahweh will not pass over the opening without holding back the Slaughterer—who enters to deal death in your home."

⌖

In awe, the people lowered themselves; they were prostrate.

⌖

Now it was midnight; Yahweh struck all the first sons in Egypt, from the son of the Pharaoh who sits on the throne, to the son of the prisoner who squats in the hole—to every beast firstling. Pharaoh awoke in the night—he, his officers, all Egypt—to a great scream: there is no house in which there is not a dead man.

In that night Pharaoh summoned Moses: "Awake, go out from my people—you and the Israelites—go, serve Yahweh according to your words. Your cattle, your sheep—take them too, as you've spoken, and may you say a prayer for me as well." Now the Egyptians hurried the people in their going out from the land—desperate, they were saying,

"We are dead men." Before it was even leavened, the people were loading the dough; the clothes carried on their shoulders were wrapped around the kneading bowls.

⊠

Now the Israelites traveled from Ramses toward Sukkot, about six hundred thousand adults on foot, besides children. And others went out with them, along with large numbers of animals, cattle and sheep. They baked the dough they brought from Egypt into matzah cakes—since it was unleavened and they had rushed out from Egypt without proper time to prepare their provisions.

⊠

They moved on from Sukkot, marked out their camp at Eitam, at the border of the desert. Yahweh walks ahead of them each day in a pillar of cloud, marking the way: at night, in a pillar of fire. Day or night, the people can walk. Ahead of them, it never disappears: a pillar of fire by night, a pillar of cloud by day.

⊠

Meanwhile Pharaoh, with his officers, changed heart again. "What have we done, sending our slaves, Israel, away from us?" He demanded his chariot and his men, took all with him.

⊠

Pharaoh was near, the Israelites saw him, saw Egypt moving behind them. Scared, shouts burst out of them.

⊠

Moses spoke to the people. "Do not show fear. Draw together. You will see the freedom Yahweh creates today. This Egypt you look upon you will never see again. Yahweh will fight for you. Watch yourself, hold still."

⊠

The pillar of cloud moved from in front to the rear of them. It comes between the two camps, Egypt and Israel; a spell of darkness is cast, the two lose touch through the night.

⊠

It is the dawn watch and Yahweh looks down on the Egyptian camp, in the pillar of cloud and fire. Egypt panicked, saying, "We must get away from Israel, Yahweh fights for them."

⊠

But Yahweh had fleeing Egypt rocked into the sea.

⊠

On that day Yahweh freed Israel from Egypt's hand and Israel saw it in the bodies of Egyptians, dead on the distant shore. Israel saw Yahweh's great hand in the work he made of Egypt. As the people saw Yahweh, fear changed heart to belief, in Yahweh and in Moses who served him.

⊠

Then Moses and the people sang to Yahweh: Sing to Yahweh overcoming   He overflows our hearts   Driver and chariot   turned over in the sea

⠿

Moses led Israel from the Sea of Reeds, entering the desert of Shur. They walked three days into the desert without finding water. They arrived at Mara yet couldn't drink there. The water was bitter; Mara, they called the place. The people grumbled about Moses, saying, "What will we drink?" He cried out to Yahweh. Yahweh revealed a tree to him; he threw it into the water, and the water turned sweet. It was there he turned the law concrete, putting them to the test.

⠿

They came to Elim and there: twelve springs of water, seventy palm trees. There they marked out their camp, beside the water.

⠿

Later, at Rephidim, in the desert, they were thirsty again for water. The people grumbled about Moses. They would say, "Why did you lift us out of Egypt? To die—me, and my children, and my livestock—of thirst?"

⠿

There were further trials. The place was called Massa and Meriba: one name for the quarrels of the people Israel, the other for their testing, saying, "Is Yahweh near—with us—or not?"

Then, at Mount Sinai, Yahweh summoned Moses, "Ascend, you and Aaron, Nadav and Avihu, and seventy of Israel's elders; prostrate yourselves from a distance. Moses will come near Yahweh alone, the others remain afar. The people will not ascend with him." Moses returned to the people with the words of Yahweh, the laws. In a single voice, all responded, "All the words and laws Yahweh desires, we will keep."

⌗

Mount Sinai was wrapped in smoke. Yahweh had come down in fire, the smoke climbing skyward like smoke from a kiln. The mountain, enveloped, greatly trembled.

⌗

So Yahweh descended to Mount Sinai, to the summit. He called Moses to ascend to the top. Moses climbed up and Yahweh spoke to him, "Descend, hold the people's attention: they must not be drawn to Yahweh, to destroy boundaries. Bursting through to see, they will fall, many will die. Even the priests who approach Yahweh must be purified— so they are not drawn to destruction."

⌗

Yahweh spoke further, "Descend, arise with Aaron. The priests and the people shall not come up, as boundaries destroyed will be their destruction."

"They must be ready for the third day, the day Yahweh goes down, before the eyes of all, on Mount Sinai. The people will be a boundary, warn them to watch themselves, approach but not climb up, not touch the mountain. For those who overstep boundaries, death touches them, steps over their graves."

※

So Moses came down and spoke to the people.

※

Then Moses ascended, and with him Aaron, Nadav and Avihu his sons, and with them seventy of Israel's elders. They saw the God of Israel. Under his feet a pavement of sapphire was created, a likeness pure as the substance of the sky. He did not lay a hand on them, the noble pillars of Israel. They beheld God; they ate and drank.

※

Yahweh spoke to Moses, "Carve two stone tablets and at dawn prepare to ascend Mount Sinai. In the light of morning you will present yourself to me, there on the top of the mountain. No one goes with you, no one is seen anywhere on the mountain, no cattle or sheep are seen near it." In the morning Moses ascended to the summit as Yahweh desired, two stone tablets in his hands. Yahweh descended in a cloud and stood with him there, calling to him, "Yahweh, Yahweh." Moses fell to the ground, prostrate.

※

"I mark this a covenant," Yahweh said. "Watch yourself, do not march into covenants with those already in the land. Walking among you, they will destroy your boundaries. You will sweep their altars away; their sacred pillars leveled, their poles cut down. You will not fall prostrate to another God, as if Jealous One is my name, Jealous Yahweh. You must not be drawn into a covenant with the inhabitants; they seduce their gods with slaughter; they will beckon you to their sacrifices and you will eat. Their daughters will give you sons yet still embrace seductive gods: your sons will also."

⊠

Now Yahweh concluded. "So be it: I will disperse a nation in your path, broaden your road and borders; so no one dreams he can embrace your land on your way to Yahweh; as you go up to face your God three times a year.

"You write these words," said Yahweh to Moses. "On the speaking of these words, I have cut with you a covenant—and with Israel."

Now look: he is there beside Yahweh for forty days, forty nights.

He did not eat bread, he did not drink water, as he wrote on the tablets the words of the covenant.

⊠

Now look: as Moses approaches the camp he sees the calf, and dancing abounds. His bitterness knows no bounds. He heaves the tablets from his hands, smashing them against the mountain.

The calf they cast—he has it melted down, pulverized to a fine ash, then scattered upon the drinking water. He calls the Israelites to drink; they swallow it.

"What could this people have done to you?" Moses asked Aaron. "Why open the door for them to such a great contempt?"

"My lord, do not be consumed in anger's flames," said Aaron. "You know this people, their memory quickly melts away. 'Make gods to go in front on our way,' they said to me. 'This man Moses, who led us up from the land of Egypt—who knows what has happened to him.'

"'To those with gold,' I said, 'remove it and give it to me.' I cast it into the fire; out of it came the calf."

※

So it was: Moses goes back to Yahweh. "Heaven forbid, this people has shown great contempt, making gods of gold.

"You will forgive their contempt, perhaps; if not, erase me—bless heaven—out from the book you are writing."

"I will erase the one with contempt for me," Yahweh answered Moses, "from my book. Now you will go, lead the people to where I said: follow the words I spoke."

The time in the Sinai desert rendered in Exodus was less than two years; the remaining 38-plus years of the journey there is covered in Numbers. The realities of life in the desert come forward; there is no meat or fish to eat, as there had been in Egypt. The blandness of diet and days sets the Israelites' teeth on edge, and a longing to return persists.

There is much less identifiable J writing in Numbers than in the previous books. What J there is has turned more ironic: her Yahweh borders on sardonic, her Moses satiric, and the people sarcastic. All this is conditioned by the harsh realization that time is inexorably passing and a sense of the miraculous is dwindling. The reality of the writing here, enmeshed in the struggles between Moses and a recalcitrant following, may have been too much too bear, and much of J seems to be replaced by a plainer rendering of the original sources. In J's hands, the rebellions both literal and symbolic would have been modulated, but much of Numbers has resorted to the raw sources. These are told in stark mythic fashion, and it's to be expected that the original audience understood them in that way—and not as realistic and subtle accounts, as would have been written by J. In other words, the killings and avenging we encounter from other writers are exaggerated, in line with necessity of imposing law—and the awe of judgment.

In J, however, Yahweh's judgment is tempered with irony; he deigns to argue with Moses and match wits: "Is the arm of Yahweh too short?" And Balaam's talking ass is the height of literary amplification. We might find one of several possible traces of the author's personality here. If, in the several layers of irony, the ass's mouth is opened to speak for the hidden narrator, it is clear who is riding whom.

Yahweh's wordplay takes many forms, so when the people go whoring in Moab and end up intermarried, they "lay prostrate with them, before their gods." The conjunction of "laying" with the women and "prostrating" before their gods—condensed into one act of "laying prostrate"—is breathtaking.

J's original document probably went to the death of Moses, which is missing here. In its place we have the later account of the book of Deuteronomy, written in quite a different style by the writer known as D, along with fragments of other sources. One of these, briefly describing the death of Moses and his burial by Yahweh, bears the subtlety of J, and I've appended it to the end of this chapter.

numbers

After these things passed, listen: "We are beginning a journey, to the country Yahweh spoke of. 'I will give it to you,' he said." Moses was speaking to Hobab, son of Reuel the Midianite—who was his father-in-law. "Join us on the way, join in our good fortune: Yahweh has joined together good words for Israel."

"I will not be going," came the reply, "but will return to my own country, my homeland."

"Please," Moses interjected. "We would not have you leave. You know this desert well and where we may make camp in it. Be our eyes; what good fortune Yahweh makes us see will make you fortunate as well—if you would only accompany us."

Now they started out from Yahweh's mountain, traveling for three days, Yahweh's covenant-ark in front of them, escorting them toward the place for making camp.

Now look: as the ark sets out, Moses says, "Arise Yahweh, your enemies disappear like stars; your haters fade before you." When it rests, he says, "Come back, Yahweh, you who embody Israel's countless thousands."

⊠

Now the rabble among them craved flesh; and soon the Israelites also were grumbling. "Who will fill our yearning for flesh? We can see the fish we used to eat in Egypt, so freely available, like cucumbers and melons, like leeks, onions, like garlic.

"But now our spirit dries up from looking at nothing— nothing but manna."

Moses heard the people weeping, all the different families, the men standing there at their tent doors. It was scalding to Yahweh; to Moses, his heart was singed.

"Why do you hurt your servant?" asked Moses of Yahweh. "How have I made your heart so heavy you push the burden of this people on me?

"Could I have conceived this whole people? Did I give birth to them? You say to me, as if I bore them: 'Hold them to your breast, the way a nurse cradles a baby, until you arrive on the earth which I vowed to your fathers.'

"How would I get flesh to feed this whole people? They are crying for it: 'Give us flesh,' they say to me. 'That is what we want to eat.'

"I am unable to bear this whole people alone; they are too heavy for me.

"If this is what you want of me, strike me dead with mercy; if I have warmed you, let me rest from seeing my breaking heart."

✂

"You will say to the people," Yahweh said to Moses: "'Purify yourselves, tomorrow you will eat meat. Your weeping words—"Who will feed us meat as good as we ate in Egypt"—reached Yahweh's ears. Yahweh will deliver your flesh, for you to eat.

"'And not for just a day or two days, not even for five or ten days, even twenty days—but for a whole month, until it comes out from your nostrils, until you loathe the smell of it.

"'For you have denied Yahweh, who is in the midst of you, wailing in his ears, "Why did we ever come out from Egypt?""'"

But Moses responded: "I stand in the midst of six hundred thousand wanderers—and you want me to say you will have meat for them—enough for eating a whole month of days?

"If all the cattle and sheep were slaughtered, could that begin to be enough? Could all the fish in the sea be caught for them?"

Now Yahweh answered Moses: "Is the arm of Yahweh too short? Soon you will see what becomes of my words."

⌖

Now a boy came running to Moses: "Eldad and Medad are prophesying in the camp."

"Prohibit them, my lord Moses," appealed Joshua son of Nun, a follower of Moses from his youth.

"Do you think I should show myself jealous?" said Moses to him. "If only the people were all Yahweh's prophets; if only Yahweh would make them bear his spirit."

⌖

"Go up through the Negev," Moses instructed the scouts sent into Canaan, "and into the mountains. Look around, scout the land and the people settled on it—their power, their weaknesses; how thick, or how thinly spread they are.

"And the land that holds them—worthy or bad. And the cities in which they collect—unwalled or strongholds?

"And the shape of earth itself—fat or sparse, dressed in forests or not. Gather your wits, collect some fruits of the land."

Now it was the time the grapes first ripen, and when they reached the Eshkol valley they cut a section of vine packed with grapes; loaded onto a stretcher, it took two of them to carry it back. They carried off as well pomegranates and figs.

They called that valley Eshkol: the section of vine cut by Israel's sons was packed as a *school* of *fish*.

⌧

After forty days of scouting the land they returned, presented themselves before Moses, Aaron, and the whole congregation of Israel. There in the desert of Paran, at Kadesh, they presented the fruit and word of the land.

Now this is what they said: "We found the land to which you sent us full with earth's milk and honey—an overflow of grain, flowing wine. Look, this is its fruit.

"But it must be said the inhabitants are strong, the huge cities walled; we even saw the breed of giants there. Amalekites live in the Negev desert, Hittites in the mountains—the Jebusites and the Amorites there too—and by the sea, Canaanites, as well as by the Jordan.

"All the people we saw were stunning in their power. The giants are the children of Anak. We felt like grasshoppers, and in their eyes we were."

A loud sigh heaved from the congregation; the whole people wept that night.

They complained and murmured about Moses and Aaron. "We were better off dying in Egypt," the congregation moaned, "or dying in this desert, than finding out Yahweh delivers us to that land. Are we here just to fall under swords, our wives and children delivered up? We would be better off descending to Egypt.

"Let's make a leader," they were whispering among themselves, "to deliver us back to Egypt."

Now Yahweh spoke to Moses: "How long will this people affront me? How long until they attend me, and see the signs I put in front of them? I will put disease in front of them, erase their inheritance. I will make a nation out of you alone, grander than they, enormous."

But Moses said to Yahweh: "Egypt will hear what you have done to the very people your power brought out from them. And then it will reach the inhabitants of the other land."

Speaking to Moses and Aaron, Yahweh said, "To this people you will say, 'So says Yahweh: "Surely as I exist, what you have said for my ears I will be sure you hear spoken of you. The little children you said will be delivered up—those I will deliver to the land, to conquer it, just as you have belittled it. Yet your carcasses will fall in the desert. Your children will wander the desert forty years, conquering your giant words, until your bodies have wasted away in this wasteland."'"

⋈

After these things passed, now look: Yahweh had become inflamed that Balaam would go with contemptuous men. Yahweh's angel put himself in Balaam's path, like an adversary. Balaam was riding on his ass, two servant-boys in attendance.

As the ass saw Yahweh's angel standing in her path, sword unsheathed in his hand, she stepped off the road into a field. Yet Balaam whipped the ass, to get her back on the road.

Then Yahweh's angel put himself in a narrow path ahead, through vineyards fenced in on either side. As the ass saw Yahweh's angel she swerved into the wall, pinching Balaam's foot against it; he whipped her again.

Once more Yahweh's angel put himself ahead, in a narrow spot with no room for turning either right or left.

The ass saw Yahweh's angel again and sat down under Balaam; he was furious, whipping the ass with his stick.

Now Yahweh opened the ass's mouth. "What did I do to you," she said, "to make you lash out at me on three occasions?" "Because *you* have been riding *me*," Balaam said to the ass. "If I had a sword in my hand, it would whip you dead this time."

"No! Aren't I your own ass? I'm the ass you've been riding on as long as you've owned me," said the ass to Balaam. "Have I been trying—to this day—to make an ass of you?" And he: "No."

Now Yahweh opens Balaam's eyes; he sees Yahweh's angel standing in the road, the sword unsheathed in his hand—and falls prostrate, flat on his face.

"Why did you strike your ass these three times?" says Yahweh's angel. "Look: at the sight of your wayward path, I came as your adversary.

"The ass sees me and shies away three times—if she had not swerved, I would have killed you by now and spared her."

"I was contemptuous," Balaam said to Yahweh's angel. "I couldn't imagine that you would cross my path. Seeing I have crossed you, I will turn back at once.

But Yahweh's angel said to Balaam: "Continue on your way. But not a word to those men—except what I will tell you to say."

※

Now Israel was staying at Shittim when the people entered the arms of Moabite daughters.

They were beckoned to sacrifices for their gods. Soon the people ate, then lay prostrate with them, before their gods.

As Israel is yoked there, embracing Baal-peor, Yahweh is inflamed. "Round up the heads of the people," said Yahweh to Moses. "Hang them before Yahweh, in broad daylight, until Yahweh's fury is burnt away, away from Israel."

To Israel's leaders Moses then said: "Each of you must kill those of your men who yoked themselves nakedly to Baal-peor."

⧓

"Look: your deathday arrives," Yahweh said to Moses. "Summon Joshua, and direct yourselves to the tent for encounter, so I may appoint him." Moses and Joshua go to the tent for encounter, as directed.

Yahweh came down to the tent through the pillar of cloud. The pillar of cloud covered the tent entrance.

Now he appointed Joshua, son of Nun: "Summon strength and audacity, as you will direct the children of Israel to the land I vowed—for I will attend you."

⧓

Moses ascends from the Moab valley to Mount Nebo in the direction facing Jericho. There Yahweh reveals all the land, from Gilead to Dan; then all Naph-tali, the land of Ephraim and Manasseh, and now all the land of Judah to the Western Sea; then the Negev, past the oasis of palms that is Jericho, and out through the valley to Zoar.

"This is the land I vowed to Abram, Isaac, and Jacob," Yahweh said to him. "'To your seed I will give it,' were my words. It is revealed to your eyes, though your body cannot follow."

Moses, servant of Yahweh, died there, in Moab's land, following Yahweh's word.

Now he buries him there, in the clay of Moab's land, in a gorge facing Beth-peor: no man has ever seen his grave, to this day.

part 2

SEEING

the prophets

The presence of prophets who sustain the narrative, primarily Samuel and Nathan, places the two books of Samuel with the Prophets. The literary portion in 2nd Samuel is known as the "court history." The rest includes some brief literary episodes among the historical legends, many of them famous but few of which evidence an eminent author behind them.

In Jerusalem, nearly three thousand years ago, a forgotten author designated as S—working as a writer, translator, and companion of the author of Genesis, J—composed a biography that has helped determine the cultural consciousness of Western civilization: a life of David. We possess a coherent portion of that work, embedded within 2nd Samuel. Throughout his biography of David, S's Yahweh stands in the background, rushing forward at crucial moments to encourage his beloved one, or to discipline him for his mistakes.

Although we cannot know the exact circumstances under which the work was written, we can observe the resemblances and differences in style, in content, and in art, between S's narrative and J's, as well as between S and other biblical authors. Recently, some scholars have become obsessed with separating S from other authors in Samuel, denoting them S1, S2, S3, and so on. But this must be considered an academic exercise, since there is only one author whose artistry has been claimed by generations of scholars: the "Court Historian," or S.

The courtier S, at the court of King Solomon's son, Rehoboam, was not more unusual a writer than those of a later renaissance in Elizabethan England—Sidney or Raleigh, Wyatt or Ben Jonson— who were also courtiers or near-courtiers writing for a small, elite audience of peers, and who rarely bothered with publication.

What kind of career would S have had, given his talents? Most likely he was a prodigy and trained at court in languages. All court writers would also have been translators, as the work of absorbing the older tradition and other cultures into the new alphabet and changing language required knowledge of cuneiform, perhaps even pictogram. As a prodigy, S would have won the notice of J, the older woman who was writing the fresh cultural history that began with the life of Adam and ended with the death of Moses. J was a Solomonic princess, one of many and perhaps daughter of a court scholar, whose fame had elevated her authority above the need to teach at court. Yet she might have cherished the role of tutor to S.

The image of Yahweh in S's court history is an image suggestive of J herself, a powerful presence largely in the background, great enough to forgive David his flaws with a constant belovedness, a "lovingkindness"—in Hebrew, the word chesed, *which weds love to ethics. David was beloved, loved as no man before him—by Yahweh.*

J's mandate had been to help create a unifying culture for Judah, so that Solomon's many foreign wives and their cultures could be assimilated. Lovingkindness was a Davidic theme she shared with S as she delegated to him the role of writing the court history of David.

In his last work Sigmund Freud writes, "The history of King David and his time is most probably the work of one of his contemporaries." On a page earlier in that book, Moses and Monotheism, *J is described as "the author in which the most modern research workers think they can recognize Ebjatar, a contemporary of King David." Freud goes no further in imagining the relationship of J and S, but he had imagined their common culture at a time, more than fifty years ago, when most biblical scholars were afraid to even mention a biblical writer.*

Freud hypothesizes the Egyptian influence at the Davidic court, and in an earlier book of my own, The Lost Book of Paradise *(1993), I followed his hint in imagining the Hebraic scholar Devorah Bat-David. She was integral to a court culture made up of hundreds of translators and writers—especially translators, since the dominant activity in building the Hebraic culture was translating the cuneiform classics (including Mosaic writings and oral tradition) into the new Hebrew alphabet. I did not speculate about its origins, but I find now, as I reread Freud, that he conjectures "that early Israelites, the scribes of Moses, had a hand in the invention of the first alphabet."*

By the time of Rehoboam's court, when I believe J and S were in their prime, the elite who could read and write were no doubt distraught about their present, yearning for a golden past that David already represented, having succeeded Moses. It was precisely this longing that both J and S could play upon, and it allowed S the freedom to embody in David a combination of the happiest and most tragic of Hebraic characters.

Prior to its archaic experience of exile, when Jacob's sons, in Genesis, are described as settling in Egypt during a famine, no other culture in history more resembles an indigenous one than that of the Hebrews. The literary sophistication of the Hebrew Bible, like no other in its region, is based on the cultural wish to override an archaic, aboriginal past. Thus the Hebraic renaissance of David and Solomon was accompanied by the will to play down the humble, aboriginal origins behind the early Jewish tribes. It's natural enough. All civilizations create mythic origins for themselves—then, as now, aboriginals are viewed as primitive, and no advanced civilization would want a primitive label attached to itself. The ancient Egyptians and Greeks and even Phoenicians were not going to respect a civilization of aboriginals.

Can a renaissance bury the past? The origins of the Bible in the biblical writers of David and Solomon's time is most likely a renaissance, the Jews having recovered an earlier period in which they were at home in their land. In the third millennium BC, cultures from the east were invading Canaan, continuing into the second millennium, when the Philistines and Hittites followed, pushing some of the Hebrew tribes to the margin while others fled to Egypt, only to become enslaved at some point. At the time around 1000 BC, when they formed a monarchy of their own, the Israelite tribes from Egypt had returned and been absorbed among those who had won much of their land back from the foreign invaders that are imprecisely called Canaanites by tradition. It was in Israel's interest to make them seem a settled unity in order to create a powerful tale of conquering the land. The tale is not a lie; it is probably a strong sublimation of a truth, which is that the Hebrews had become exiles in their own land—in much the position Native Americans find themselves today.

Imagine S's written sources. In the palace library he would have found many old scrolls about the pre-Davidic period, scrolls about David's ancestors and youth—such as the Book of Ruth, which has survived—and court documents from David's time. From all of these he might have lifted telling details that become ironic when retold in the context of his court history. S's David may not seem as ironic a character as J's Yahweh because he is confined to the human, but within those confines he is continually surprising us with what appear to be extreme actions. Whether it is the sudden disappearance of grief when his son by Bathsheba is pronounced dead, or the interminable grief that Absalom causes, the narrative leads us to accept that David's actions are sagacious—and it is our very willingness to accept it, awed by the dimensions of this David, that is ironic, an irony S most exploited in many satisfying ways. We might call S's narrative a transformation of a typical royal chronicle for a knowing audience, bestowing an ironic sense of character as destiny and reflecting the individuality of the culture itself.

2nd samuel

"Is there no one left from Saul's family—" David began, "one to accept my lovingkindness, in Jonathan's name?"

An attendant remained from Saul's retinue, one Tziva. "Your servant am I," he said, after he was called to David and the king asked, "Are you that Tziva?" The king continued: "Is anyone left from Saul's family, to whom I may grant lovingkindness, in God's name?"

"Jonathan has a son left," said Tziva to the king, "one whose feet are lame."

"Can you tell me where he is?" the king inquired. "It is nothing," Tziva responded. "In the camp of Machir, son of Ammiel, in Lo-devar." It was nothing for David to send for him. Out of Machir's settlement, who was the son of Ammiel, he appeared before the king, out of Lo-devar.

Mephibosheth, son of Jonathan—grandson of Saul— arriving in fearful submission, touched the ground with his face. "Mephibosheth," David said. "Your servant," he answered, "nothing more."

"Fear not," David continued. "In Jonathan's name, your father, I am devoted to you, in lovingkindness. The fields of your grandfather, Saul—I grant you everything. From now on, you will break your bread at my table."

He fell prostrate. "Your servant asks what service can a dead dog merit—one such as I?"

But the king affirmed to Tziva, Saul's attendant: "Everything that belonged to Saul and his line I grant to your master's son. You, your sons, your attendants—all of you will work the land for him, bring in his bread and set the table before him. Yet your master's son, Mephibosheth, will break his bread in my house."

Fifteen sons and twenty attendants—these were Tziva's. "Everything my king and master sets before his servant," said Tziva to the king, "your attendant will fulfill."

"And before Mephibosheth," said the king, "is my own table, where he eats as a king's son."

Mephibosheth had a little son, Mica, and all who lived with the family of Tziva served Mephibosheth's line. In Jerusalem it was that Mephibosheth himself lived, since he ate at the king's table from then on. He was one whose feet were lame.

⋈

After all this, Ammon's king died, and ruling in his turn was Hanun, his son.

"Now I will grant lovingkindness to Hanun, son of Nachash," said David, "since his father's devotion was granted to me." David's hand was extended to him in consolation by his attendants, on behalf of his father. These servants of David proceeded to the land of the Ammonites.

But Ammonite leaders had advised Hanun, their ruler. "Will you believe David loves your father," they asked, "and sends friends? Are these servants of David not here instead to penetrate, explore, and expose the town?"

Hanun seized David's servants, shaved off half their beards, cut off half their battle dress—their buttocks exposed to the air—and booted them out.

When David got wind of this, he sent comfort to the men—they were humiliated. "Stay in Jericho while your beards grow back. Come back yourselves."

The Ammonites soon understood the stink before David was theirs, and they sent contracts to the Aramaeans in Beth-rehob and the Aramaeans in Zoba for twenty thousand foot soldiers, as well as a thousand more from King Maacah and twelve thousand men from Ishtob.

When David got word of this, he sent out Joab and all the veteran military.

The Ammonites marched out of their town gate and opened a front right there, while the Aramaeans of Zoba, Rehob, Ish-tob, and Maacah were organized by themselves in the field.

Joab could see himself exposed from behind if he met the front, so he chose the pick of all Israels men and assembled them against the Aramaeans. The remaining troops he put under the hand of Abishai, his brother, to array opposite the Ammonites.

"If the Aramaeans are too strong for me," he said, "you will come back to help."

"If the Ammonites are too strong for you, I will come

to back you up. Be bold and boundless in the eyes of our people and beyond the cities of God, and Yahweh can do as he pleases."

Joab and all his men advanced into position for battle, and the Aramaeans fled before his eyes. The Ammonites saw it—the Aramaeans fleeing—and fell back before Abishai, into their city. Joab returned to Jerusalem, the Ammonites overcome.

The Aramaeans then understood they were outdone in the eyes of Israel, and they pulled themselves together.

Hadadezer contacts the Aramaeans who are on the other side of the river and orders them to come to Helam. Shobach, captain of Hadadezers army, was at its head.

As David hears of this, he gathers all of Israel's men, heads across the Jordan, and also comes to Helam. The Aramaeans fall back into position against him, and battle David.

Before Israel's eyes the Aramaeans turned to flee, but the men of seven hundred Aramaean chariots were cut off by David, along with forty thousand horsemen—Shobach, their head, was cut down there.

All the kings in service to Hadadezer beheld their downfall. They turned to peace, turned into servants of Israel. The Aramaeans turned away from the extended hand of the Ammonites after this.

⌘

Here we are: a year was passing, and it is the season best for the wars of kings. David sends out Joab, his own retinue, and all of Israel's army, and they bring the Ammonites to their knees, besieging Rabbah. Meanwhile, David lingered in Jerusalem.

It happens one late afternoon that David rises from his bed, takes a walk around the palace roof, and from there, his glance falls upon a woman in her bath. The woman appeared very beautiful in his eyes.

David sent messengers to uncover more about the woman. "Of course, that must be Bathsheba," someone said, "the daughter of Eliam and wife of Uriah, the Hittite."

Now David sent his assistants—they besieged her—and she enters before his eyes. He lay with her in his bed, since her period had passed and she was purified, and then she returned to her house.

The woman conceived and sent word—"I am pregnant," she revealed to David.

Now word from David reaches Joab—"Have Uriah the Hittite sent to me"—and Joab conveyed Uriah to David.

David questions Uriah when he enters, wanting to know how Joab fared, how the forces were doing, how the war was going.

"Go home and bathe your feet," David directed Uriah, and as he went out of the king's palace a spread of meats from the king was sent down to him.

But Uriah bedded down at the palace gate, in the quarters of his king's courtiers, and did not descend to his own house.

David was told—"Uriah did not proceed to his house"— and confronted him with these words: "Haven't you come from the road? Why didn't you return to your house?"

"The ark rests in a tent," Uriah said to David. "Israel, Judah—they are encamped—my commander, Joab, and your own regiment camp in the open. Do I just go into my own house, eat and drink, and sleep with my wife? On your life—and as flesh breathes—I cannot do that."

"Then rest today as well," said David, "and tomorrow you will go out." So Uriah lodged in Jerusalem the rest of the day and next, when David had him summoned to eat and drink in the king's presence until he was made intoxicated. Yet in the evening, instead of going home, Uriah returns to bed down among Israel's courtiers.

Here we are: in the morning, David composes a letter for Joab, sending it by Uriah's hand. "Move Uriah into the spearhead of the fighting," his letter read, "and then fall back until he's laid bare to his death."

So it happens: Joab explores his siege of the city and moves Uriah into a probing unit of fighters. The defenders of the city thrust out and attack Joab, and some of the lives of David's servants are lost, Uriah the Hittite fallen among the dead.

Presently Joab conveyed to David a thorough account of the fighting, directing the messenger to say: "When you finish telling the king everything about the war, the king may be furious and ask, 'Why did you approach so close to the city when you struck—too dumb to remember they could shoot from the wall? So who killed Abimelech, son of Jerubbesheth—if it wasn't a woman dropping a piece of millstone on him from the wall at The-bez, blotting him out? Why advance so close to the wall?' Now you will add: 'Your servant Uriah the Hittite is among the dead.'"

Out the messenger went, arriving before David and announcing precisely what Joab had directed. "It seemed their men were succeeding against us," recounted the messenger to David, "coming out to attack us in the open, but we pushed them back to their gate. Their archers then shot at your men from the wall, and some of the king's servants fell. Your servant Uriah the Hittite is among the dead."

Said David to the messenger, "Tell Joab this: 'Do not become disturbed about it. The sword cuts down one as well as another.

Strengthen your attack on the city, penetrate it.' And offer him comfort."

As Uriah's wife comprehends the words telling of her husband Uriah's death, she wails for her husband. The period of mourning passes, and David conveys his wishes: he has her conveyed to his palace, where she becomes his wife and bears him a son.

It was a disloyal thing David had done before the eyes of Yahweh.

⌘

Now Yahweh sent Nathan to David. Nathan went to him, to tell: "Two men were in the same city, one rich, the other, poor. The rich man had a legion of sheep and cattle—the poor man had nothing but a little ewe lamb that he had bought. He cared for her, and it grew up together with him and his children. It shared his own morsels of food, drank from his cup, and snuggled in his lap—it was like a daughter to him.

"It happened a traveler visited the rich man, but when it

came to making a meal for this visitor stopping with him, he spared his own flocks and herds and took instead the poor man's lamb. And then he fixed it for the man who had come to him."

David's face was ablaze with fury against the man. "As Yahweh lives, the life of the man who did that will not be spared," said David to Nathan. "He will replace the lamb four times over, because he spared no gesture of kindness in this deed."

But Nathan said to David, "You are that man. Here is what Yahweh, the God of Israel, says: 'I anointed you king over Israel, I released you from Saul's grasp. I gave you your master's house, your master's wives fell in your lap. I gave you the House of Israel and Judah, and if that is not enough, I would double and quadruple it. Why then have you defied Yahweh's desire—disloyal before his eyes? You have dispatched Uriah the Hittite with sword, turned his wife into your wife, cut him down by the blade of the Ammonites.

"'So be it: the sword will never depart from your house, because you have been disloyal to me, grasped the hand of the wife of Uriah the Hittite to be your wife.'

"So says Yahweh: 'Look well: I will uncover disloyalty for you in your own house. I will deliver your wives, before your very eyes, to your neighbor, and he will lay with them under this very sun. Since you did this in secret, I will make it happen before the eyes of all Israel. It will be broad daylight.'"

David said, "I have betrayed Yahweh." And Nathan answered David, "Yahweh has dispatched your disloyalty away from himself—you will not die. Still, your deed bears out contempt before Yahweh's enemies—the child born to you will have to die."

As Nathan walked back home, it turns out Yahweh encounters David's child, born of Uriah's wife—it is deathly ill.

David besieges God for the child: he fasted, hid himself, lay all night on the ground. The senior advisers in the palace stood over him and tried to coax him up but he could not bear them now, nor would he eat with them.

Look: seven days pass and the child is dead. But David's attendants are panicked to tell him the child has died—and among each other, they say, "He couldn't bear us when we spoke while the child was alive—what terror will grip him when we tell him the child is dead?"

Noticing that his servants are whispering, David understands that the child is dead. "Is the child dead?" he asks. "Departed," they say.

David rises from the ground, bathes and oils himself, changes into fresh clothes, and goes to the House of Yahweh, prostrating himself. He returns to his own house, requests food—they set it before him, and so he eats.

"Why do you bear yourself in this way?" asked his courtiers. "You fasted and wept for the child when he was sick, and now when he is dead, you go out and eat a meal."

He replied, "I fasted and wept while the child was still alive, because I thought, 'How can one know if God will spare some kindness for me, and allow the child to live?' Now that he is dead, what is the use of fasting? Can I bring him back again? I may go to him, but he can never come back to me."

David consoles Bathsheba, his wife—he goes to her and

lays with her—she bears a son whom she named Solomon—and Yahweh loves him, sending a name by the prophet Nathan's hand: Jedidiah he calls him, beloved of Yahweh.

Meanwhile, Joab had struck the Ammonite city of Rabbah, imperiling the royal grounds. Messengers from Joab arrived before David, saying: "I have struck Rabbah and captured their water supply. Assemble the rest of the army, besiege the city and capture it, or else my name will be linked to it, if I take it myself."

David summons the rest of the army, besieges the city and takes it. Then he takes the gold crown from the head of the royal idol, weighing about a hundred pounds, and from it the jewel—to be fitted on the head of David. He also bears off a massive amount of spoils from the city.

The citizens within were conveyed out, and he put them under the rule of saws and sledges and iron axes, or settled them into brickmaking. All Ammonite cities were treated equally, until David and the army could depart for Jerusalem.

⚶

Much has happened, but now look closely: it becomes clear that Absalom, David's son, has a beautiful sister, Tamar her name, and a son of David, Amnon, loves her. But Amnon is sick with a mess of feelings for his sister Tamar—she is a virgin, besides—and it is a forbidding task to imagine what to do with her.

However, Amnon had a friend in Jonadab, the son of David's brother Shimah, and Jonadab was quite an intelligent man. "You are a prince," he told him, "so why are you just dragging yourself through these days? Can't you tell me?"

"I love Tamar, the sister of Absalom, my brother," Amnon told him.

Now Jonadab says, "Lie in your bed and make believe you are sick, and when your father comes to see you, say to him, 'Allow my sister Tamar to come and make my supper. Permit her to fix a meal in my presence, so I can see what it is, and grant that she serve me with her own hands.'"

Amnon lay down and made himself sick. The king came to see him, and Amnon pleaded, "Please, allow my sister Tamar to come and fix some cakes before my eyes, and permit her to feed them to me."

David sent word for Tamar at home: "Go to your brother Amnon's house, and make him a meal." Tamar goes to the house of her brother Amnon, while he is lying in bed—then, she prepares dough and kneads it into cakes while he watches, and she bakes the cakes. She finds a pan and serves them, but he turns down the food.

"Let the men all leave," Amnon says, and the servants depart.

"Bring the food to my room, so you can feed me," Amnon implores Tamar. But as she brings them into the room to eat, he embraces her: "Come lie with me, sister," he says.

"No, my brother, do not rape me," she said, "these things are not done in Israel. Do not embrace contempt. Where would I go with such a smear? And you, you will become a joke in Israel. Please, speak to the king, and he will not turn you away from me." But he will not listen to her, stronger than she, he pushes her down and lies with her.

Afterward, Amnon felt a great disgust with her—now his dislike of her was greater than the love he had borne. "Get dressed and leave," Amnon said to her.

"No, not now," she replied, "to send me away is a coarser thing than the first contempt you held me in." But he would not listen to her.

He called his personal servant, and said, "Take this woman out of my sight, and lock the door behind her." She is wearing a many-colored gown, the customary clothes for princesses who are still virgins—as the servant takes her outside and bars the door behind her.

But Tamar puts dirt on her head, and rips the gown of many colors she is dressed in—and she tears at her hair, and goes away screaming.

"Was your brother Amnon the one who did this?" asked Absalom, her brother. "For now, sister, be silent about it—he is your brother. Do not dwell on it." Tamar stayed in her brother Absalom's house, but she was crushed.

Word came to King David of all these things, and he was furious. Absalom would not speak to his brother Amnon, neither a good word nor bad, yet Absalom was disgusted with Amnon for raping his sister Tamar.

What happens now—a full two years later, when Absalom is having a sheepshearing in Baalhazor, which is next to Ephraim—is that he invites all the king's sons. Absalom goes to the king and says, 'Your servant is making a major sheepshearing. If it pleases you, will the king and his courtiers accompany your servant?"

"No, my son, we should not all go," the king said to Absalom. "It is too burdensome for you." Absalom urged him to go, but he would not, bidding him farewell.

"If not," said Absalom, "please allow my brother Amnon to accompany us."

The king replied, "Let him not go with you." But Absalom persisted, and he let Amnon and all the princes go with him.

Absalom gave these instructions to his men: "Pay attention to Amnon, and when the wine goes to his head and I say strike, then kill him. Show no fear and remember: haven't I ordered you? Be strong and act with confidence."

Absalom's servants do to Amnon as Absalom instructed, alarming all the other princes, who climb on their mules and flee.

Now it happens they are still on the road when this news reaches David: Absalom has killed all the king's sons and not one survives.

Alarmed, the king rises and rips apart his clothes and lies on the ground, with all his attendants standing over him in their torn coats. But Jonadab, the son of David's brother Shimah, declares: "My master must not believe all the young princes are dispatched. Amnon alone is dead, as was Absalom's intention ever since he raped his sister Tamar. So the king my master cannot believe for an instant that all the king's sons are dead, when only Amnon is departed."

Meanwhile, Absalom had departed with his life.

Now the sentinel spots a large group as it suddenly appears coming around the back side of the hill opposite.

"Look, the princes," says Jonadab to the king. "As I am your attendant, my words accompany the men." It happens, when he has hardly finished speaking, that the princes arrive and burst into tears, and the king broke out sobbing, as did all his retinue, uncontrollably.

But Absalom had fled, gone to Talmai, King Ammihud of Geshur's son. Yet David grieved for his son day after day. Absalom remained in Geshur three years. King David's heart ached to see Absalom but he was consoled by now for Amnon—what was the use, seeing he was dead.

⬯

When Joab son of Zeruiah noticed that the king's heart would not bend from Absalom, he sent word to Tekoah and hired a wise woman, and instructed her: "Act like a mourner and dress in mourning clothes and without makeup—play a woman who has grieved long days for someone vanished. Go to the king and perform this part for him." Now Joab puts the words in her mouth.

The woman of Tekoah speaks to the king, but first prostrates herself, and calls out—her face to the ground—"Save me, Your Majesty."

"What's wrong with you?" the king asks.

"I am a widow, my husband is dead," she begins. "Your humble housemaid had two sons, who began to fight out in the field, and there was no one around to stop them, until one of them knocked the other down, killing him. And now the whole family has turned against your humble housemaid, and they cry, 'Turn over the one who struck down his brother, so we may take his life for taking a brother's, even if we have to extinguish the heir as well.' That is how they would extinguish the last coal left burning on my hearth, and leave my husband without name or vestige on the face of the earth."

"Go home," said the king to the woman. "I will rule on your behalf."

"Your Majesty the king," said the woman of Tekoah to the king, "let the stain be mine and on my father's line—let the king and his throne remain clean."

The king replied, "Let anyone say another thing to you—I will have him brought here, and he will not touch you again."

"Let Your Majesty remember Yahweh, your God," she said, "and hold back the unbound hands of revenge, before they smash my son."

The king replied, "On Yahweh's life, not one hair of your son's will touch the ground."

"Let your humble housemaid say one word more to Your Majesty," the woman said. "Say it," he said.

"Why have you acted in the same way you yourself played out a similar plot against God's people?" the woman began. "In the judgment you have made for me you condemn yourself—since you turn away from your own outcast.

"No man escapes death—we are like water drained into the ground that cannot be collected again. But God will not turn from a life that can make this judgment: no man should remain an outcast.

"That is why I have come to appeal to Your Majesty, alarmed by those people. Your humble housemaid thought, 'I will speak to the king and what I ask, be granted by a king. The king may listen, and sever the grasp of those who would sever me and my son from their God-given inheritance.'

"Finally, your humble housemaid said to herself, 'The word of His Majesty may bring peace. He sees right from wrong like God's own angel.' May Yahweh, your God, be with you."

Now the king says to the woman, "Do not withhold from me what I may ask." And the woman answers, "Speak, Your Majesty."

"Is Joab behind you in any of this?" asks the king.

"As sure as you live, Your Majesty, I cannot turn from what you say," she says. "True, your servant Joab directed me, putting all these words in the mouth of your housemaid. To shape the true purpose of these words, your servant Joab withheld his role. But Your Majesty is wise as an angel who can see through all earthly things."

Turning to Joab, the king says, "It is done. Depart, and return my boy Absalom again."

Joab kneels to the ground, then prostrates himself, thanking the king. "This day," says Joab, "your servant knows he has your faith. The king has performed his servant's purpose."

Now Joab proceeds and arrives in Geshur, bringing Absalom to Jerusalem. "To his own house take him," said the king, "and to my face may he not be taken." So Absalom returned to his house, and did not see the king's face. Yet throughout Israel there was none to be admired as Absalom was, for his beauty. It was said that from the sole of his foot to the hair on his head there was no defect in him.

And when he cut his hair, which he had to do every year, as it grew too heavy, the fallen hair weighed two hundred shekels by the royal weight.

Absalom had three sons, and a daughter whose name was also Tamar, and she too was a beauty. He lived in Jerusalem two years without appearing before the king. Then Absalom sent for Joab, who could arrange for him to be presented to the king, but Joab would not come to him. He sent for him again, and again he would not come. He turned to his servants: "You know that Joab's field is next to mine, and he plants barley there. Go and set it on fire." Absalom's servants set the field on fire.

Now Joab comes right away to Absalom's house, saying to him, "Why have your servants set fire to my field?"

"I sent for you to come here," Absalom replies. "I want to send you to the king to present my words: 'Why did I leave Geshur? I would be better off if I were still there. Now I would be taken to the king, and if there is some defect in me, why then, take my life.'"

Joab goes to the king, presents all this, and in response, Absalom is summoned. He comes to the king and throws himself facedown to the ground before him. The king kissed Absalom.

⊠

Sometime afterward, Absalom provided himself with a chariot, horses, and fifty men to run before him. He took to rising early and stationing himself by the road to the city gates, so when a man had a case that was pending before the king, Absalom called out to him, "What city are you

161

PART II

SEEING

Samuel

from?" When he heard, "Your servant is from one of the tribes in Israel," Absalom said, "I am sure that your claim is fair and just, but no one is assigned to you by the king to hear it. If I were made judge in the land," Absalom went on, "everyone with a legal dispute that came before me would be sure to get fair justice."

Further, if a man approached who bowed to him, Absalom extended his hand, took hold of him, and kissed him. He did this to every Israelite who came to the king for judgment. With this practice, Absalom won the hearts of the men of Israel.

Here we are: four years have gone by. "Allow me to go to Hebron and perform the vow to Yahweh I have made," Absalom said to the king. "Your servant vowed these words when I lived in Geshur of Aram: 'If Yahweh takes me back to Jerusalem, I will serve him.'" The king answered "Go in peace." He set out for Hebron.

But Absalom sent his attendants to all the tribes of Israel to say, "When you hear the sound of the horn, announce that Absalom has become king in Hebron." Meanwhile, two hundred men left Jerusalem with Absalom. Having been invited, they went in good faith, suspecting nothing. Absalom also asked Ahithophel the Gilonite, David's counselor, to come from Gilo and be present as the promised sacrifices were fulfilled. The conspiracy gained strength, as the numbers swelled at Absalom's side.

One of them, however, comes to David: "The hearts of Israel are turned toward Absalom." David turns to all the courtiers with him in Jerusalem: "We must be prepared to run, or none of us will escape from Absalom. We must get out fast, or he will intercept us and we will meet with disaster, the city turned to the sword." And the king's courtiers say to a man, "Whatever my lord the king judges, your servant is prepared."

Now the king went out, followed by his entire household. But he left ten of his women, concubines, to look after the palace. As the king was going, the people following behind, he stopped at the last house.

All his followers marched past him, including Cherethites and Pelethites and Gittites, all of them—and six hundred men who had accompanied him from Gath, also marched by the king.

The king said to Ittai the Gittite, "Why should you too go with us? Go back and stay with the new king, for you are a foreigner and you are also an exile from your country. And you arrived only yesterday. Do I make you wander around with us today, when I must run wherever I can? Go back, and take your companions with you, and lovingkindness go with you."

"As the Lord Yahweh lives and as my lord the king lives," said Ittai to the king, "wherever the king goes, whether in death or life, there your servant will be."

"Then go on by," said David to Ittai. And Ittai the Gittite and all his men and the children who were with him passed by.

The whole landscape was weeping aloud as the army passed by. The king crossed the Kidron Valley, as all the troops had crossed it, on the road to the wilderness.

Look well: Zadok was there also, and the Levites carrying the Ark of the Covenant of God, which they set down until all the people had passed out of the city. Abiathar also had appeared.

But the king said to Zadok, "Take the Ark of God back to the city. If Yahweh looks kindly on me, he will bring me back and show it to me again—and in its resting place. But if he should say, 'I do not want you,' I am ready. He can do with me as he pleases."

The king spoke again to Zadok the priest: "Are you not a seer? Return to the city in peace, with your two sons—your own son Ahimaaz and Abiathar's son, Jonathan. See well. I will stay in the protection of the wilderness until word comes from you to inform me."

Zadok and Abiathar brought the Ark of God back to Jerusalem, and they stayed on there, while David went up the slope of the Mount of Olives, weeping as he ascended, his head covered and walking barefoot. And all the people who were with him covered their heads and wept as they went up.

Now David heard: "Ahithophel is among the conspirators with Absalom." And David responded, "May it please Yahweh to turn the sagacity of Ahithophel into lunacy."

David reaches the top of mount, where people have kissed the ground before God, and now look: Hushai the Archite is there to meet him, but with his coat ripped open and earth upon his head. "If you go on with us, you become our burden," David says to him. "But if you go back to the city and say to Absalom, 'I will be your servant, O king. I was your father's servant in the past—as I will now be yours,' then, on my behalf, you may undo the sage advice of Ahithophel.

"Besides, the priests Zadok and Abiathar will be there with you, and with everything that you hear in the king's palace you may inform Zadok and Abiathar, the priests. Listen well: their two sons are there with them, Zadok's son Ahimaaz and Abiathar's son, Jonathan, and through them you may inform me of everything you hear."

So it is: Hushai, the friend of David, reaches the city as Absalom was entering Jerusalem.

⊠

David passes a little beyond the summit and now look: Ziba the servant of Mephibosheth is coming toward him with a pair of saddled asses, and upon them two hundred loaves of bread, one hundred cakes of raisin, one hundred cakes of summer figs, and jar of wine.

"What are you doing with these?" the king asked Ziba. "The asses are for Your Majesty's family to ride on," Ziba answered, "and the bread and figs are for your attendants to eat, and the wine is to drink by those who are exhausted in the wilderness."

"And where is your master's son?" the king continued. "He is staying in Jerusalem," Ziba told the king. "He said to us: 'Tomorrow, the House of Israel will give me back the throne of my grandfather.'"

"Then all that belongs to Mephibosheth will now be yours," the king said to Ziba. And Ziba replied, "My lord, may it please Your Majesty that I deserve such graciousness, a minion such I.

King David approaches Bahurim, and now look: a member comes toward him of Saul's family. His name:

Shimei son of Gera, and he is hurling curses as he comes. He throws stones at David and all King David's courtiers, while all the people and all the warriors stand at his right and his left.

"Get out, get out, you beast, you outcast," are among the curses that flew. "Yahweh is paying you back for all your crimes against the family of Saul, after you took his place. Yahweh is delivering your throne to your son Absalom, and you are on the run because you are an outlaw."

Abishai son of Zeruiah said to the king, "Why let that dead dog abuse my lord the king? Let me go over and take off his head."

"What has this to do with you, you sons of Zeruiah?" the king stepped in. "He is abusive only because Yahweh told him to curse David, so who is to say, 'Why did you do that?'"

David turned to Abishai and all the courtiers: "If my son, out of my own loins, is hoping to kill me, how much more this Benjaminite. Let him go on with his curses, since Yahweh has told him to. It may happen that Yahweh will look upon me kindly in my punishment and reward me for the curses spoken today."

So David and his men continued on their way, while Shimei walked alongside on the slope of the hill, cursing him as he walked, and throwing stones at him and flinging dirt.

The king and all who were accompanying him arrived exhausted. They rested there. Meanwhile, Absalom and all the people, the men of Israel, arrived in Jerusalem, together with Ahithophel.

When Hushai the Archite, David's friend, appeared

before Absalom, Hushai said to him, "Long live the king. Long live the king."

But Absalom said, "Is this your kindness to your friend? Why didn't you go with your friend?"

"No," Hushai replied. "I am for the one whom Yahweh and this people and all the men of Israel have chosen, and I will stay with him. Besides, whom should I serve, if not David's son? I was your father's servant in the past—as I will now be yours."

Absalom turned to Ahithophel, "What would you advise us to do?"

"Have intercourse with your father's concubines," Ahithophel advised him, "these whom he left to mind the palace. When all Israel hears that you have challenged the anger of your father, all who support you will be strengthened in resolve."

So they pitched a tent for Absalom on the roof, and Absalom lay with his father's concubines before the eyes of all Israel.

In those days, a man accepted the advice Ahithophel gave as if he had asked an oracle of God. That is how the advice of Ahithophel was respected, both by David and by Absalom.

⋈

"Let me pick twelve thousand men and I will proceed tonight in pursuit of David," Ahithophel was now saying to Absalom. "I will come upon him when he is sad and exhausted, and I will put him into a panic. As all the forces with him run away, I will kill the king alone.

"In this way I will bring all his people back to you. When

they have all come back—except the man you are after—all the people will be at peace."

The advice was pleasing to Absalom and all the elders of Israel.

"Summon Hushai the Archite as well," Absalom was saying, "so we can hear what he too has to say."

When Hushai appeared before Absalom, he heard: "This is what Ahithophel has advised. Shall we follow his advice? If not, what do you say?"

"This time the advice that Ahithophel has given is not good," Hushai said to Absalom. "You know that your father and his men are brave fighters," Hushai continued, "and they will be as desperate as a bear in the wild robbed of her cubs. Your father is too experienced a soldier to sleep among his men.

"Open your eyes and you will see that even now he must be hiding in one of the pits or in some other place. And if any of our men fall in the first attack, whoever hears of it will say, 'The forces that follow Absalom are being slaughtered.' Even if he is a brave man with the heart of a lion, he will be shaken—for all Israel knows that your father and the soldiers with him are ferocious fighters.

"Thus I advise that all Israel from Dan to Beersheba, that number as the sands of the sea, be called up to join you, and that you yourself march into battle. When we find him in whatever place he may be, we will fall upon him as the dew falling on the ground. No one will survive, neither he nor any of the men with him.

"And if he retreats into a city, all Israel will bring ropes to that city and drag its stones as far as the riverbed, until not even a pebble of it is left."

Absalom and all Israel agreed that the advice of Hushai the Archite was better than that of Ahithophel.

"Such and such is what Ahithophel advised Absalom and the elders of Israel," Hushai told Zadok and Abiathar, the priests, "and such and such is what I advised. Now send this message right away to David: 'Do not spend the night at the fords of the wilderness, but pass over at once, or else the king and all his forces will be overwhelmed and sunk.'"

Jonathan and Ahimaaz were staying at En-rogel, not wanting to risk being seen entering the city, and an outcast girl would go out to bring them word, and they would then go and acquaint King David. Yet a boy saw them and acquainted Absalom, so they left right away and came to the house of a man in Bahurim who had a well in his courtyard. They got down into it, as the wife found a cloth, spread it over the mouth of the well, and scattered groats on top of it, so that nothing would be noticed.

Absalom's servants came to the woman at the house, asking, "Where are Ahimaaz and Jonathan?" The woman said that they had crossed a bit beyond the water. They searched, but found nothing before they returned to Jerusalem.

Now look: they are gone, and the two come up from the well and go to inform King David. "Be prepared to cross the water quickly," they said to David, "for Ahithophel has advised such and such concerning you."

David and all the people with him pass over the Jordan, and by daybreak not one is left who has not reached the other side.

When Ahithophel saw that his advice had not been followed, he saddled his ass and went back to his hometown, where he ordered his affairs and then hanged himself. He was buried in his ancestral tomb.

David had already reached Mahanaim when Absalom and all the men of Israel with him crossed the Jordan.

Absalom had made Amasa army commander in place of Joab. Amasa was the son of a man named Ithra the Israelite, who had lain with Abigail, daughter of Nahash and sister of Joab's mother Zeruiah. Now the Israelites and Absalom made camp in the district of Gilead.

So it happens: David reaches Mahanaim, and Shobi son of Nahash from Rabbath-ammon, Machir son of Ammiel from Lo-devar, and Barzillai the Gileadite from Rogelim present couches, basins, and earthenware, along with wheat, barley, flour, parched grain, beans, lentils, honey, curds, a flock, and cheese from the herd for David and the people with him to eat. "The people must surely have grown hungry, and exhausted, and thirsty in the wilderness," they say.

※

David assembled the soldiers who were with him, naming captains for troops of thousands, and captains of hundreds. Out went the troops, one-third under the command of Joab, one-third under the command of Joab's brother Abishai son of Zeruiah, and a third under the command of Ittai the Gittite. "I myself will march out with you," David said to the troops.

"No!" they said. "For if some of us flee, the rest will not be concerned about us; even if half of us should die, the others will not be concerned about us. But you are worth ten thousand of us. Therefore, it is better for you to support us from the town."

The king said to them, "I will do whatever you think best."

So the king stood beside the gate as all the soldiers marched out by the hundreds and thousands. The king gave orders to Joab, Abishai, and Ittai: "Deal gently with my boy Absalom, for my sake." All the troops heard the king give the order about Absalom to all the officers.

The soldiers trooped out into the open to confront the Israelites, and the battle was fought in the forest of Ephraim. The Israelite army was routed by David's followers, and a great slaughter took place there that day—twenty thousand men.

The battle spread out over that whole region, and the forest seemed to devour more soldiers that day than the sword. Absalom encountered some of David's followers as he was riding on a mule, and as the mule passed under the tangled branches of a great terebinth, his hair got caught in the tree: he was suspended between heaven and earth but the mule under him kept going.

One of the men saw it and told Joab, "I have just seen Absalom hanging from a terebinth."

"You saw it!" Joab said to the man who told him. "Why didn't you kill him then and there? I would have owed you ten shekels of silver and a belt."

But the man answered Joab, "Even if I had a thousand shekels of silver in my hands, I would not raise a hand against the king's son. The king directed you, Abishai, and Ittai in our presence: 'Let no one touch my boy Absalom, for my sake.' If I betrayed myself—and nothing is hidden from the king—you would have stood aloof."

"Then I will not wait for you," said Joab. He took three darts in his hand and drove them into Absalom's chest. He was still alive in the thick growth of the terebinth, when ten of Joab's young arms-bearers closed in and struck at Absalom until he died.

Then Joab sounded the shofar, and the army halted their pursuit of the Israelites—Joab kept rein on the soldiers. They took Absalom and flung him into a large pit in the forest, and they piled up a huge heap of stones over it. Meanwhile, all the Israelites fled to their homes.

Keep in mind that while he was alive, Absalom had taken the pillar which is in the Valley of the King and set it up for himself, explaining, "I have no son to keep my name alive." He had named the pillar after himself, and it has been called Absalom's Monument to this day.

"Let me run and report," said Ahimaaz, son of Zadok, "that the Lord has avenged the king against his enemies."

But Joab said to him, "You will not be the one with the news today. You may bring news some other day, but you'll not bring any today—the king's son is dead." And Joab turned to an African: "Go tell the king what you have seen." The African bowed to Joab and ran off.

Ahimaaz, son of Zadok, insisted, "No matter what, let me run, too, behind the African." Joab asked, "Why run, my boy, when you have no news worth telling?" "I am going to run anyway." "Then run," he said. So Ahimaaz ran by way of the plain, and he passed the African.

David was sitting between the two gates. The watchman on the roof of the gate walked over to the city wall, and in the distance he saw a man running alone. The watchman called down and told the king—and the king said, "If he is alone, he has news to report." As he was coming nearer, the watchman saw another man running, and he called out to the gatekeeper, "There is another man running alone." And the king said, "That one, too, brings news."

"I can see that the first one runs like Ahimaaz, son of Zadok," said the watchman. The king answered: "He is a good man, and he comes with good news."

Ahimaaz called out and said to the king, "All is well." He kneeled, face to the ground, and said, "Praises to Yahweh, your God, who exposed to us the men who raised their hand against Your Majesty, the king."

The king asked, "Is my boy Absalom safe?" And Ahimaaz answered, "I saw a large crowd when Your Majesty's servant Joab was sending your humble servant off, but I don't know what it was about."

"Step aside and stand over there," said the king. He stepped aside and waited. Just then the African arrived, saying: "Let Your Majesty the king be informed that Yahweh has avenged you today against all who rebelled against you."

"Is my boy Absalom safe?" the king asked the African. The African replied, "May the enemies of Your Majesty the king and all who rose against you to do you harm turn out like that young man!"

The king shook. He mounted to the upper chamber of

the gateway and wept, moaning these words as he went, "My son Absalom! O my son, my son Absalom! If only I had died instead of you! O Absalom, my son, my son!"

⚙

Mark well: After Joab is told that the king is weeping and mourning over Absalom, the victory day turns into one of mourning for the whole army, as they hear that very day that the king grieves for his son. They steal into town that day like an army in shame, after running away in battle.

The king covers his face and keeps crying aloud, "O my son Absalom! O Absalom, my son, my son!" Joab comes to the king in his quarters, saying, "Today you have shamed the faces of all your followers, who this day saved your life, and the lives of your sons and daughters, and the lives of your wives and concubines, by showing love for those who hate you and hate for those who love you. You have made clear today that the officers and men mean nothing to you. I am sure that if Absalom were alive today and the rest of us dead, you would have preferred it.

"Now get yourself together, come out and placate your followers. I swear by Yahweh that if you do not come out, not a single man will remain with you overnight. That would be a greater disaster for you than any disaster that has struck you from your youth until now."

The king prepares himself, sits down in the gateway, and when the warriors are told that the king is sitting there, they all present themselves to the king.

Meanwhile the Israelites flee to their homes. All the people throughout the tribes of Israel were arguing: Some say, "The king saved us from the hands of our enemies, and he delivered us from the hands of the Philistines, and just now he had to escape the country because of Absalom. But Absalom, whom we anointed over us, has died in battle—why then do you sit idle instead of escorting the king back?"

The talk of all Israel reaches the king in his quarters. So King David sends this message to the priests Zadok and Abiathar: "Speak to the elders of Judah and say, 'Why should you be the last to bring the king back to his palace? You are my family, as my own flesh and blood. Why should you be the last to escort the king back?'

"And to Amasa say this, 'You are my own flesh and blood. May God do such and more to me if you do not become my army commander once and for all, in place of Joab.'"

Amasa changes the hearts of all the Judahites as one man. They send a message to the king: "Come back with all your followers."

The king started back, arriving at the Jordan as the Judahites come to Gilgal to meet the king and to bring him across the Jordan. Shimei son of Gera, the Benjaminite from Bahurim, hurried down with the Judahites to meet King David, accompanied by a thousand Benjaminites. And Ziba, the servant of the House of Saul, together with his fifteen sons and twenty slaves, rushed down to the Jordan ahead of the king while the crossing was being made, to escort the king's family over, and to do whatever he wished.

Shimei son of Gera flung himself before the king as he was about to cross the Jordan. He said to him, "May my lord not hold me guilty, nor remember the curses your servant committed on the day my lord the king left Jerusalem. May Your Majesty give it no thought. Your servant knows that he has offended, so I have come down today, the first of all the House of Joseph, to meet my lord the king."

But Abishai son of Zeruiah interrupted, "Shouldn't Shimei be put to death for that—cursing Yahweh's anointed one?"

"What has this to do with you, you sons of Zeruiah, that you should cross me today?" said the king. "Should a single Israelite be put to death today? Don't I know that today I am again king over Israel?"

Then the king turned to Shimei: "You shall not die," on which the king gave him his oath.

Mephibosheth, the grandson of Saul, also came down to meet the king. He had not pared his toenails, or trimmed his mustache, or washed his clothes from the day that the king left until the day he returned safe. When he arrived from Jerusalem, the king asked him, "Why didn't you come with me, Mephibosheth?"

"My lord the king, my own servant deceived me. I, your servant, planned to saddle my ass and ride on it and go with Your Majesty—for your servant is lame. Ziba has slandered your servant to my lord. But the king is like an angel of Yahweh, and may you do as pleases you. All the members of my father's family deserved only death from my lord the king, yet you brought your servant to eat at your table. What right have I to appeal further to Your Majesty?"

"You need not speak further," the king said to him. "I decree that you and Ziba shall divide the property." But

Mephibosheth answered, "Let him take it all, as long as my lord the king has come home safe."

Barzillai the Gileadite had come down from Rogelin and passed on to the Jordan with the king, to see him off at the Jordan. Barzillai was very old, eighty years of age, and he had provided the king with food during his stay at Mahanaim, since he was a very wealthy man. "Cross over with me," the king said to Barzillai, "and I will provide for you in Jerusalem at my side." But Barzillai said, "How many years are left to me that I should go up with Your Majesty to Jerusalem? I am now eighty years old. Can I tell the difference between good and bad? Can your servant taste what he eats and drinks? Can I still listen to the singing of men and women? Why then should your servant continue to be a burden to my lord the king? Your servant could barely cross the Jordan. Why should Your Majesty reward me so generously? Let your servant go back, and let me die in my own town, near the graves of my father and mother. But here is your servant Chimham—let him cross with my lord the king, and do for him as pleases you."

"Chimham shall cross with me," the king said, "and I will do for him as pleases *you*—and anything you want me to do, I will do for you."

All the people crossed the Jordan. When he was ready to cross, the king kissed Barzillai farewell, who returned to his home. The king passed on to Gilgal, with Chimham accompanying him. All the Judahite forces and part of the Israelite army escorted the king across.

Then all the men of Israel came to the king, saying, "Why did our cousins, men of Judah, steal you away and escort the king and his family across the Jordan, along with all Davids men?"

"Because the king is our relative," the men of Judah replied to the men of Israel. "Why should it upset you? Have we consumed anything that belongs to the king? Has he given us any gifts?"

But the men of Israel had an answer for the men of Judah: "We have ten parts in the king [ten tribes to your two], and in David, too, we have more than you. Why then have you slighted us? Were we not the first to propose that our king be brought back?"

However, the men of Judah prevailed over the men of Israel.

※

A beast named Sheba son of Bichri, a Benjaminite, happened to be there. He blew the horn and announced:
"We have no portion in David,
No part in Jesse's son!
Every man to his tent, O Israel!"
Watch: the men of Israel leave David and follow Sheba son of Bichri, while the men of Judah accompany their king from the Jordan to Jerusalem.

David goes to his palace in Jerusalem, and he takes the ten women concubines he had left to keep the palace and puts them in a secluded place. He will feed them, but he will not have intercourse with them. They will remain shut in retirement until the day they die, in living widowhood.

"Call up the men of Judah to my order," the king says to Amasa, "and report here three days from now." Amasa goes to call up Judah, but takes longer than the time allotted. David turns to Abishai: "This Sheba son of Bichri will bring us more trouble than Absalom. Take your lord's servants and pursue him, before he reaches a walled city and escapes us."

Joab's men, the Cherethites and Pelethites, and all the warriors, march out behind him. In pursuit of Sheba son of Bichri, they leave Jerusalem, and just near the great stone in Gibeon, Amasa appears before them. Joab is wearing his military dress, with his sword fixed over it and fastened around his waist in its sheath, and as he steps forward, it falls out.

"How are you, brother?" Joab says to Amasa, and with his right hand Joab grabs hold of Amasa's beard as if to kiss him. Amasa was not on his guard against the sword in Joab's left hand, and Joab drives it into his belly so that his entrails pour out on the ground and he dies. He does not need to strike him a second time.

Joab and his brother Abishai then go off in pursuit of Sheba son of Bichri, while one of Joab's followers stands by the corpse, announcing, "Those who approve of Joab, and who are on David's side, follow Joab."

Meanwhile Amasa lays in the middle of the road, drenched in his blood, and the man sees that everyone is stopping. When he realizes that all the people are going to stand stark still, he drags Amasa from the road into the field and covers him with a garment. Once he is removed from the road, everyone continues to follow Joab in pursuit of Sheba son of Bichri.

⊠

King David was now old, advanced in years, and though they covered him with bedclothes, he could never feel warm.

"A young virgin must be found for my lord the king," his courtiers said to him, "to care for Your Majesty, as his attendant. And let her lie in your bosom—then my lord the king will be warm."

So they looked for a beauty through the whole territory of Israel. They found Abishag the Shunammite and brought her to the king.

The girl was extraordinarily beautiful. She became the king's attendant and cared for him, but the king did not enter her.

The scope of Isaiah is beyond any one poet, yet there is a core of vision holding the book together. Several poets, writing centuries apart, shared a unique sensibility manifested in oracles and other poetic forms. Scholarship used to call this sensibility "the school of Isaiah," allowing for many other poets whose work has been lost or who acted largely as curators and restorers of an earlier Isaiah's text. For example, the autobiographical section that begins Chapter 6 was clearly not written by the poet who set down his autobiographical experience at the beginning of Chapter 40.

Taken together, the chapters in Isaiah do not progress as a narrative but present a serial building up of passion and vision, an intuitive architecture of feeling. I've tried to knit together a representation of at least three of the school of Isaiah poets. The feeling for consciousness is fundamental, as it struggles to free itself from conventional pieties. To restore a sense of the original poetry's spokenness and withering irony, I attempted to bend modern poetic practice toward playing the grandiose (or prophetic) "I" against the intimacy of a conversational voice. In a similar manner, the first Isaiah lent his oracular voice to the Isaiah poets who came after.

In a central metaphor for prophecy, Isaiah represents self-knowledge as a light to others: the visionary power hidden in every man and woman, beginning with the most oppressed. Isaiah becomes a testament to self-consciousness, illustrating how language itself— the quality of listening to it—bonds poet to creator.

The poets of the school of Isaiah extend five hundred years after the original prophet in the eighth century BCE. Consider how our religious institutions today prefer their religion in more manageable prose forms. In the same way, the religious establishment during some ancient periods tried to limit poets to the realms of prayer and wisdom literature. Facing this opposition, the poets of the prophetic schools sharpened their poetics further.

The depth of poetry puzzles many readers, who still turn to prose exegesis. But take away the sound, metaphors, and images of Isaiah and we're left merely with a mummified corpse of its meaning. Or worse, we're in the hands of interpreters who take the prophetic metaphors too literally. Parts of Isaiah have been characterized as primitive for their "elaborate ferocity," for instance. Yet, as the critic C. C. Torrey wrote long ago in The Second Isaiah, "The prophet was not bloodthirsty, he was only a poet."

There is a broad emotional range to the Isaiah poets, from the fierce satire of Chapter 14 to the tender consolation of Chapter 40. A desire to transform loss into creative vision prevails. "We've papered over loss," from Chapter 52, is typical of an Isaiah poet's refusal to leave it alone. The poets writing in Isaiah's spirit project this self-awareness into the world: "we wandered away / lost in ourselves / we were all nations / servants of our own / interests . . ."

The passion is devoutly self-critical. Opening to pain, to an identity with the lowest, the poorest, the most powerless individual, the poets and prophet become one in recognizing the imaginative freedom this openness allows. For poets, the freedom yields timeless metaphors: "all flesh is grass / and the reality of love is there / wild flowers in the field . . ."

isaiah

CHAPTER I

Listen universe
and ear of earth   turn
to words of your creator

they are witnesses   tuned
to the source of memory
invisible to all that changes:

I brought up children
held them in my presence
and they turn from me

deaf and blind
when even the dumb ox knows
who holds his food

an ass
the trough
its master fills

but Israel knows nothing
of its root in me
sees nothing of where

they come from
who brought them up
nobody knew them helpless and wide-eyed

and they can't stop to remember
to think or to hear themselves thinking
lost in themselves

mindless people
so heavy with repressed guilt
they think they walk lightly when they crawl

fathers in masks of self-pity
sons in poses of self-righteous
pettiness

their backs to creation
they pushed it out of mind
and turned

condemned it as blindly as a slum
they grew up in
they see their true home as a slum

and they refuse to see it
looking through mirror glasses
walking through a false landscape

of their own making   through the rubble
of their distorted image of themselves
grossly attenuated

running away as they run out of time
from the father of their spirit
from the saving dimension of depth

and history reaching back   memory
unfolding space and time
beyond them   beyond change

what part of this people's body
isn't bruised yet
from turning away

still lusting for internal bruises
in the claws of a soulless world
a head naked to despair

a heart exposed to desperation
from bottoms of the feet
to head crown

not a spot on your body
untouched
by the painted hand of vengeance

the revenge of men
painting themselves
with raw animal pride

raw canvas bejeweled
with open wounds and blisters
open to infection

no clean hand to unroll the bandage
no tender selfless arms
to cleanse your spirit

a country totally desolate
cities of ash heaps
fields of mud

trampled by strangers
hordes of them streaming by
leaving you a bystander

in your own land
on desolation row
the daughter of Zion

dear Jerusalem left standing alone
scarecrow
a shed in a cucumber field

a shack in the sea of a vineyard
a ghetto a slum holding on
as if by its teeth

a remnant of survivors
and if the Lord of creation turned his back on us
we'd only be a painful memory   *no* memory!

a tombstone overturned face down
Sodom and Gomorrah
the dark side of the moon

listen to the words
of your creator
blind leaders of Sodom

tune your ears
to the witness of the universe
deaf people of Gomorrah

look up from the self-indulgence
of gilt-edged prayers
the sentimental eyewash

of the time you "sacrifice"
the money of your ritual donations
to make yourself feel better

this is your witness speaking
I've seen enough
of your distracted meditation and mysteries

measured in time and money
heard enough of your sheepish sighs
for a pastoral future

swallowed enough of your toasts
to institutions of repression
smelled enough of your smokestacks

felt enough bodies fall
to their knees in
bloodless words

of posed "uplift"
before monumental paperweights
pious backdrops for photographs

who asked you for pictures
of righteousness
when you come to look for me

trampling through my sanctuary
my library of unwritten
prayer from the heart

with your precious albums
your unreal books
your desperate fantasy of prayer

I want no more sacred mirrors
of yourselves
the microphones of your empty voices

praying for an answer
a travesty of sympathy
like a tape-recorded answer would be

you are so locked in yourselves
your coming out to worship
to readings of my books

becomes the ghost of true spirit
superstitions
of new moons and sabbaths

I can't stand your weird impersonations
of spiritual beings
your minutes of meditation

and Sundays off
I hate that cheap
indulgence of spirit

heavier than lead
I can't bear it
it crushes spirit

I hide from you in light
when you close your eyes
to look for me

when you bow your heads
your prayers will fall
to the floor

your ears are filled with blood
of your own hearts pounding
I won't listen to that desperation

your hands are full of blood
you turn to me
with the blood memory of your slaughtered conscience

wash yourselves
clean your desperate wish
to be loved   clinging

like cheap perfume to your soul
remove your cloaks of status
your veils of sincerity

beneath them you grope for me
like blind animals
laying hands on your brothers and sisters

climbing over them desperately
to appear self-satisfied
before the mirror

before the community of lies
but there in the bed of your hands
your evil lies

there are no roofs over you
in my sight
let me not see it

stop the oppression
learn to see it
respond openly

ask questions
love can answer
what are those beggars on your streets

those window shoppers
those like you depressed
too desperate to even know it

look at them and give
your attention
place your hope in their hands

for they are fatherless and motherless
widows and widowers
totally alone

make them your cause
reach for them
cause them to see you are human

let us come together again
openly says
your creator

though the hands of your desire
are scarlet
they will be clean as sunshine

falling effortlessly
over the city
light as snow light as fleece of lamb

if you are listening
the world will be open
to you

if you hide your heart
you will be slaughtered like cattle
by the hands of desperation

the mouth
of my creator
has spoken

How the beautiful daughter my city
clean light falling around her
has become a whore

she opened the door for love
and light came into her
and shone in her eyes

now you murderers stand naked
in her windows
your house smeared with gaudy paint

of status and power
cheap façades all
sense of proportion lost

in the violent rush for metal
the clasping of silver
to your breasts

the vintage of your heart
love pressed deep in your blood
has become cheap wine

the cream of your people
has mixed with the blood of thieves
in the dark

your leaders are like terrorists
of spirit
spilling your lifeblood

everyone loves to steal
and turn the pages of my books
into worthless money

they hide their loneliness away
in dark asylums and turn
away from orphans

turn away from the naked heart
open to me   exposed by loss
my widows and orphans

leaders lost in the cheap reflection
their metal armor casts
armor they dress their image in

to be princes for whores
lose themselves in silence
in beds of cheap clichés

and so my creator speaks
to those who've repressed him
who oppress each other

Oh I'm tired of defenses
I'm going to lean on
the world's tinsel fences

and crush them
the burden of guilt will fall
on you

with the weight of silence
I will open your hands
as if to cover your eyes from light

and the paper in your fists
will fall
the armor thin as paper

money and contracts: symbols
of the memory loss
that is repressed

instead I'll forgive
with the pure fire of feeling
remembered

you'll share the weight
of each other   with care
the burden of vision

will take form again
in words
as in the beginning

of our speaking   our book
our text of light
it will be *remembered*

with care
in order
to forgive

to forget   to need
to create again
a nation

you will come home
to see yourselves as you are
children of light

to say it in what you do
city of light city of song
city of arms that are strong

that are men and women open inside
embracing
my daughter Jerusalem

Zion will be called
an open ear will be its calling
a light in the window

of the home you can
go back to
the memory whole again

in those that are moving
moved to return
lifted on wings of care

exposed to light
committed to the page
connecting past and future

infinite page of the sky
recording this journey
present journey

from and to
desire
all your children

turning the pages
for others
disarming the blind demands

of domineering pride
the brutal suppression of daylight
for the darkness of a self-centered womb

denying the wonder of the journey
those dictators of hot air
those mindless followers

they are lost together
their memory wiped clean
they will keep nothing

of the precious stones they cling to and defend
they will return to the earth
pried loose from their pebbles

as they left their children straying
from the rock of our desire
the light of our creation

to them it's a violent explosion
they repress
secure in the general darkness

for them a violent uprooting
who put their faith in nature
and their own imitations

industrial idols   cheap paradises
blind to the light
that nourishes all

it will strip them bare
to face their wounded pride
openly

in terror
at the violence of the energy
that was repressed

for a taste of seedless fruit
a sexual knowledge
sucking light's power in

a garden of one's own making
a dream of being seduced
by pride

a dream that will fade
like leaves on dying trees
in a desert oasis

your life will dry up
of unquenchable thirst
for it is really a mirage

no water will bring that dream
to life
you are lost in that desert

the power in your hands
holds a paper doll
for the fire in your mind

your world is a map of paper
you wrap yourself in
and burn

both you and your dream world
burning up together
no one to quench the fire.

CHAPTER 2

These are the words
Isaiah found
before his eyes.

One day
far away from now
distant as the days of creation

the mountain of spirit
in which Israel found
the House of God

that mountain will be revealed
higher
than any earthly mountain

and all nations of the earth
will see it clearly
their hearts go out to it

flowing streams
cleared of fallen wood
moved to come closer

"Let's go up
this mountain of vision
to the House of Israel's God

to learn his ways
to walk
in his ways

to carry his words
books of the Bible
out of Jerusalem"

the words Israel found
before them
in Zion

then the spirit behind them
God
will come forward

to settle the conflicts between us
finally   the one
true witness

even the finality of holocaust
will melt away
like lowland snow

the military hardware
translated into monkey bars
where children play

the hardened postures
crumbled
like ancient statues

children will wave through the gunholes
of tanks
rumbling off to the junkyard

people will find hands
in theirs
instead of guns

learn to walk
into their gardens
instead of battle

Oh House of Israel
let's walk in the sunlit ways
of his presence

for you've been abandoned
the House of Israel
full of fortune tellers

provincial cult merchants
village idiots from the East
buying and selling the air we breathe

imitating the Philistines
the latest style of infantile
chant and handshake

and their warehouse filled with silver
and gold stuffs
beyond counting

their land full of horses
and bloated chariots
embroidered like doormen uniforms

totally superfluous
going nowhere
overly driven

their cities and roadstops thriving
crammed with idols
like supermarket shelves

in a daydream
where the ego glides freely
down the aisles

civilized slaves
to the ghost towns
they've bought in their heads

and they will lose it all
their bodies fall dead
in their tracks

in an incredible parody
of humility
bowing down to the idols

of their own toes
as they emptied their spirit
into objects of their fingers

praying to the ghosts
of themselves
and so they're abandoned

so you will hide
deep in stone
dark caves

you will pull a blanket
of dust over
your head

in a cold sweat
from a vision of your Lord
light

light you will never close
your eyes to
a Hiroshima for the blind

to what always was true
light behind us
creation before us

the false eyes of pride will look in
to find the humble man
behind him

the arrogant mind
kneels
to its earth

the highest imagination
will be shimmering sand
on that day

when only the Lord
like a blue sky
will be above us

that will be the day
a day
over the heads of all

that stands
and by its little height above the earth
is proud

feels endowed with highness
and tall words for what stands
merely upright   in its image

human or inhuman
or the giant Cedars
of Lebanon

all the upright oaks
of Bashan
all the straight-backed mountains

and high-rising hills
the skyscrapers
and sheer walls

the Super Powers
and their walls of missiles
stockpiled

the huge launching towers
of the Saturns
the incredibly tall masts

of the ancient ships of Tarshish
sailing to the edge of the world
all the beautiful craft

all the inflated art
the high-priced picture frames
and gilt-edged imitations

all the high-sounding ideas
and high-minded poses
will fade to nothing

on that clear day
will melt away
like dew on the ground

men and women
in the statues and masks
of their pride

will topple over
like carved chess pieces
in a gust of wind

the little board
on which they lived for power
swept away with sand

when only the Lord
like a blue sky
will be above us

and the idols of dark thoughts
like dreams
passed away   utterly

and men will go deep
into caves and to the depths
of darkness   holes

holes in the ground
to hide from the terrible truth
of the Lord   light

deep beauty and power
shaking the earth to its core
with the simple fact of light

men will toss away fortunes
like flaming embers
in their laps   on that day

their mind-forged status
the gold-lettered names they worship
as if their hands alone conceived them

the idols of themselves   self-inspired
the brilliant paint
on their gods and monuments

will fade in the light of that day
all the coveted possessions
become molten in their hands

and they will fling them away
to moles and bats
in a fit of inspiration

and creep into cracks
and crawl into
dark corners

in fits of desperation
clinging to stones
to petrified wood

to a cold bed to hide under
from the terrible truth
of the Lord

clear beauty and power
shaking the earth to its core
with the simple fact of light

beyond the grasp of a man
who reaches for power
and cannot hold

the breath in his nostrils
who cannot grasp it
whose sum total is less

than that little wind
blowing through him
and the naked sail of his heart.

CHAPTER 6

It was the year King Uzziah
died and the year
I saw the Lord

as if sitting in a chair
the true throne
as it was very high

so high
the train
of his robe flowed down

to fill the Temple
where I was standing
the sanctuary

seraphic beings   burning
shone around him
six wings

each had six wings
two covering the face
enfolding it

two covering the torso
and enfolding the sex
of its body

and two unfolded
in space
flying

and each was calling
to each other
and the words were saying

a chorale   a fugue
an endlessly unfolding
hymn

Holy   Holy   Holy
is the Lord   beyond
all that is

and filling the world
with the substance of light
unfolding creation

the doors the windows the foundation
were shaken
moved by each voice calling

singing out
and the House was filling
with white smoke

clouds
and I heard myself
I was saying

Oh my God!
this is the end of me
my lips are a man's

unholy
I live among men and women
who give their lips falsely

give their lips to darkness
and now my eyes are given
blinding truth

inner and outer   the one
king: Lord beyond all—
and I'm uncovered   primitive

in horror of my darkness
in terror of inhuman space
exposed to a private death

totally vulnerable on the surface
of earth's
material matter . . .

then one of the seraphim
flew toward me
a live coal in his hand

a fire from the interior
of the earth
the core of my being

it was a burning stone
from the fire
on the altar

with the priest's tongs
he reached in the holy altar
and took it

and touched my lips
with it
and he was saying

you are seeing
the purifying fire of creation
burn up your past

and abstract fear and guilt
of light   of losing yourself
your small and only light

now abstraction turns concrete
on your lips
to feel the universe

the private guilt gone
purged   lanced
like a boil

erupted around your body . . .
and I was clean
and whole

and I heard the voice
of my creator
it was saying

who will I send
to be a witness—
here am I   send me

I heard myself saying
and he said
go and say to this people

hear over and over
and understand nothing
look again and again

and again you don't see
the whole body:
of language, sound

of action, history
of memory
imagination

of matter, light
they can't even feel
the energy inside them

the material of their being
and you will make their hearts harder
like ignorant fists of matter

and their ears
heavy earrings for their mind
and their eyes shut

like a censor's eyes
before a naked soul
in front of them

their thoughts become glinting swords
to hide their narrowness
to reflect away light

they will stay out late
like stubborn children
bleary-eyed

heaven forbid they should see
with their eyes clear
hear with open ears

and understand by feeling
with that sacred metal cow
of their heart

and so be moved
to turn and become
wholly human again

how long I said how long
this shell this wall
and he was already saying

until cities have fallen
to the ground   not a house
with a person or statue standing

countryside a wasteland
until this king has driven men
away   the whole country

blown down like a primitive pile of stones
some forgotten sacred place
wiped out like royal contracts etched in sand

even the promise of a remnant of survivors
will slip from mind
like the hollow ring of a cliché

like leaves from a blighted oak
ripped in a hard wind
crumpled as the tree falls

the pages of that high pride
the record of its worldly dealings
will be smooth as a stump

the stump
the holy seed
remains.

Roll this testimony up
in a scroll   this revelation
hidden in the inner library

of hearts still open
to the word mind
open to the ear

I am turning in   to wait for him
to look up from his reading
in the book

his face is hidden in
as if his people had become
a history book

a book ignorantly dropped
from sight
by Israel

like a mirror   absently swept away
a shattering insult
but the pages the pieces I will keep

before him
and I will look for him there
when he turns again to face us . . .

Listen to me because I
like my children
are signs of his reality

children of Israel
as it was and will be
in touch with his presence   in Zion

knowing where we come from
where we're going
where we are

on the map   the signs
our lines pass through
in the vehicle of his word

but when you hear
the consoling voices
of stylish intelligence and mass appeal

the religions of faithless men and women
trying to sell you on yourself
in the disarming pose of

generous free advice
urging you to consult ghosts
and articulate machines

the mindless testimonials
of spiritual ventriloquists
hearing the ghosts of themselves

and the assorted animal screechings
of sophisticated machines
running their metal tongues

by all means consult the machines
they are superior to us
like the dead

and listen to the motor
of your own cheap power
over others

as it drowns out self-doubt—
and why shouldn't we trust the gods
we make of ourselves—

and they will become oracles
in the dark   in the spiritual trap
of their own shadows

knocking wood
tossing coins
wishing on stars

beyond light
from the hand that put his word
in theirs   hand of light

utterly open daylight
and the warmth
of faith in its coming

they will pass through it like one
locked in the reflection of his shadow
going deeper into depression

he will walk and walk
and arrive nowhere as in a dream
going hungry

for something real
his mind growing bitter
he turns on his gods and kings

turns in on himself
cursing himself senseless
until his sky and his earth

are one
until he is floating
in the naked terror of space inside him

until he is a planet spun free
into total darkness
his mind in the grip of bottomless pain

his body desolate and airless
totally vulnerable
to the forces of darkness.

The people walking on
through darkness
will be overcome by light

those who were locked in the shadow
of death
are released by light

you have increased the nation
not in numbers
but in the joy of rebirth

they are rejoicing in beautiful weather
in the fullness of light
in a full harvest

in the simple joy of a windfall
they are carrying home the inner prize
of a deep victory   a selfless pride

like a liberation army coming home
an underground resistance coming out
their own home the spoil

openly yours
because you lifted the impenetrable lid
the selfish pride the manhole cover

the armor of all oppression
you have broken the iron grip
of repressed guilt

and we have broken through
in touch again
with the day at Midian

the original victory made new
the scrap of centuries peeled back
in the light of your presence

penetrating the manhole
of material pride   unearthing
the deep wonder of memory

preserved in the fullness
of time and space   earth
we walk on and carry within

every military boot
putting its mindless scrawl
on earth's drawing board

every uniform soaked in blood
or steeped like thoughts
in the smell of blood

will be tossed in the bonfire
and in miraculous transformation
become a fuel for peace   hearts lightened

to see a child being born
to see the future
being given to us in the moment

of wonder   to be in touch
with the inner strength of seeing
our own past lifted   to be uplifted

in the clean air of justice
to see the transforming   the shaping
that is constant reality

to feel the weight of constancy the longing
that is light as a baby
in our arms

growing in our love
the suspended sentence of guilt
our children will wear like summer clothes

and we will see it with real eyes
of earth   not in the stars
we are children of reality

struggling to give justice a name
as if it were a child
born to us

like a king
bringing the world to him
like blood flowing through the heart

as if the heart of the world's body
were on a line
descended from David

in the miracle of time
unfolding space
to realize ourselves in

in the insistence of struggle
to stay in touch   holding
a lifeline into the deep past

to touch
the infinite
within   and live

children of a free nation
struggling in the name
of Israel

to reclaim our birth
to open the window
of our ancient home

and say we're here to stay
defending justice to the stars
integrity to the light of dawn.

CHAPTER 14 (4–21)

One day you'll pick up this satire
of Babylon and its king
and sing:

How the storm of power
has passed
stormed off the cliff

into an endless pit
how quiet after all
the dramatic thunder

the Lord has snapped the golden crutches
of pride   cracked the whips
of despots in their own faces

who lashed the people
from an imperial seat
no country beyond reach

and now they break out singing
the whole earth is lying on its back
peacefully humming to itself

the fir trees are laughing
in the wind at you
and the cedars of Lebanon are whispering

since you lay down
the men have stopped coming
to chop us down beside you

(Oh graceful long-limbed trees
silent before the slaughter
by greedy men

who stumbled over the hills drunk
like a sunshower
that now is suddenly gone!)

the waiting room below
is all astir
at news of your coming, Babylon

all the shadows are gathering
of all the dead kings
of the world

they all stagger up to their high thrones
like ghosts of mountain goats
all the stubborn world leaders

they are all muttering they are saying
not you too
welcome to the club

so you've decided to join us
to amount to absolute zero
to bend your knee to nothing

the big parade of your pride
pushed by insatiable will
has come to the edge of the grave

to do a nose dive
all the royal trumpets
and inner noise of power

has come to play for maggots
as you stretch out on your bed of worms
and pull the blanket of worms over you

how did you fall out of bed
in heaven bright morning star
Ishtar   Lucifer

the immortal king
now reigns over sleepers
sprawled over the nations at his feet

like the shadow of The Thinker
on a plaza of flagstones
you who thought to yourself

I will climb into heaven
and set my throne on the floor
of its stars

I'll be king of the mountain
where the gods meet
utter North

I'll burst through the clouds
to make myself
god of thunder

I'll be Most High
light
will kiss my feet

but you've burst like the heaviest headstone
through the bottomless pit
utter hole

those who've been there long enough
to be accustomed to the darkness
still squint and stare at you

skeptically
like at a dim and badly painted
likeness

is this the king who made nations shake
at his feet like trembling diplomats
they say scratching the top of their skulls

who blitzed through cities
in a storm of terror
smoothing the world before him into desert

who swallowed the keys to prisons
whose bowels (they said privately) were so hard
keys came through broken in pieces

who sneered at humor
who taught the world to laugh
at humility and tears

to cry in desperate secrecy
to doubt the liberty
of their hearts in crying

who spit in the eye of kings
no foreign subject allowed to return
his last address: unknown

now all the world's kings reside
in their own plush tombs
and sleep at prominent addresses

but you've been kicked out of the mausoleum
you've been clubbed
like a Nazi collaborator

raised high above the crowd
by your heels
dressed up in royal scarlet

you and your henchmen's blood
and flung into a hole
like a horribly disfigured fetus

your head has been cracked
against the marble of your headstone
and that stone has been ground to fine powder

scattered in the wind
like the inhuman seed of your pride
unfit to be buried

in your land (incestuously exploited)
with your people (purged)
with the dignity of even a name

I will not dignify it with sound
and even your family
will be stone before it can mouth it

they will pay the sins of their father
in simple seed: their lives
extorted from the whole family

of man in the spirit of incest
in the rape of spirit itself—
let their seed be spilled

in the hole of their father
let weeds possess the earth
before that breed returns.

TYRE, PHOENICIA

Pick up your lyre
and walk through the city
whore no one remembers

pick the strings gently
sing all your songs over
until you've remembered: desired

Once again Tyre
will be handsomely paid
like a whore

open for hire
to every self-serving kingdom
on the leering face of earth

like a royal taxi
much of the world's commerce
done inside her

its traffic
passing through her
heavily breathing

but her trade her obscene profits
will become a true vehicle
this time reopened

to the core
filled with light
nothing held back

nothing under the table
no self-reproducing capital
no closet deals

no treasures secretly hidden
but totally opened for love
for pure service   a wealth untouched

all the desperate merchandising
of life and blood and the air of a song
all the face-saving prostitution

will be a way for the Lord
the profits and losses a highway
prosperity will build a house

for those who live in his presence
who breathe in his air
there will be food for all

all human desire
will be clothed
with dignity

all will be moved
to fill their place at his table
to sing his grace.

Come out of yourself
and take this down
print it in a book

so it can't be erased like dust
from the blackboard of people's minds
so it's engraved in their genes

because this is a stubborn race
erasing the truth in front of them
before they even read it

spoiled children: little liars
refusing to sit still
for the testimony that really frees them

saying to their open-eyed teachers: go to sleep
to their poets and prophets:
no piercing visions please

of uncensored truth
seduce us with surfaces
touch up the pain in our lives

with a little rose color
show us the movie of the future
so we can sit back and enjoy it

turn off the camera of reality
and make us like ourselves
under the glossy coats of postcards

turn off the words of the Lord
get out of the way
drown out those primitive feelings

with the upbeat popular tunes
of car radios
as we drive on landscaped expressways

over the naked parts
and around the unpainted sections
of hard times

even concentration camps
can be pruned
for respectable tourists

we can make anything
look easy
with modern minds and machines

but the Lord of Israel
has something to say
over all

you have swept the truth
under your consciousness
and let yourself hate

shamelessly
these words
I am speaking

you despise them
with the clenched teeth
you hide behind smooth lips

used to deceive
and to set an example of trust
in cynical salesmanship

and moral bankruptcy
relying on the cheap paper
of politics

the secret darkness
you wall in yourselves
is a fatal flaw

a fault line
nobody sees and easily forgets
under intense pressure

a trace of steam
a slight rumbling
is vaguely there until the

instant shock
the earth cracking as simply
as a china knickknack

knocked from the shelf
in the deeper quake
of his justice

your inflated careers
mere figurines
of rigid selfhood

will fall like tiny porcelains
from a tower
bursting totally apart

not a piece recognizable
mere traces of fine powder
as total as the sudden shocking

explosion of a zeppelin
not even a bolt or propeller
left for salvage

not even a photograph
a scrap of paper—
so irretrievably present

so decisive
is his presence
in his speaking

these are his words
precise pieces of language
making up the one

over Israel
over all
in my speaking

a secureness is found
as one slows down
a quiet confidence

in hearing and seeing
building strength
to open oneself

in the strength of trust
but not this people
only their mouths are open

saying not us
we've got fast horses
we can escape any danger

and they will escape
and they will ride
into the jaws of danger

saying we are so clever
as the teeth flash
behind them   unclenched

in a terrible smile
one of those smiles
will set a thousand fleeing

ten bared lips
and all will be running
as if they could escape themselves

as if they could escape
up the self-made mountain
of themselves

until what is left of them
stands free in the breeze
like a flag left on a mountain

like a warning light still flashing
in the wind-racked unearthly solitude
of a deserted runway

from some forgotten war
a tin flag in a strange wind
left behind on the moon

but even now   as then
the Lord is waiting
to embrace you

you will open to him
as pure mountain air
totally surrounding you in an embrace

there is a just voice speaking
in the quiet strength of those
listening

to his presence unfolding
around them
like a scroll of overwhelming poetry

you are survivors of the future
in Jerusalem in Israel
your tears have fallen like rain

in the desert of the past
where he hears you crying
he responds in the flowing

of your own voice
and though your mouth is dry
from the suffering you've recorded

and your hand weak from the journey
from the inner severing
of the hands you've had to let go

the teacher you've carried deep within
in the seat of your conscience
will come out

passing memory and thought
and the huge mirror of imagination
to stand in front of you

in the light of your eyes
your teacher your life
in front of you

you will see yourself
alive in the future
you will come out to meet it

and the words will come over you
a voice will be there
that was within you

and your ears will embrace it
and your arms will reach out
and sweep away the precious idols

your poets will be prophets
vehicles on the one road
in front of you

a real road
and when your mind wanders
they will call you back

to the present
to the space and time
we create together: *dialogue*

of creation
wind and rain
on the open faces

pleasing the deep roots
cleansing the leaves
that bear his message

you will bite into the sweet
miraculous rainbow
of real fruit

and spit out the bitter fruit of self-made power
the dry self-worship
greased with gold and silver

worked up like sexual fantasies
into illusions of success
over the dead bodies of others

those dreams will be wiped out
real for only an instant
returned to the earth as manure is

enriching it for the rain
he sends
to wash away the decaying past

to open the infinite eyes of
the living past:
the seeds we plant

as each living thing does
and so there is always bread
and meat

and if we let our eyes fully open
to ripen in the air
we are planted in

we can grow up and see
beyond it
into the infinite universe of stars.

CHAPTER 40 (I–II)

Console my people
comfort your people
my Lord   speaking

in my voice   saying
speak to the heart
of Jerusalem tenderly

in a voice embracing her
call to her
that her exile is over

come home
the sentence is over
that knocked the voice out of her

her guilt has been paid
into the firm hand
that is the Lord's

into which she paid more than herself
and now that hand of justice
is still open

to support her
listen a voice is calling
to open a road through the desert

clear a highway for the Lord
straight through the desert
and through your throat that is parched

deep stone valleys
you struggle through
will be filled in

lifted to your feet
to make a smooth way
a plain rolled out before you

stubborn obstacles
mountains and hills
will be swept away like dust

and a new carpet laid out
level
for all flesh to see

and to walk on together
to feel the firm reality
of his way

spread before us
direct and clear
as words spoken through air

touch all that is there
and we will see the Lord clearly
as these words from him

a voice said speak
and a voice said
what should I say

say
all flesh is grass
and the reality of love is there

wild flowers in the field
and all flesh blooms
no longer than a flower

the grass shrivels and dies
the flowers curl up to paper
in the wind

that is an undying breath
of the Lord
surely the people are grass

grass shrivels flowers fade
but the word of our God
stands in the wind forever

stand up prophets and speak to Jerusalem
your tired litany reawakens as poetry
embrace her with good news

speak to her
heart of Zion
from the top of a mountain

let your voice rise to the mountains
with the strength of love
fearless headline of truth

let all the cities of Israel see
and hear the true
Here I am!

Here is your God
here
see how he is strength itself

and vision is his arm
ruling hearts
with the power of feeling justice

to see we are here
we are our own reward
his words make us a priceless vehicle

carrying his work forward
in our arms like books
that is the air we breathe

and we are carried in it
like lambs
gently breathing

in the arms of a shepherd
in the law of life itself
in the justice of air itself

we look around and
there are pastures
and leaning against his arm new mothers

giving suck
and he is leading the ewes
to water.

CHAPTER 52 (13–15)

Listen to this vision
and know my poorest servant
my student most despised

overcomes   uplifted and held
above material honor a tower
an immovable mountain

a model of strength that makes
faces of worldly power pale   masks
over wills of mere steel

the many who turned aside in their superior air
appalled at his uncivilized
state his wild appearance

as if he had no human parents
as if he came from beyond humanity
out of some ancient ruins

a wild-eyed student
starved and sickly
from a condemned ghetto

those many appalled nations
"civilized" and "progressive"
will find their eyes glued

and their imaginations riveted
on him
the mouths of world leaders

will fall open
in amazed silence
before their own ignorance

of something so real their
lips turning to rubber
before their false education

their ears burning
with the fact
of what they've never listened to.

Is there anyone to believe
what we've listened to
as we report it

who is there
who's actually seen the Lord's
arm around the shoulders

of the despised   this richness
incredible support
freely given to him

who would have believed
seeing we were as unconscious of him
among us as a common tree

a weed tree in a lot
junk-strewn in a poor section
of the city

what could have been there
to attract us   no handsomeness
nothing to divert the eye

how could we even turn our heads
for something so poor in our eyes
so uninspiring

he was a thing rejected
despised for being human
in an offensive suit of clothes

the clothes of suffering
a shirt of pain
a cloak of sorrow

a coat the solid color
of loss   worldly indifference
like leprosy written across his face

so densely it hurt to look
as if we'd only see
ourselves reflected in it

as in a dense layer of dust
over a window
in an ancient place we've long forgotten

we don't want to remember
we loathe that place
we despise weakness

and he meant nothing to us
a blight on our existence
we couldn't even condone his existence

but it was our
loss and our
pain he bore

our hidden fear and indifference
he wore
openly for us

while we wrote him off as beneath us
as an example of God's vengeance
as being even our own self-vindication

he was punished
tortured by disease
to condone our fear

hidden under a worldly cloak
thrown over our unconscious
we've swept it out of sight

we wrote it off
with the hurt and loss
as if struggle and pain

were not a human bond
a mirror in which to see
ourselves

not an unreflecting
stone
fear symbol

but he was shattered
for our heart of stone
he was locked in ghettoes

for our hidden guilt
and we are made human
together

in the punishment and contempt
he wears in the world
on this earth for us

in black and blue
our eyes can see it
and we are healed by that seeing

he makes us real
we were all victims
we were all sheep

we strayed   we were lost
we wandered away
lost in ourselves

we were all nations
servants of our own
interests

we made our own selfish way
slavishly alone
each with our own patch of lust

in the unconscious pasture
of self-indulgence
trespassers of spirit

silent accomplices of thugs
on the highway of feeling
that is the Lord's

that is his word
and the Lord has chosen
his servant to carry it

a burden of pain on his naked back
beyond power of men to lay on him
it is the guilt of us all

made real
the guilt inside us
the abyss we were losing

our richness of feeling in
and now we see how cheaply
we've papered over loss

how openly it's borne
beyond our power to pay
he was a low animal in our eyes

a carrier of disease
and we treated him
lower than dogs

but he didn't open his mouth
for bitterness
he was open to the core

he was a lamb
led to slaughter
he was an innocent sheep

as his coat is shorn from him
but he was human   he suffered
and like a lamb his mouth didn't open

out of bitterness
and he was led away
stripped of his rights

shorn of his humanity
not a shred of justice for him
not a mouth opened for him

he was deported
he was sentenced
out of existence itself

like a nation marked for death
he was led into the fire
of bitter hatred

he was led alive
into ovens   he burned
as indifferently to the world as an ordinary lamp

turned on at evening
a lamp of skin
and no one gave it thought

he was a flame
lit in the darkness of terror
he was a light

to the truly guilty
those who deserved to be lost
in their own land

in their own bitter darkness
in the abyss
of their hidden guilt

my own people were blind
but his eyes were true
suffering the world for them

and the world gave him a grave
unmarked like a criminal's
like a mass grave

the way cattle are buried
the way refuse is disposed of
the way a rich man

orders cut flowers
like common flowers crushed beside a highway
he was nothing he was in the way

he was banned from sight   victimized
by a decadent justice
a worldly masquerade

of men dressed up in power
he was naked   innocent of crime
not guilty of even a common lie

but the Lord allowed him to feel
pain   to be open
to injustice as to disease

to be vulnerable as an animal
given in spirit of sacrifice
a faith in a human future

and out of that death march
through the fire
out of that holocaust

out of the deepest abyss
beyond torture and despair
out of sheer hell furnaces

he comes through
piercing through the guilt
deep fear and self-contempt

of all the world
because he gave himself whole
persistently human

transcending spears of bitterness
and for his pain
the pain of all creation

he will have children again
and he will see them
as sure as they will feel

his soul
and the deep consolation spoken
in the openness allowed

by the Lord
by his hand
through his words

through the pure insistence
to bear his words
in human hands   his servant

out of the massive depths of pain
into the daylight
of a living nation

that is his future illuminated
as real and warm as a body
lit by the color of feeling

my servant an example
lighting the steps up
from deep depression beneath the surface

everywhere
a struggle for the merest foothold
in the mass of people and nations

and out of the inhuman scars the clawing
he made his heart a vessel
out of the storm the raging

of primitive pride
he carried my justice a lightness
in his nameless heart   open

a room without walls
room for the lowest and highest
guilt   all that is borne within

and without: the world is his
to share with the richest nations
in the present

I make his future present
and the mouths of worldly power
fall open in awe

at the beauty
the utter reality laid bare
of life itself

because he opened his heart
totally   putting it in the hands
of death

speaking straight through a transparent life
from his soul
and his nakedness was a menace

he was judged for his skin
what is visible to the lowest
a disgrace to worms

dressed in material
of pride
a crime to those human eyes

locked up in themselves
and he was given the final clothes
of death   dust of the earth

and he wore the deaths
of those with murder in their hearts
and the criminal thoughts

of all in self-hating prisons
and he was stripped of his self
for sheer integrity

of the deeper language
of creation
and as he was scarred

in his openness
beyond worldly recognition
for the self-debased to see

their disease in him
and as he was crushed by weight
of their hidden guilt revealed

he heard it is the creator speaking
words of life
you will survive by them

your voice: lightness of breath itself
clothe the cold and hidden
hearts of stone

and warm in the dark
the unborn   vulnerable as you were
your light into the future.

CHAPTER 58 (1–12)

Open up and speak from the heart
a voice rushing through you
startling the air

a lover
rushing to the side
of a wounded mate

wind opening the door
of a deserted mountain cabin
a wounded mountain ram

lift your voice
like a horn
to your lips

calling to my people
they are guilty
they are wounded

hiding their wounds
inflicted on each other
within   in pride

indifference and self-righteousness
shout it openly   jar the doors and windows
of this House of Israel

because they're still looking for me
daily   finding pride
in looking like they're searching

all dressed up
in clothes of righteousness
like a moral nation

wearing the moral law on their sleeve
and acting
as if their integrity depends on it

as if they're beyond acting
so may approach me
like a judge over their house

asking for direction
in the immoral streets
anxious for approval of their way

anxious children
impatient to please
tugging at the sleeve of justice

why are we fasting a day
if you won't take a moment
to notice they ask

why are we humbling ourselves
dressed in mourning
sacrificing body

baring soul
if you won't know it
answer us

here it is
you ask for answered prayers
when you won't stop to think

thinking with your feet
carrying you to the marketplace
only of yourself

how to further your business
on the shoulders
of others

thinking with your stomach
the day you're fasting
an empty stomach-mind

unable to get past yourself
pushing and shoving
unable to stand still inside

turning the intensity of this day
up like metallic car radios
playing mindless words and music

geared to desperation
to turning a profit on silence
an assembly line of minutes

on which you turn out
cheap images of yourself
material to digest with an iron stomach

making you more irritable
grasping for words of spirit
to swallow like bitter pills

to make yourself feel better
about turning your soul
inside out like another pocketbook

turning openness around
with a gun at its back
like a desperate criminal

"sacrificing" your precious time
at the primitive altar
with the money of your ritual donations

turning on a figment of imagination
in a pagan death-cult act of "self-sacrifice"
in which you offer a hollow shell

going through mechanical motions
impressing hollow religious phrases
on metal

you fast with a vengeance
pushing past the inner voice
too bruised to rise and be heard

is this a day for rising
standing in my presence
expecting a reward

for physical sacrifice   for your fasting
bowing heads like royal footmen
like rows of bulrushes

parting for the heavy prow of ritual
self-serving ghost ship
with its real cargo of slaves

instead of your soul you save
face by fasting
and I can't see through *that?*

wake up to a day
beyond acting
for yourself

the Lord's voice speaks
for itself:
act for others

not with faces but hands
opening
locks of injustice

sophisticated knots
tied mentally and physically
around the poor and powerless

like a harness
to break their spirit
free them   break the locks

cut the reins of oppression
rise to the occasion
fast to free man's spirit

make a day for opening
your cupboards
sharing with the poor

open your house your heart
to the homeless
open your eyes

instead of filling your stomach
instead of harnessing the weak for it
look at the hopeless around you

put your hand through that invisible curtain
and throw a coat around their shoulders
those are men and women

flesh like you   desperate and blind
outside the walls you've built to hide in—
the otherness you reach for is *there*

all around you
nakedly human
to a soul undressed by kindness

bare hands
untying the cloak of self-serving pride
and wrapping it around a naked body

and then all around you
as sudden as light
to eyes opening in the morning

the light inside you breaks open
as certain and irrevocable
as dawn

you will see yourself
healed by a human warmth
in the reality of daylight

a sky clearing over you
like new flesh over a wound
your body will be whole

and you will see it in the light
of others   revealed
in care for the hurt you've left behind

and openness to those you find
on the way of your future
like lost memories of your creator

memory repressed
oppressed   dispossessed
now yours from which to speak

sing out openly
and the Lord returns
your voice

call into empty space
for help
and he answers "Here I am"

and if you open
the locks of injustice around you
rip open the curtain of suspicion

remove the ring from the finger of status
you point at the poor
and open your mind to them

removing the insults from your tongue
and if you open your hand
dropping your body's show of pride

showing compassion sharing your gift of life
pouring the milk of your kindness
for the starved and hopeless

then the light inside you
will rise like the sun
from the dead of night

and the depression hidden within you
will walk out openly a child free
under an afternoon sky

the Lord will be behind you
always around you
water in the desert of your need

meat and strength for your bones and
over you gentle rains
your life a fruitful garden

a mountain spring
always running
under a clear sky

and many from among you will walk out
to build on your ruins
firming the shaken doors and windows

reaffirming the ancient foundations
of your ancestors
on earth

and you will walk out
in the universe
deep in the firmament

building from the ruins
of planetary bodies
renewing the foundation

of the changing universe
continually
by your presence

water of your body
unchanging air
of your soul

you will be spoken of
openly and everywhere
as discoverer of lost ways

restorer of faded memories
nurse to broken dreams
surveyor of a universal highway

landscaper of sandswept paths irrigator of deserts
plasterer of broken walls rebuilder of broken defenses
archaeologist of morning

making a world
to live in   secure
in the infinite light of reality.

The Lord speaks
this way
the sky

and all ways behind it
is a royal seat for me
space

is where I rest
and the earth my footrest
in time

where could you build a house
for me
where a place

especially for me to rest
as if I would sleep or abide
there   or there

when I made all this
all of it comes from my hand
all that is came into being

from me
my Lord
is speaking

but I look at man especially
for the man or woman oppressed
poor and powerless

when he knows he is
brokenhearted and
filled with humility

his body trembling with care
open to the others
to my words.

Most of the book of Jeremiah, as with Isaiah, is composed of poetry; the key exception consists of a prophet's autobiographical passages in prose. The poet's main form is the prophet's oracle—but he is still a poet, just as a composer of songs is not necessarily a singer. And as with Isaiah, we are probably talking of several poets.

It is hardly different today when it comes to the profession of the poet. Sometimes he or she is a college professor, but we still call him or her a poet, not even a poet-professor. The most eminent English-language poet alive and writing in 2009, for instance, John Ashbery, is also a professor. In his earlier career, he was a prominent art critic and an editor. Ashbery wasn't called an art critic-poet, and neither were the poets of Jeremiah called prophet-poets, as far as we know. Actually, we don't know how they fit into the lost Hebraic culture of their day and what they were called, especially when writing "in the name of" a prophet, such as Jeremiah. Many of the biblical writers likely held one or more positions, especially prophet, priest, or prince, or else were in their employ, such as Baruch. We might imagine Jeremiah's text in the passage I've translated as late Walt Whitman, during the Civil War, when he worked as a nurse. Although "poet-nurse" is not a term we employ, it is perhaps here applied aptly to Jeremiah.

It's important to think of the poet, divinely inspired or not, deriving his work from sources, which are themselves written as poetry. Several oracles of Isaiah are transparently played upon in the book of Jeremiah. The poet's forms and rhetoric also draw upon the wide world of ancient literature, current and classical. Poets also embody the historical Hebraic culture as they play with and upon the Hebrew language. How the Hebrew language was spoken and written, and in what relation to other languages, is perhaps more crucial to know than deconstructing "prophecy."

Baruch names and designates himself the prophet Jeremiah's secretary, supposedly setting down his master's words. One can't help but feel that Baruch's fidelity is to a range of Jeremiah's moods—sometimes raw, sometimes elaborated with great sophistication—rather than to a specific text. It might help to imagine the original prophet Jeremiah in his lamentation as a soul singer; when transcribed, the illusion of spokenness to Jeremiah's words becomes artful in Baruch's subtle settings.

Later, other poets in the school of Jeremiah added passages and chapters to the book, while perhaps editing earlier portions. The chapter from which I've translated appears written by one of these later poets, based upon some lines attributed to the original Jeremiah. The vision of a return from exile seems to have been written in retrospect, long after the Babylonian captivity that Jeremiah experienced. It's a poignant vision for a reader who knows of the real hardship and poverty encountered in the return. In fact, few returned to Jerusalem at first, and this passage was probably meant to be read by those still living in Babylon. Alternatively, if it was written in the following century, it would be directed to those who had already assimilated the shock of returning. They would have accepted this text with a fondness toward an earlier, more idyllic age (as an Israeli poet today might look back longingly on the idealism of Zionist pioneers).

The key to the vision—one that later, hard-bitten realists might still accept—is the promise of children (and a new audience), an exaggerated echo of Abraham's original blessing. As God remembers Ephraim (a term of endearment for the northern kingdom of Israel); as Jeremiah remembers a mother of Israel, Rachel; and as we remember the words, "there is new life for your labor, remembrance / in the presence of children"—so we become aware, as readers "listening," that we were the children. Just as Ephraim and Rachel are breathing presences in Jeremiah's poetry, the blessing is redeemed in the eyes and ears of "the children alive."

jeremiah

CHAPTER 31

Listen to words the Lord has spoken:
A people discovered grace
when they had run away

a consoling treasure
when they had escaped an enslaving power
into the desert

immeasurable richness in front of their eyes
opening their hearts and minds
when you had looked only for rest, Israel

the Lord reveals his words to me
as he was then, in that desert
ages ago, saying

a love that lasts forever
I revealed to you
and you always will carry that loving-kindness

the love that drew you to me
will rebuild your nation
will draw you home, dear Maiden Israel

again you will fasten on timbrels
leading the dance   keeping time
to the rhythm of seasons

again you will clothe the mountains with vineyards
the hills of Shomron will sparkle
with the jewelry of vines

and you will live to pluck the fruit
to raise it to your lips
to praise it, singing

for there will be a day
when watchmen on the hills of Ephraim
will shout, the way is clear

we may go up to Zion
the mountain of vision
walking in the presence of the Lord

for these are the Lord's words:
raise a song to your lips for Jacob
let the startled nations hear it

let their watchmen turn to it
on every hilltop listening post
of the world

let it be music to their ears:
am Yisrael chai
the people of Israel live

I am bringing them back from the north
and gathering them
from the ends of the earth

look, the blind and the lame are returning
women heavy with child, and yes
even those already feeling birth pangs

a great congregation is coming
weeping openly, and among them little cries
of newborn infants—sweet and gracious tears

and I will lead them beside rushing waters
on fertile ground, on soil so smooth
not a foot will stumble on the way

their path is straight, clear before them
for I am Israel's father
Ephraim my firstborn son

nations of the world, listen
to the word that is the Lord's
turn and tell it to the islands

islands, send it to the coasts
the one who scattered Israel
is a shepherd who never sleeps

and will bring them back
gathering his flock tenderly
unchanging as the sea

for the Lord has redeemed Jacob
paid the ransom into the worldly hand
that was too strong for him

they will come home with songs
singing from the mountaintop
that is Zion

the land will be beautiful in their eyes
the earth's goods abundant
in their hands

the fullness of their hearts
will reap wheat
and wine and oil

flocks of sheep
giving birth to healthy lambs
vigorous herds of cattle

and the people will take root
thrive and stretch themselves
like a watered garden

they will not be confined
not imprisoned in exile again
not steeped in sadness

the maiden will dance unashamedly
young men and old men
will join in together

I will turn their sighing
into breaths of excitement
their sadness into blushes of joy

and they will relax by fountains
of imagination, clearing the air
of dank grief

their mourning changed into music
of birds alighting in trees, by windows
thrown open to new mornings

the priests will have their arms full
with gifts for the sacrifice
the hunger of the people will be filled

with the goodness of the world
and their hearts thrown open
to hear these words again

like fresh air to comfort them
for the Lord has given his word—
just as now you hear his words:

listen, a voice sobbing in Ramah
bitter weeping, open
inconsolable

Rachel mourns her children
refusing all comfort, all soothing
all her hope gone blind:

her children gone—
yet these are the Lord's words:
your voice will cease its weeping

your eyes brighten behind the tears
that dissolve into crystal-clear vision
of the children alive

returning home
from the lands of enemies
from beyond anguish to hope revived

vision is your reward
there is new life for your labor, remembrance
in the presence of children, eyes wide open

turning to the future
that is also yours
within the borders of a reality

and beyond them your descendants
are walking freely
by the strength of an unfailing imagination

an unbroken integrity
a listening   dedicated
to the words that bade them live.

As I have heard Ephraim crying
as I hear him rocking in grief:
my heart has been trained

like a wild bull, an unbroken calf
all my desire set on returning
remembering in the turning

trusting in the memory
for you are the Lord
and were always my God

and when I opened my eyes in exile
my stomach turned, I knew my loss
and when I repented and learned

to bear the burden
and when I knew I had been tested
I broke down, I struck my forehead

aware of my arrogance
ashamed of the ignorance
blinding my youth

and I lived to face it
to blush with the disgrace
to embrace my past

Is Ephraim not my dear one
says the Lord dear
as an only child

that whenever I speak of him
I am filled with remembering
and my heart goes out to him

to welcome him back
to receive him with love
with mercy, says the Lord

mark your path well
plant guideposts and road marks
set your desire by the highway

your thoughts to the road leading home
turn back on it, my Maiden Israel
come back to these your cities.

PART II

SEEING

Jeremiah

Composed during the period of return from Babylonian exile, in the sixth and fifth centuries BC, *the imagery used by the poet reflects a cosmopolitan influence in its representation of a heavenly court. The poet also revives older Jewish imagery, as in the representation of the Temple Menorah. Yet here the Menorah has become a powerful image in a dream while the heavenly court is suffused with down-to-earth details, including political attitudes toward the governing head, Zerubbavel. It appears that Zechariah was decidedly more poet than prophet—or that a sophisticated poet in his camp set his works in writing. There are several poets who composed different chapters of the book, some less sublime than the one I've chosen.*

In this portion of Zechariah, the coming together of state (symbolized by Zerubbavel) and religion (symbolized by Joshua) echoes back to earlier mergers, starting with the ark in Sinai built by Moses and the temple built by King Solomon (where the creation of the Menorah is first described). There are parallels with earlier prophets, particularly Ezekiel. Yet this poet in the circle of Zechariah is different—he has learned complex literary techniques during his stay in Babylon. His dialogues between God, prophet, and interpreting angel encompass a literary style that conceals nuances of criticism toward both politics and religion—but especially toward contemporary poetry, echoing back to the much older poetics of northern Israel, such as E's dream sequence of Isaac's near-sacrifice.

The night visions are hallucinatory scenes and even though a prophetic symbology is counterpointed by political allegory, the poet's craft has overtaken the prophet's. Most biblical scholars miss the poetry for the allegory and pursue meanings secondary to the text's imaginative power. It is more likely that in Zechariah we are in the presence of a renaissance in Jewish poetry, a poetry of Exile that will culminate in Jonah.

zechariah

Sing like a skylark
happy being home
daughter of Zion

because I am coming
to join you
with the sky you hoped for

over you
sky of your deepest dream
infinite sky

of reality
you dared to see
in the midst of a fogbound world

I will be in the midst of you
as true as your eyes
see through a clear blue sky

and I will be inside of you
as you were open to me   light
in a world suppressed in darkness

leadenly earthbound
giants in their mirror
hearing only themselves

and the gargoyles of their unconscious
but light is the voice of your creator
breaking through you

in the midst of the world
and many nations will see it
dawn breaking on that day

all will join me in the light
of reality   warm
beneath an infinite wing

and you will know my breath is sent
the man who is speaking to you
by the Lord our creator

who will breathe in Israel
once again enfolding his daughter
Zion in the holy land

holding Jerusalem
small reflection
in the pupil of an eye

beholding him again
beneath an azure sky
calm inside

be quiet be still
all people of flesh
before the Lord

a sky of promise is unfolding
before us
the horizon expands

to include earth and sky
and the small voice within
will break out singing.

⬲

Then the Lord allowed me to see
in a vision
the high priest Joshua

in a court in heaven the judge
the Lord's angel
(the word for divine agent)

to his right the satan
(the word for accuser)
accusing him .

and the word of the Lord
said to the satan
May the Lord reject your words hard accuser

the Lord who chooses Jerusalem
rejects your flood of venom
this man is but an ashen stick

plucked from the fire—
Joshua's clothes were filthy
as he stood before the angel—

who was saying to those in the heavenly court
take off his poor and filthy clothes
and turning to him was saying: look

I have removed your guilt
and dress you in clean robes—
and then it was I who was saying:

let them put a clean turban on his head!
and they did
and he was splendidly dressed

as the Lord's angel watched
then to Joshua slowly said
(matching the depth of his attention)

these are the words of the Lord
if you will walk through your life
in my ways

and keep my presence there
in the people's life
you will be head of my house

and present in my court
free to come and go
in this heavenly court

listen Joshua   high priest
you and your new pioneers
are signs of the growth coming

you are like new shoots
and I will bring you
a new branch a new line

the man growing from my promise
as from a root
in the promised land

look at this stone it has eyes
I reveal to Joshua
seven facets seven eyes

cornerstone of a new day
on which I engrave
the living inscription the promise

that on that one day
I will remove
the dirty clothes and guilt

from the shoulders of this land
and in your lightness
you will see every man your neighbor

and call to him
(the words of the Lord are speaking)
come sit on this good earth with me

beneath my fig tree
(each will be truly at home)
and my ripening vine.

⊠

Then the angel returned
startling me with words
as if life was a dreamy silent movie

until an angel spoke to me
saying what do you see
and my words like an unblinking camera

showed me a golden menorah
a golden bowl above it
brimming with oil

fed from two olive trees
standing on each side
there are seven lights

fed by the golden oil
so that it's always lit
by the trees

seven golden flames
lit by trees
like a blazing fountain

then I turned to the angel
speaking again
in words of conversation

what are these things my Lord
I've described
through the camera of vision

you don't know how to read then
what you've written?
spoke the angel that was there

conversing with me
and I was saying
no my Lord

then he answered
and was saying
these words

this is the word of the Lord
(immediate vision)
to Zerubbavel the governor

not by force
not by power
but by my spirit

says the Lord
what are you
worldly mountain

of all material things
and earthbound forces
compared to Zerubbavel?

you are nothing a false shrine
leveled to the ground
and he will hold up the crowning headstone

that was highest once beneath the sky
and it will be a cornerstone
of azure

and all will step back deeply in awe
of pure beauty
singing the grace of spirit.

A recent biblical critic, when confronted with poetic exaggeration, wonders whether readers in antiquity believed what they were reading. If this critic had been a poet himself, he might have understood that poets naturally inhabit conventional forms so that their readers may suspend disbelief. The late Chilean poet and novelist Roberto Bolaño inhabited the "detective novel" in his major work, 2666 (2008 in English translation). In similar manner, the poets of written prophecy inhabit the oracle and other poetic conventions—and in particular, when it comes to the book of Jonah, the "prophetic call" or divine inspiration itself.

As with the contemporary poet or novelist, the writing prophet of Israel embodies prophecy as a seer of cultural direction—a prober of conventions and not a fortune-teller. In order to get closer to this or any biblical writer, we have to ask who was the intended reader or audience? What was the writer's culture probing or obsessed with, especially in relation to other cultures? These are questions only barely asked today. Yet only by getting closer to imagining the writers, whether in Torah, Prophets, or Writings, will we properly approach the text.

Most commentators, religious and secular, strain to place Jonah among the books of the Prophets. It fits most naturally as a critique: a sympathetic but intricate satire of the Jewish prophets (a precursor of the anti-heroic genre that is typical of great cultures in exile). Later parallels abound, down to modern Yiddish literature.

The author is worldly, and in the manner of biblical poetry the text appropriates older verses about a prophet Jonah into a new tale. But only an outsider among prophets could unite so many critical dimensions in one narrative. At the time of writing, in the fifth century BCE, the women of the elite classes educated in Babylon might hold a cautionary view of the increasingly male conventions of prophecy. Jonah *exhibits a soulful critique of these conventions.*

The institution of official prophecy would find itself in turmoil as a result of exile, and an exaggerated backlash against the old fixture of women prophets would have been likely—and also require countering. At the same time, new schisms between elite and priestly classes would have arisen. The educated woman who probably wrote Jonah *in its present form nevertheless sympathizes with honest piety. She is perhaps related to ancestral women prophets, or to a male prophet held in derision (of which there were many after the nation's downfall)—or even more aptly, to a family of the ruling class under criticism from religious quarters.*

Like a typical book of a prophet, the book begins with the call to witness. But in place of Jonah's words, we're suddenly in the realm of narrative, as the prophet's failings are characterized as bluntly as any common man's. This is especially surprising because Jonah is, after all, the recipient of a call. An essential difference is established between this book and the legends of similar date recalled in the later collections of Midrash. Even more extraordinary than the fantastic imagery of fish, plant, and naive Ninevites, is that this is prophecy unabashedly about prophecy.

The primary commentary in Jonah *is on biblical language itself, and the customs of prophecy and prayer. The elegiac language in Jonah's psalm at the bottom of the sea—and within the roundly figurative fish belly—serves as caricature to self-possessed prophecy. Everywhere, literalism is under attack. Consider the Hebrew word for "great"—this same word is applied to the fish, to the city of Nineveh, and to the hurricane. The verbatim quality of the diction in* Jonah *is subverted by the context the poet presents, beginning with Jonah's error in taking God's call too literally (as if he could escape it by crossing a border, which is what the words required of him in the call to Nineveh).*

The poet of Jonah *is calling on men and prophets to listen to themselves self-critically. It's not the castor-oil plant that is the object* lesson in the last chapter, but imagination itself. We have to absorb the irony of the imagery in order to grasp the emotional core—as Jonah feels kinship with the plant. At this core is the representation of a mothering God (cried out to, from a womblike belly) and the deity's way of speaking to poets in their own language (the language of both poetry and creation).

Jonah uses some terms in common with Isaiah and turns them inward, personalizing them. The familiar word for "call" also becomes "cry in its ear," since it's a word depicting human conversation (it's the same word used by the captain of the ship in the mundane act of waking the napping Jonah). The most emphatic contrast is in Jonah's usage of it, within the fish belly, and the impersonal utilization of it in the command to cry to Nineveh. This is one of many instances in which the poetic language parallels the drama of Jonah finding his identity in listening to—rather than separating from—the mothering God who perhaps resides within him.

jonah

CHAPTER I

And the word of God came to the prophet Jonah
saying to him, Jonah ben Amittai: rise
go to Nineveh, the great city
and cry in its ear
because its hard heart stands out before me
like an open sore

Jonah rose, but to go instead
west to Tarshish: far away
out of the Lord's presence
to the ends of the earth, for good measure

Jonah went down to foreign Jaffa
found a ship going all the way to Tarshish
bought a one-way ticket
(paid in cash on demand)
went below like any other passenger
as the crew set sail for distant Tarshish
away from the Lord, out of his demanding presence

But the Lord threw a great wind
over the sea—a hurricane so great
the ship thought she'd be broken to pieces
all the sailors were scared to death
each trembling soul
crying to one god or another
then throwing all the cargo overboard
to lighten the load

Meanwhile Jonah, having already lain down
in the hold below, was fast asleep
the captain himself came down to him
and cried in his ear: what does this mean
this sleep of ignorance—rise ·
cry to your god
perhaps the god will turn his ear
and kindly spare us our death

Among the sailors each consulted his neighbor
and agreed: we must cast lots
revealing the source of this bitter fortune
so they cast lots, fortune continuing to unfold
as Jonah drew the cast lot

Turning to him they said: now tell us—
now that you've brought your bitter fortune
on all our heads—why are you here?
where did you come from?
what country, what people
do you belong to?

And he answered: I am a Hebrew
and I tremble before the Lord
God in heaven, creator of this sea
as well as dry land

And the men were struck with a great terror
their lips trembling as they asked: what
is this bitter fortune you've created?
because the men already knew Jonah's fear
of the Lord—of being in his presence
he has told them as much

And they asked: what can we do
for you, that might calm the sea
around us? for the sea was growing
into a great hurricane

And he said: lift me up, like a sacrifice
throw me into the sea
this will calm the sea for you
it was on account of me, I'm sure
this great hurricane surrounds you

But the men desperately rowed for dry land
yet couldn't—the sea grew even more
into a great hurricane

And they cried to the Lord
Please Lord hear us
we don't want to die for this man's soul

along with him—please don't hold us guilty
of spilling his blood into the sea
for you are the Lord who has created
this fortune unfolding here

And they lifted Jonah up, like a sacrifice
and threw him into the sea

Suddenly the sea stopped its raging
the men trembled in awe
a great fear of the Lord engulfed them
right there
they slaughtered a sacrifice, sacrificing to him
they cried vows, vowing to him.

CHAPTER 2

And a great fish was waiting
the Lord had provided
to swallow Jonah

And Jonah was a long time
within the fish body
three days three nights

and Jonah prayed to the Lord
within the mothering fish body—
he prayed to his God, saying

I cried out within my despair
I called to the Lord and he answered me
I implored him within the belly of death itself

Yet he heard my voice—
I was flung into the abyss
swept into the sea's bottomless heart

Devoured by rivers
all your waves and walls of water
fell over me

And I was saying I am lost
cast away, driven out
of your presence, from before your eyes

How will I see
your holy Temple again
if I am gone?

Water was all around me
penetrating to my soul: I was almost gone
devoured by a flood

Seaweeds were tangled
around my head
I sank to the depths

I went down to the roots
of mountains
the earth shut her gates

Behind me
it was the end of the world
for me—and yet

From destruction you brought me to life
up from the pit
Lord my God

My soul was ebbing away within me
but I remembered the Lord
and my prayer came up to you

Up to your holy Temple
as if I were there
in your presence

Those who admire mists of illusion
to hide their fears
abandon the compassion of openness

But I with a thankful voice, not fearing
will make of sacrifice a thanksgiving
I will pay with gladness every vow I make

It is the Lord who delivers us
alive
he is the captain of our praises

I will pay my fare gladly
I am his
precious cargo

And the Lord spoke to the fish
and it vomited Jonah out
onto dry land.

CHAPTER 3

And the word of God came to the prophet Jonah
for the second time, saying: rise
go to Nineveh, the great city
and cry in its ear
with the words I give you to cry

Jonah rose, and went to Nineveh
as the word of God had said
now Nineveh was a great city
even in God's eyes—so wide
it took three whole days to walk across

And Jonah walked right in
walking one day's worth into it
then cried out, saying
just forty days more
and Nineveh falls

And the people of Nineveh believed the Lord
they cried out, calling for a fast
then all of them dressed in sackcloth
from the greatest on down
to the smallest

And God's word reached the King of Nineveh
and he rose from his throne
removed his robes
covered himself in sackcloth
and sat down in ashes

And it was shouted throughout Nineveh
as the word of the king
and all his great men, saying
of man or beast
of flock or herd
none shall taste food or graze
none will feed, none drink water

They will cover themselves in sackcloth
the man and the beast
crying out to the Lord
with all his might—
and will not bear injustice

And each will turn away
from his hardhearted way
from the grip of illusion
that frees his hands from violence only—
who knows, the god may turn
and repent
and turn from his burning wrath
and kindly spare us our death

And the Lord saw
what they had made of themselves
how they turned from their bitter ways
and the Lord repented from the bitterness he said
that they would bear
he didn't make them bear it.

CHAPTER 4

And this appeared like a bitter justice to Jonah
a great bitterness grew inside him
it hurt him deeply

And he prayed to the Lord, saying
Oh Lord, wasn't this the exact word and vision
I had always delivered and known you by
when I was still in my own country?
this is exactly why
I wanted to leave your presence
for Tarshish, before you would call me
a second time
because I knew you as a gracious God
compassionate, long-suffering
and of great kindness
and would repent bitterness

Now, Lord, take my soul from me
for me it is a good thing to be dead
and leave the presence of the living

and the Lord said
can it be a good thing
that you are hurt so deeply?

And Jonah left the city
walking all the way through it
and beyond it on the other side
where he sat down, east of Nineveh
having made a *sukkah* for himself in the desert
to sit in the shade, in the fragile booth
until what is made of the city
is revealed

And the Lord God had provided
a castor-oil plant, making it grow large
up over Jonah's head, a cooling shadow
to save him from bitterness
to soothe him

And Jonah began to feel happy
with the castor-oil plant
a great happiness came over him
changing his mood

And the Lord had provided
a worm in the night
and by the time darkness had risen away
it attacked the castor-oil plant
which wilted, was already dry

And then, the sun already shining
the Lord had provided a desert east wind
blistering
and the sun grew fierce, attacking
Jonah's head, he was falling
into a daze, wishing he was dead
already, saying
for me it is a good thing to be dead

And the Lord said to Jonah
can it be a good thing
that you are hurt so deeply
and because the castor-oil plant
no longer can soothe you?
and Jonah was saying
it is a good thing to be hurt deeply
until I am dead like it

And the Lord said: *you*
may feel compassion, may identify
with the castor-oil plant
for which you did not labor
to bring here, did not provide for its growing
into a great plant—a sudden child of a night
yet in one night it was gone

And may I not feel compassion
for Nineveh, the great city
which has grown up here with more than

a hundred and twenty thousand men and women
all of them innocent of knowing
the difference between right (the hand that provides)
and left—and likewise
many, many animals?

Jonah

part 3

WRITING

the scrolls

We've explored the relation between contemporary and ancient poets in earlier chapters, especially in the introductions to Prophets, and in particular, Jonah. In the twenty-one psalms I've translated here, there may be almost as many poets. And within the psalms themselves, there is an abundance of "quotation": bits and pieces of other works and ritual sayings that add a dimension of emotional immediacy, as if to bridge any gap of thought—or the need for original thinking. Another aspect of quotation resembles the methods of contemporary poets, where it's not specific words but rather a manner or image that is quoted. For these reasons, many scholars make the mistake of assuming the psalms contain additions and subtractions by other hands, including editors. Familiarity with today's poets can help to see through this common misunderstanding about quotation, yet even the literary critic who translates a psalm may fail to convey its drive for immediacy. It's in the intensity of that drive for spokenness that all manner of quotation can be enjoyed and forgiven.

One day, translating a psalm that I thought was driven by anger and is usually presented as such, I suddenly realized it was not anger at all but an intense depression, a self-conscious awareness of failure. The psalmist was facing depression and not allowing himself to respond with anger. Instead, even as his voice speaks bitterly, he overcomes despair with his song's ironic sense of never-ending, echoing into eternity, like a blues.

Psalms was written by as many as a hundred poets over seven centuries. Hebraic culture went through many changes in that span, and consequently the Lord appealed to in one psalm may seem a different deity from the Lord in another. A unity is nonetheless maintained in the personal bonding with that Lord, and this relationship is clearest in the ancient Hebrew, where God's original names were used. Normally we think of relations with a lord or king as highly formal, so the personal intimacy is striking.

When I was still in college, I was provoked to reencounter the Bible by the psalm translations of Philip Sidney and his sister, the Countess of Pembroke, made in Elizabethan England. I hadn't imagined the original poems to be as sophisticated in idiom as their translations suggested. Although Sidney and Pembroke worked from Latin, they adapted all manner of Italianate forms— they were playing with their own language, a relatively new language then, as Hebrew was for the earlier psalmists.

What better analogy for the court of King David than Queen Elizabeth's, who was not only a patron of poets but known to have written verse herself. As the lyrics of Renaissance Europe were often free variations on the classical Latin originals, many of the psalms seemed to me spirited transformations of Canaanite, Mesopotamian, and Egyptian liturgies.

Although sometimes formally intricate, a speaking voice penetrates the texture of many psalms, often punning on officious religious phrases. The resemblance to a modern poem's texture of phrasing is prevalent, where even collage methods can seem to echo ancient parallelism. And the psychological situation of a poet struggling to hear himself—to let his voice counterpoint the poem's texture—parallels a psalmist's simulated dialogue with his or her Creator.

In early translations by English poets, the tones of classical convention—of invoking the muses—amplify the Hebrew conventions of speaking to deity. At its origins, however, the biblical psalm exhibits an even greater range of speaking tones. Today, poetry mostly sheds the ghosts of the muses. Without standard criteria of diction, a poem is almost an act of faith itself as it gropes toward discovering its own inclusive form. As a poet, in that act of discovery, I'm both speaking and listening to myself speak. And in that way I draw closer to the psalmist's enactment of voice.

The drive toward realism in the psalmists is remarkable. A series of seemingly unrelated images in a given psalm creates not a tapestry, but a psychological atmosphere of reality. It's a self-conscious realism, and I imagine it as music, and in particular the blues, whose sobering irony often developed from spiritual hymns. Some of the early psalmists appear to be musicians as well, their texts serving as lyrics; many of their names indicate musical collaboration, Korah and Asaph the most prominent. Other psalmists seem to me fundamentally writing poets.

When the literary specialist approaches the Bible in our day, a crucial component of his or her education is often missing: an empathy with the biblical author's poetic engagement of the Hebraic cosmic theater. The critic Jack Miles, for instance, writes in Christ: A Crisis in the Life of God (2001), that "there are very few Psalms that do not, at some point, allude to a fight in progress and ask God's assistance in winning it." For his example, Miles offers Psalm 139:

> Do I not hate them that hate thee, O Lord?
> And do I not loathe them that rise up against thee?
> I hate them with perfect hatred . . .
> . . . lead me on the path everlasting!

Miles describes this passage as "virulent hatred . . . almost conventional when the Psalms were written." The problem is that he reads exclusively for meaning rather than poetic depth, and without awareness that the biblical writer is a poet. The psalmist uses "hate" not to hate but to cancel out hatred—he wishes his hatred to erase the hatred of God. Within the Hebraic cosmic theater, the poet-psalmist speaks like a son identifying with his father. He doesn't wish that all his father's enemies be killed; his wish is to cancel out their hatred. No loving child wishes to see his father hated, nor is he drawn to murder in response. But literary critics can miss this when they ignore the sublime drama of the Hebraic cosmic theater—one in which man and God are on intimate terms—and treat the text as if primitive.

The Hebrew poet's sense of drama, however, is mature and most often concerns the Covenant. Thus, the "path everlasting" he aspires to in Psalm 139 is the negotiation and interpretation of the Covenant *(he would wish to go on interpreting forever!). It's not a Covenant of wars and victories as Miles describes it, but one in which history can be dramatized: it becomes a stage upon which whatever happens must continue to be negotiated and interpreted. When Israel is defeated and when God's Temple is destroyed, neither history nor the story ends. The ancient losses to the Assyrians and the Babylonians are faced up to, and history goes on. Israel survives and the mighty Babylonian empire turns to dust, yet no victory is celebrated—other than the continual and life-renewing interpretation of the Covenant, upon which Jewish literature of all genres is usually based.*

It is hardly different when another literary critic, Robert Alter, in his recent translation of Psalm 139, renders God as a slayer whose enemies deserve "utter hatred":

> *Would you but slay the wicked, God— / O men of blood, turn away from me! . . . Why, those who hate you, Lord, I hate / and those against you I despise. / With utter hatred I do hate them.*

In the lines preceding this passage, the poet-psalmist has fallen asleep trying to count the "weighty" thoughts of God: "Should I count them, they would be more than the sand. / I awake, and am still with you." Thus the lines above that follow seem to wish slaying and hatred. What is lacking, however, is the poet-psalmist's sense of drama, moving from the breathtaking thought of Creation to the awareness that, since the Maker gives breath, he can also withdraw it. And thus the translations above obscure the psalmist's poetry; he sounds merely vengeful.

It's not the hatred of men but rather the hatred of lies that the poet-psalmist evokes. To account for this in my own translation, I began with the same counting of thoughts and then called to mind— with the use of "breath" and "face"—the inadequacy of human language in itself:

. . . like grains of sand I try to count
I fall asleep and awake
on the beach of your making

My Lord—stop the breath
of men who live by blood
alone and lie to your face . . .

___

___

___

___

p s a l m s

PSALM I

Happy the one
stepping lightly over
paper hearts of men

and out of the way
of mind-locked reality
the masks of sincerity

he steps from his place at the glib café
to find himself in the word
of the infinite

embracing it
in his mind
with his heart

parting his lips for it
lightly
day into night

transported like a tree
to a riverbank
sweet with fruit in time

his heart unselfish
whatever he does
ripens

while bitter men turn dry
blowing in the wind
like yesterday's paper

unable to stand
in the gathering
light

they fall
faded masks
in love's spotlight

burning hearts of paper
unhappily
locked in their own glare

but My Lord opens
his loving one
to breathe embracing air.

PSALM 6

Lord, I'm just a worm
don't point to me
in frozen anger

don't let me feel
I more than deserve
all your rage

but mercy, Lord, let me feel mercy
I'm weak, my spirit so dark
even my bones shiver

my shadow surrounds me—I'm shocked
how long, Lord, how long
till you return to shine your light

return to me dear Lord
bring back the light
that I can know you by

because those that are dead
have no thought of you
to make a song by

I'm tired of my groaning
my bed is flowing away
in the nights of tears

depression like a moth
eats from behind my face,
tiny motors of pain push me

get out of here all you
glad to see me so down
your every breath so greased with vanity

My Lord is listening so high
my heavy burden of life floats up
as a song to him

let all my enemies shiver
on the stage of their total self-consciousness
and all their careers ruined in one night.

PSALM 8

My Lord Most High
your name shines
on the page of the world

from behind the lights
covering the heavens—
my lips like infants

held to the breast
grow
to stun the darkest thoughts

when I look up
from the work of my fingers
I see the moon and stars

your hand set there
and I can barely think
what is a man

how did you spare a thought for him
care to remember
his line

descending through death
yet you let him rise
above himself, toward you

held by music of words . . .
you set his mind in power
to follow the work of your hand

laying the world at his feet
all that is nameable
all that changes through time

from canyons to the stars
to starfish
at bottom of the sea

all that moves blazing a path
in air or water
or deep space of imagination on paper

My Lord Most High
your name shines
on the page of the world.

PSALM 12

Help, My Lord
where's the man
who loves you

where's the child
with human truth
behind him

helping him walk—
he grows into a lie
with his neighbors around him

speaking from made-up hearts
he becomes an empty letter
his lips sealed

tongue dried up
in its coat of vanity
its web of pride

"our lips belong to us
do what we want
to rise in the world

we don't want to hear
anything higher"
"I'm called I appear

by the human voice
the conscious victim
I send words to lift

whoever's waiting
I release him from lips
swollen in authority"

these words are free
like released energy
without violence

finite matter
broken open
with the tenderness of dawn

these words were always yours
My Lord, you sent into the present
lifting us from the inhuman

you are behind us
with every step in the infinite
through the swollen crowd around us

living lies
in a chain of lips
holding their children.

The universe unfolds
the vision within:
creation

stars and galaxies
the words and lines
inspired with a hand

day comes to us
with color and shape
and night listens

and what is heard
breaks through deep silence
of infinite space

the rays come to us
like words
come to everyone

human on earth
we are the subjects
of light

a community
as it hears
the right words

creating time
the space of the sky
the face of the nearest star

that beats like a heart
in the tent where it sleeps
near the earth every night

then rises above the horizon
growing in our awareness
of the embrace

of inspiration
we feel as we turn
toward the warmth

starting at the edge of the sky
to come over us
like a secret love we wait for

love we can't hide
our deepest self-image
from

nobody holds back that fire
or closes the door
of time

words My Lord writes shine
opening me
to witness myself

conscious and unconscious
complex mind
warmed in an inner lightness

that moves me
to the simple beat
of time

testimony
of one author
speaking through history's pages

commanding my attention
bathed in light
around me

clean perfect notes
hearts play
make us conscious

we become the audience
amazed we can feel
justice come over us

our minds become real
unfold
the universe within

silence becomes real
we hear
clear words

become the phrasing of senses
lines of thought
stanzas of feeling

more lovely than gold
all the gold in the world
melting to nothing in light

sweet flowing honey
the right words
in my mouth

warming your subject
as he listens
breaking through his reflection

his image in the mirror
what mind can understand the failure
waiting in itself

silent self-image
created in the dark alone
to hold

power over others!
but justice comes over us
like a feeling for words that are right

absolutely
a mirror is pushed away
like a necessary door

we're free to look at everything
every shape and color
light as words

opening the mind
from nightmares of social failure
desperate routines

we're inspired above
the surface parade
of men dressed up in power

we see the clear possibility
of life growing
to witness itself

let these words
of my mouth
be sound

the creations
of my heart
be light

so I can see myself
free of desperate symbols
mind-woven coverings

speechless fears
images hidden within
we are the subjects of light

opening to join you
vision itself
my constant creator.

PSALM 22

Lord, My Lord, you disappear
so far away
unpierced by my cry

my sigh of words
all day My Lord
unheard

murmur of groans at night
then silence
no response

while you rest
content
in the songs of Israel

in the trust of fathers
you delivered
who cried to you

they were brought home
warm and alive
and inspired

but I am a worm
subhuman
what men come to

with a hate of their own futures
despised
and cheered like a drunk

staggering across the street
they howl after him
like sick dogs

"Let the Lord he cried to
save him
since they were so in love"

you brought me through the womb
to the sweetness
at my mother's breasts

no sooner my child eyes
looked around
I was in your lap

you are My Lord
from the time my mother found
me inside

make yourself appear
I am surrounded
and no one near

Psalms

a mad crowd
tightens a noose around me
the ring of warheads

pressing ravenous noses
the mad whispering of
gray technicians

the water of my life evaporates
my bones stick through the surface
my heart burns down like wax

melting into my stomach
my mouth dry as a clay cup
dug up in the yard

I've fallen into the mud
foaming dogs surround me
ghost men

pierce my hands and feet
my bones stare at me
in disbelief

men take my clothes
like judges
in selfish dreams

make yourself appear
My Lord show me
the power

to free my life from chains
of bitter command
from the mouths of ghost men

trained on my heart
like a city
save me from mindless

megaphones of hate
you've always heard me
from my human heart

allowed me to speak
in the air of your name
to men and women

all who know fear
of losing yourselves
in vacant cities

speak to him
Israel's children
sing with him

all seed of men
show your faces
amazed in love

he does not despise them
he has not disappeared
from the faces of earth

from the ground of the worm
or the ear of the victim
I will always repeat

this song of life
with my hand that is free
from men who need victims

may our hearts live forever!
and the furthest reaches of space
remember our conscious moment

inspiring light
like those disappeared from memory
returned to the planet's earth

everyone has to appear
at death's door
everyone falls to the ground

while his seed carries on
writing and speaking
to people still to come

who remember to sing
how generous My Lord appears
to those hearing.

The Lord is my shepherd
and keeps me from wanting
what I can't have

lush green grass is set
around me and crystal water
to graze by

there I revive with my soul
find the way that love makes
for his name   and though I pass

through cities of pain, through death's living shadow
I'm not afraid to touch
to know what I am

your shepherd's staff is always there
to keep me calm
in my body

you set a table before me
in the presence of my enemies
you give me grace to speak

to quiet them
to be full with humanness
to be warm in my soul's lightness

to feel contact every day
in my hand and in my belly
love coming down to me

in the air of your name, Lord
in your house
in my life.

PSALM 30

High praises
to you who raised me
up

so my critics fall silent
from their death wishes
over me

Lord Most High
I called you
and I was made new

you pulled me back
from the cold lip of the grave
and I am alive

to sing to you
friends, play in his honor
band of steady hearts

his anger like death
passes in a moment
his love lasts forever

cry yourself to sleep
but when you awake
light is all around you

I thought I was experienced
nothing was going to shake me
I was serious as a mountain

Lord, you were with me and then
you were gone
I looked for your face in terror

my body was made of clay
My Lord, it is now
I call you

what good is my blood my tears
sinking in the mud
is mere dust singing

can it speak
these words on my tongue, Lord
help me

turn my heavy sighing into dance
loosen my shirt and pants
and wrap me in your glow

so my heart can find its voice
through my lips to you
warm and alive

rising
above all bitterness
high praises.

PSALM 36

Inside my heart I hear
how arrogance talks
to himself without fear

hidden from eyes
he flatters himself
but we see him on the faces

of false faces and words
thinking—even asleep—
how to squeeze love out

from feelings from words
how to put wisdom on her back
then hold his miniature knowledge back

your love fills a man, Lord
with a kind of air
making him lighter

he rises in measure of your judgment
above the mountains of thought
above the clouds of feeling

the strength of his measure stays
in the eyes returning to mountains
from the surface of the sea

he falls like any animal
standing up only by your mercy
his children grow in the shadow of your wings

feast on gourmet fare in your house
with water that sparkles from wells
beyond the reach of a mind

the fountain of life
is lit
by your light

you extend your embrace
to those who feel you are there
keep holding the loving

keep us from being crushed
by arrogant feet
by the hand of pride

the powerful are falling over themselves
their minds have pulled them down
there they will lie, flung down.

PSALM 49

Now hear this, world
all who live in air
important, ordinary, poor

my lips are moved by a saying
my heart whispers
in sound sense

I measure with my ear
this dark message and it opens
around my lyre

why should I make fear
dog my steps
growl in my thoughts

when the masters of vanity
breed in public for attention
rolling in scraps of money

no man can build a way
to God outside his body
to buy his continual release

to pay a ransom in every moment
for the gift of living
the price higher than his power to think

so that he could live forever
.blind to his own falling
into the pit of death

but we all can see
the wisest man dies
along with the cunningly petty

their fortunes pass like mumbled words
among others
above their graves

it is there in hardened silence
the inheritors will join them
their bodily measure of earth

and though they put their names
on spaces of land,
their inward thoughts like words,

the mouths wither around them—
prosperous men
lose their intelligence

remember that in its saying
like animals who leave nothing to quote
those men pass on totally self-centered

like sheep gathered into the earth
their followers headlong after them
death's herd

their flesh stripped in death's store
and the big show made standing upright
erased in the sunrise

but My Lord holds the ransom
for death's vain embrace
as this music holds me—inside

don't be afraid of the big man
who builds a house that seems to grow
to the pride of his family

nothing will lie between
his body with its pride
and the ground he falls to

the life he made happy for himself
"so men may praise you
in your prosperity"

will find the company
of his fathers
around him as total darkness

his inward thoughts like words
the mouth withers around—
prosperous men lose their intelligence.

Can this be justice
this pen to hold
they that move my arm

to follow them—blind stars?
They think I have submitted
to the vicious decorum of fame?

Oh generation come from dust
Oh no: you steel yourselves
to write; your hands

weigh, like a primitive scale,
selfish desire unfulfilled . . .
strangers from the womb

no sooner born and here
than chasing after
impulsive wishes

for which they will lie, cheat, kill.
Cancerous cold desire
gnaws in their brain

as the doctor
the greatest virtuoso specialist
numbs their consciousness

cutting into the chest
exposing the vital organ
totally blind to the truth.

Lord, cramp their fingers
till the arms hang limp like sausage,
grind down to sand

the teeth of the power-hungry
and let their selves dissolve into it
like ebbing tide on a junk-strewn beach

and when they in profound bitterness
unsheathe the sharpened thought
cut it out of their brain, Love!

make them disappear like snails
slime of their bodies melting away
or like babies, cord cut in abortion

to be thrown out as discharge
eyes withered in the daylight
though they never looked at it.

And let the children of greed like weeds
be pulled from their homes
and their parents blown away like milkweed . . .

The loving man will be revived
by this revenge and step ashore
from the bloodlust of the self-righteous

so that every man can say
there is justice so deep
a loving man has cause to sing.

PSALM 73

My Lord is open
to Israel, to all hearts
within hearing

but I turned and
almost fell   moved
by flattery spoken

through transparent shrouds
impressing me
with the power of imagery

and fame of the mind
loving to strut
in its mirror

with its unfelt body
smooth as a machine
without a care in the world

prosperous mouthpieces
in their material cars
of pride

and suits of status
covering up
crookedness

their eyes
are walls
for wish-images

their mouths big
cynical
megaphones

self-made gods
whose words envelop the heads of men
hiding their fears

they go through the world
in self-encasing roles
in which they will die

lowered in heavy caskets
they made themselves
out of words

but meanwhile they suck in
most people
draining their innocence

until everyone believes
God isn't there
no wonder these men prosper

they push through the world
their violence
makes them secure

it seemed I opened my heart
and hand
stupidly

every day had its torture
every morning
my nerves were exposed

I was tempted to hide
to kill the moment
with pride

instead I tried to know you
and keep your song alive
but my mind was useless

until my heart opened
the cosmic door
to a continual presence

that is you
lighting the future
above the highway

down which self-flattering men
travel in style
to prisons of mind-locked time

they have their pleasures
cruelly pursued
and you urge them

to their final reward
you let them rise on dead bodies
so they have to fall

like a bad dream
the moment you awake
they are gone forever

my mind was dry thought
my feelings drained
through dusty clay

I was blindly
eating through life
like a moth in wool

I was crude
too proud
to know you

yet continually with you
take my hand
in love

it sings with you
inspired advice
leading to your presence

what will I want
but continual inspiration
in the present with you

what else will I find
in the blues of the sky
but you

and me in you
where am I in what universe
without you

my body dies of exhaustion
but you are the mountain
lifting my open heart

higher than a mind can go
into the forever
into the future

men who hide in their hearts
have bitter minds
they will lose

those people become no one
leaving you for an ideology
for a material car

but I waited for you
I was open, My Lord
to find my song

I found you here
in music I continue
to hear

with each new breath
expanding
to give me space.

PSALM 82

My Lord is the judge
at the heart
in the infinite

speaking through time and space
to all gods
he let be

"instead of lips
smoothed by success
and appearances

defend your silent critic
locked in barred categories
his conscience

painfully opened
by vicious systems
release him

let him speak
break the grip
of the prosperous

whose things enclose them
from the lightness of knowledge
the openness of understanding

they build in darkness
burying justice
digging at the foundation

of earth and men
the orbit
of trust"

I was thinking
you too are gods
heads of nations

thoughts of My Lord
but you will disappear
like the spirit you silence

your heads fall
like great nations
in ruins

My Lord, open
their consciousness
to share your judgment

all nations are men
you hear
beyond categories.

PSALM 90

Lord, you are our home
in all time
from before the mountains rose

or even the sun
from before the universe
to after the universe

you are Lord forever
and we are home
in your flowing

you turn men into dust
and you ask them to return
children of men

for a thousand years
in your eyes
are a single day

yesterday
already passed
into today

a ship in the night
while we were present
in a human dream

submerged
in the flood of sleep
appearing in the morning

like new grass
growing into afternoon
cut down by evening

we are swept off our feet
in an unconscious wind
of war or nature

or eaten away
with anxiety
worried to death

worn-out swimmers
all dressed up
in the social whirl

you see our little disasters
secret lusts
broken open in the light

of your eyes
in the openness
penetrating our lives

every day melts away
before you
our years run away

into a sigh
at the end
of a story

over in another breath
seventy years
eighty—gone in a flash

and what was it?
a tinderbox of vanity
a show of pride

and we fly apart
in the empty mirror
in the spaces between stars

in the total explosion of galaxies
how can we know ourselves
in this human universe

without expanding
to the wonder that you are
infinite lightness

piercing my body
this door of fear
to open my heart

our minds are little stars
brief flares
darkness strips naked

move us to see your present
as we're moved to name each star
lighten our hearts with wonder

return
and forgive us
locking our unconscious

behind the door
and as if it isn't there
as if we forget we're there

we walk into space unawed
unknown to ourselves
years lost in thought

a thousand blind moments
teach us when morning comes
to be moved

to see ourselves rise
returning witnesses
from the deep unconscious

and for every day lost
we find a new day
revealing where we are

in the future and in the past
together again
this moment with you

made human for us
to see your work
in the open-eyed grace of children

the whole vision unlocked
from darkness
to the thrill of light

where our hands reach for another's
opening to life
in our heart's flow

the work of this hand
flowing open
to you and from you.

PSALM 101

The city of your love
sings through me
before you, My Lord

you hold my writing hand
that makes my living
creative act

won't you come to me?
I sit here in my house
with an open heart

no willful image
blocks the door,
I just won't see

the theatrics of personality
crowding
the openness you allow

this art that hurts
those with ears for only jewelry
they go far away

locked within themselves
their self-flattery
I've reduced to silence

their narrow eyes
inflated pride
blown away

I'm always looking
for your people
to share this space

the contact of imagination
inspired
by necessity

beyond the stage doors
of weak characters
cut off from real streets

no more precious actors
costumed in sound
to litter this town with clichés

every morning
I silence with your light
desperate images

they run away
from the city of your name
that calls an open heart.

PSALM 114

When Israel came out of Egypt
like a child suddenly free
from a people of strange speech

Judah became a home
for the children of Israel
as they became a sanctuary

for the God of their fathers:
Once, this House of Israel
stammered into the open

and as the sea saw them coming
it ran from the sight
the Jordan stopped dead in its tracks

mountains leaped like frightened rams
hills were a scattering flock
of lambs

What was so alarming, sea?
Jordan, what vision
drained your strength away?

Mountains, why did you quake
like fearful rams?
Hills, why did you jump like lambs?

Earth, tremble again, again
in the presence
of your maker's voice

it was the God of Jacob
and he is here
all around you

a sudden pool of water
from a desert rock
a fountain from wilderness stone—

life from a heart of stone
and from bitter tears
sweet-spoken land.

PSALM 121

I look up and find a mountain
to know inside
then light appears

inspired from most high
My Lord, creator
of earth and sky

we shall not be moved
this power inside
never fell asleep

over Israel
My Lord is in the light
the atmosphere

the power that moves my hand
through the sunlight that doesn't melt me
and by the moonlight

that moves us inside
to be inspired
above burning pride

desire
which is the mountain of our life
held in his air

and by his hand
we're free
to be moved

we may come and go
from now
to forever.

PSALM 130

I am drowning
deep in myself, Lord
I'm crying

I'm calling you
hear this voice, Lord
find me in your ears

the mercy of your attention
as it looks through the shell
of my selfishness

if you see only
vain impulses
marking the body's surface

the lines in the face
then there is no one
who'd hold up his head

but you allow us forgiveness
allow a song
coming through us

to you
as I call to you
as I rely on these words

as I wait
for you
more certain than dawn

through the steady ticking till morning
wait, Israel
even when watches seem to stop

My Lord comes to me
in a rush of love
setting my heart free

into a bright sky
we are lightened
in the mercy of his attention.

PSALM 133

It's so good, the turn of a season
people living for a moment as equals
secure in the human family

as sweet as spring rain
making the beard silky
Aaron's beard

his robes sparkle
rich with heaven's simple jewels
like the crown of dew

on Lebanon's Mount Hermon
shared equally on the hills
of Israel

where the Lord graces our eyes
fresh from reborn wonder
as if we'd live forever.

PSALM 137

Into the rivers of Babylon
we cried like babies, loud
unwilling to move

beyond the memory
the flowing blood
of you, Israel

to an orchestra of trees
we lent our harps
silently leaning

when the enemy shoved us
"asking" tender songs of Israel
under heavy chains

"give us songs of Israel!"
as if we could give our mouths
to a strange landlord . . .

If I forget thee
sweet Jerusalem
let my writing hand wither

my tongue freeze to ice
sealing up my voice
my mind numb as rock

if I forget
your kiss
Jerusalem on my lips . . .

My Lord
remembers you, Edomites
Jerusalem raped vivid as daylight

you who screamed to strip her
strip her naked
to the ground

Oh Lady Babylon
Babylon the destroyer
lucky man who holds you

who crushes you
who opens your mind
to wither instantly in air

who holds up your crying babies
as if to stun them
against solid rock.

PSALM 139

There's nothing in me, My Lord
that doesn't open to your eyes
you know me when I sit

you note when I arise
in the darkest closet of my thought
there is an open window of sunshine for you

you walk with me
lie down with me
at every move await me

at every pause
you know the words
my tongue will print in air

if I say yes
you have already nodded
no—and you have shaken your head

in any doubts I lose my way
I find your hand
on me

such knowledge so high
I can never reach with a mind
or hold any longer than a breath

to get away from you
I could let my imagination fly
but you would hold it in your sky

or I could sleep with the dead in the ground
but your fire from the depths
would awaken me

I could fly on gold ray of sun
from dawn in east
west to stars of night

and your hand
would point the way
and your right hand hold me steady

however close I pull the night around me
even at midnight
day strips me naked

in your tender sight
black and white
are one—all light

you who put me together
piece by piece in the womb
from light

that work shines
through the form of my skeleton
on my song of words

you watched as my back steadied
the still-soft fuselage of ribs
in primitive studio deep within

you saw me as putty
a life unfashioned
a plane at the bottom of the sea

and the great book of its life
this embryo will write
in a body you have sculpted

My Lord—your thoughts
high and precious
beyond logic like stars

or like grains of sand I try to count
I fall asleep and awake
on the beach of your making

My Lord—stop the breath
of men who live by blood
alone and lie to your face

who think they can hide
behind the same petty smile
they use to smear your name

My Lord—you hear me hate
back your haters
with total energy

concentrated
in one body
that is yours and mine

My Lord—look at me
to see my heart
test me—to find my mind

if any bitterness lives here
lead me out
into the selfless open.

PART III

WRITING

Psalms

L A M E N T A T I O N S

There are several laments that comprise Lamentations, each most likely from a different poet. There were probably many laments and elegies that were not as pertinent but that helped create a Hebrew elegiac tradition.

The poet who composed the third and most personal chapter of Lamentations may have written psalms and prophetic poetry as well, since this poem radiates formal mastery. The daughter of Zion whose voice laments throughout the book seems a particularly vulnerable sensibility in this poem, and it seems worthwhile to imagine the author as a woman. At the time of writing, her poem was passed from hand to hand, her seal a mark of genius. Not yet a chapter in a book (scroll), this poem may have been collected by the circle of poets returning to Jerusalem from exile in Babylon.

The lament was already an ancient form when this great Hebrew poet lived, and it was central to the ancestral tradition of women prophets. Long before, Sumerian laments over the destruction of cities were being composed as Abram left Ur for Canaan; usually these compositions were put into the mouth of the ruined city's goddess. The Jewish poet of Lamentations assimilated this form to a Hebraic vision. She transformed the patron goddess of ancient cities into the daughter of Zion, who is no goddess but only a metaphor to convey feelings of loss—the loss of people, first, and then homeland.

The voice in Lamentations faces a God who allows his one Temple to be destroyed. The poet makes his loss intensely personal, probably within a generation of the actual event in 587 BCE. There is no justifying the catastrophe, and no easy comfort in absolute answers. As Jerusalem personified, the poet does not turn suffering into a condition for redemption. We are losers, she admits, yet we share the disaster with the deity. In worldly terms, the poet remains alive to the reality of an imperfect world, and that worldview was probably assimilated in Babylon along with the complex acrostic form of the poem.

This poet founds her work on typically Hebraic calls to prophecy: the need to bear witness and to dramatize vulnerability. The unspeakable is given a peculiarly Jewish voice that confronts the mysteries, silences, and abandonments of the ancient religions of that time with personal testimony. No event could be too sacred for such poets, who now found themselves writing in exile in Babylon.

Although born into the literate upper class, the poet might have been a widow or orphan of a Levite (a class of liturgical scribes and musicians) and any religious prohibitions against her authorship would have been broken in the devastation of exile. Centuries later, tradition would ascribe her poem to the prophet Jeremiah, but I've tried to restore the original author's poem in its idiomatic yet strict stanzas. Formally complex, the poem manages to contrast the daughter of Zion's intimate speech with a choric response—a vestigial chorus—in its refrain.

The liturgical use of Lamentations as the central scroll of Tisha B'Av, an ancient fast day commemorating the devastation of the Temple, was reinforced after the destruction of the second Temple by the Romans. Many additional poems were composed for historical catastrophes on up through the Middle Ages and European pogroms. These are collected in a book of Kinot, or laments, that quote and adapt Lamentations to contemporary events. A Holocaust lamentation would not be out of place.

lamentations

It is I who have seen
with just human eyes

suffering beyond the power of men
to know is there

a wrath so deep
we are struck dumb

and we are sheep
seized by animal terror

defenseless before a world unleashed
from anything human

we have seen its frenzy raised like an arm
but we feel our shepherd's blow

BET

He has led me into darkness
a valley no light can reach

nothing to illumine the smallest step I take
though I follow what he alone may teach

he has turned against me
with the arm that pointed my way

it is I alone who felt his hand
all sleepless night and day again

he reduced me to skin and bones
my skin was paper for his heavy hand

I was under siege
I was herded into ghettoes

GHIMEL

My mind was utterly stranded
surrounded by seas of poverty

he let me sit in the dark
until I could not think

I was sealed up in a tomb
with the ancient dead

I was fenced in like sheep
I was locked in an empty room

I was bound in chains
I could not turn around

I could not stand up to pray
he had turned away

DALET

I would cry after him for help
my throat was dry as clay

all my hopes came to roadblocks
all my dreams to barbed wire

inside myself I was exposed in a desert
all my ways arrived at despair

he was a scorpion in my path
a lion crouching in the brush

he had become my nightmare
a mad bear in my tracks

a cancer waiting inside me
a fear of being torn to pieces

HEY

He had mauled my confidence
I was a living horror

all the world turned its eyes away
I crawled in the desert

I was his target
I was pinned in the center of his sight

I was pierced in my vital organs
I had lost control of my bowels

I was a laughingstock to the world
he made me their crudest joke

he passed me the cup of bitterness
he made me drunk with tears

VAV

I was dazed with wormwood
I was in a deadly stupor

he pressed my face in the dust
I had ground my teeth to bits

I have woken with my heart in pieces
I have breakfasted on ashes

my life was pulled from my grasp
my soul was in exile

I was a hollow shell
I was a stranger to myself

peace was a dry husk, an empty word
I was blown in the wind

ZAYEN

I forgot what goodness means
shalom meant nothing to me

and I thought: my spirit is dead
hope in God is beyond me

I was broken down, mumbling
I was shattered by anxiety

the more I thought about my suffering—
remembering the agony of my losses—

the more I tasted wormwood
turning to poison within me

and now, still, I remember everything
my soul staggers into exile:

Memory the weight on my back
and deep in my breast every crushing detail

I cannot close my eyes before it
I cannot rise from my bed

and yet I do each day
and I rouse my heart

that the memory itself so vividly lives
awakens a deathless hope

loving-kindness like air
cannot be used up

though I breathe heavily, locked in a room
beyond the wall a wind blows freely

TET

The Lord's mercy brings a new morning
each day awakens the thought of him

though I'm buried in nights of doubt
day returns faithfully—he's always there

"The Lord is all that I have"
calls my soul and my heart responds

my hope lives within, infinite as mercy
how else could I *remember* it!

the Lord is good to me
because I do not turn and run

his goodness does not disappear
to the heart turning to him:

Y O D

Remembering in the turning
trusting in the memory

how good to find patience
to let rejected hope return

and how good to learn
to bear the burden young

to sit silent and alone
when the weight falls on your shoulders

to feel the weight of your maker
as all hope seems lost

to put your mouth to dust
(perhaps living is still worthwhile)

⬓

To turn your cheek to its striker
to be overwhelmed by abuse

to face the worst
to drink your fill of disgrace

to swallow mockery of things held dear
to survive the poison of humiliation

⬓

KAPH

How good to be desolate and alone
because the Lord does not reject forever

after the intensity of anger
mercy returns in a firm embrace

because his love lasts forever
beyond anything we can know

no matter how far away
he does not abandon his creation

we were not tormented lightly
yet nothing in him desired suffering

he didn't desire to make us earth's prisoners
returning to the dust at our feet

LAMED

And when men lower us in their eyes
cheapen our right to be ourselves

when we are brutalized by "universal" justice
subverting the word "justice" itself

because men believe they are not seen
are not in God's presence when they judge

(even with their hands laid upon Bibles
their interest devout self-interest)

and when we are tormented for being different
by laws of idol or human supremacy

his justice is brutally mocked
he has not desired it:

MEM

His own creation abandoning him
is a horror

but men can say and do as they want
they can act like gods: speak and it comes to pass

but they become heartless idols speaking
they will pass into dust and silence

they couldn't have opened their eyes
if the Lord did not desire it

and they strut in iron over us
yet the Lord does not will it—

because the words for good and evil
both came from him

N U N

We the living have a complaint
ignorance

a strong man or woman remembers
their weakness

instead of running from the past
turn to face the source

open your heart on the rough path of knowing
open your mind on the hard road of understanding

the solid ground supports
firm trust

let us search our ways
examine the difficulties within:

SAMECH

Where the will and faith turn bitter
repent that loss, return to him

take your heart in your hands
lift it high

sweetness flows from a broken heart
to heaven

we have hurt and destroyed
in self-righteous ignorance

Lord, we were lost in clouds of our own making
you could not forgive this

you knocked us down
you exposed us to your anger:

PEY

You were hidden behind it
we were slaughtered without mercy

the earth was a vast pen for us
you were hidden beyond the clouds

our prayers were hollow echoes
our hopes were crushed flowers

littering the ground like discolored pages
ripped from prayer books

you had made us garbage
in the world's eyes

human refuse
reeking in a senseless world

A Y E N

Our misery only enraged them
all our enemies gathered to jeer us

we were beaten as a whining dog
our blood pounded in our ears

their mouths were opened wide
pouring our hatred

the world in open chorus
blind and shameless

we had fallen into a hole
the world was a hunter's pit

death was our horizon
terror as far as our eyes could see

TZADDIK

A dam burst in my eyes
to see the heart of my people broken

the daughter of my people terrorized
her defenses breached, pride swept away

all the built-up pressure released
like a river that runs forever

until the Lord looks down
to me

what I see with my own eyes
floods my mind, sickens me

I am swept up in the wake
of my daughter's despair

QOPH

I was brought down for no reason
like a bird with a stone

by people who hate me just for being
again they bring me down, again

I am thrown into a pit
a stone is rolled over me

I who sing to the sky
am not to breathe

the nations of the world were like water
flowing over my head

to whom could I turn
I said to myself "I am gone"

RESH

In the deepest pit, Lord
I was drowning, alone

in the depths of abandonment
yet your name was on my lips

and you knew I was there
do not turn your ear from my groaning

whenever I turned to prayer
I felt you suddenly near

as if you said "do not fear"
Lord, you restored my soul

you were there and I knew
I could never be disowned

SHIN

You gave me the right to be myself
and you've seen men take it away

you've seen the hands across my mouth
Lord, speak for me and clear my name

even words have been subverted
I was brought to the bar of injustice

you saw their barbarous vengeance
you saw their final solution

my life was a living death
I was butchered for you

my death was the solution to all their problems
all their imagination was brought to my dying

TAUF

You heard their hatred crafted against me
as shameless as daily prayers

holy alliances condemning me
you saw the papers drawn up openly

their minds and their mouths fastened on me
like bloodsuckers

behind my back or in their company
I was spittle on their lips

in conference or on the street
I am the scapegoat uniting them

I lighten their labors
I am the guinea pig of their salvation

⌖

For the hands they raise to slaughter us
with your hand, Lord, strike them deeply within

let their pride be the poison they swallow
their hearts are stones, their minds tombstones

etched there forever let all their words mock them
with their bloody thoughts spilling into silent dust.

⌖

Although I've designated it Song of Songs, *as it is known in Hebrew,* Shir ha-Shirim, *I prefer the resonance of the traditional title,* Song of Solomon, *because it suggests a single author. There are no doubt "quotations" from other poems in* Song of Solomon, *but the singular sensibility of the poem is what I would emphasize.*

The Aramaic targumim *(ancient translations) of the* Song of Solomon *are allegorical, taking the kind of liberties with the Hebrew that we might call fictionalizing. The text is easily allegorized because it already embodies a transformation of imagery in the plausibility of King Solomon's original composition. Some of the imagery comes from ancient Canaanite ritual songs for mythological marriage rites. By transforming a pagan liturgy into a poem of passion, human and divine, Solomon—or a "Solomonic poet"—demythologized it.*

It's fashionable among some biblical scholars to read the preferred title of Song of Songs *as if it were a collection of secular love songs. Marcia Falk's translation does it best, yet it can't help turning the poem into another allegory, a modern one of sensuality. The imagery in the original text, however, reflects a powerful and characteristic type of early Jewish irony, a provocative appropriation of pagan liturgical style in which the lovers were gods, and the occasion of anxiety, fertility rites. The imagery, as transmuted in the* Song of Solomon, *comes free of its ritual usage; the emotional anxiety of the lover is personally felt.*

I find the poem to be sophisticated, the narrator assuming the dream persona of his lover as well as the voices of a chorus (in order to satirize those ancient conventions, as Greek poets often did). I've translated the fifth chapter of the Song of Solomon, *although I don't believe the original was divided into chapters. In fact, I would suggest that we have only a fragment of the original poem, much of it edited by later, priestly hands.*

The editors did not forget that the great king was the putative author. It makes sense that Solomon was a serious poet, given the reputation of his father, David. And unlike his father, he had the benefit of a court education. He no doubt encouraged a large retinue of poets at his own court, of which more than one may have collaborated with him on the Song of Solomon. These professional poets would also have found exotic sources for the poem in Canaanite forms, knowing Solomon's reputation as lover to his many wives (in political marriages) of non-Jewish origin.

In this portion of the poem, the female protagonist's anxiety about Solomon suggests the poet was familiar with longing. And yet I can also imagine him as a father, consoling a lovesick daughter. I suspect the poet received much support (if not direct help) from the woman in question. She would have appreciated the way the king personalized the customs of mythical and earthly love, and how he localized the scene in Jerusalem. But if not Solomon or his court poets, Hebraic poets of a later date added as well a dimension of threat or loss to Jerusalem personified.

song of solomon

I will be in my garden
as I am deep within you
my bride

as if you are my sister
I am rich in spices—
as if my bride, I pluck fresh myrrh

I am rich with honey
and I will eat the honeycomb whole
as well

I will have my wine, my bride
and it is pure, my sister
as milk and honey

friend, you will eat
you will drink deeply, lover
you will be rich with love, my dearest friend

I was asleep
but the soul within me
stayed awake

like my heart—true to a timeless rhythm
to which I still respond—
listen, a gentle knocking

like my heart's beating—
Open to me, my love
my purest image, sister, dove

all I can imagine—my head is drenched
with dew, all my memories
melt into you

I would walk through nights of blinding rain
all doors locked to my presence
I would be happy in blackest exile

knowing you alone would not reject me
never forget
not turn away—

⋈

But I've undone the robe of devotion
where I wrapped my naked heart before you—
how can I rise to your presence?

I've washed the feet that were tired and dirty
when I walked in the reality of your presence—
how can I stand and face myself?

⌘

My love who came inside me
whom I held firmly
whose hand was on the lock of my being

removed his arms
pulled his hand away—
I awoke and

I was drawn to him
a softness spread in me
I was open within

and then I was desolate and empty
he had gone
my heart leapt from my breast

I ran to the door
my soul overwhelmed me
my hands were drenched, as if with perfume

it was my love for him—
the lock was wet with the myrrh
of my devotion

I opened for my love
I alone was open to him
but he had gone

the one for whom I trembled
heard it from my lips
how I had turned from him when

I thought I was alone—
suddenly my soul no longer knew me
just as I had forgotten him

I was riveted with anxiety
I was as lifeless as an empty robe
I couldn't move

my feet were a statue's feet
I was lifeless clay
I was naked earth

then I wandered through the streets
looking for signs of his nearness
seeing nothing

I called, I cried
desperate for his closeness
hearing only silence

only my enemies heard me, like watchmen
patrolling my city's walls
who found me in night gown

who saw me vulnerable and alone
who struck me down
I was wounded for my distraction

my robe my dignity stripped away
I could not even pray
my heart was in my mouth

but now, nations of the world, I warn you
when you see my love
when you turn toward Jerusalem

you will say I bore all for him
the pain and loss was love for him
I was his to the core

"But what makes your love any better than ours
what makes you so beautiful
that he leaves you, and you search for him?

How is your love better than any other
that you stoop from your ivory tower
daring to warn us?"

My love is white with radiance
red with vigorous strength
unmistakable—a banner leading the way

over the heads of a great army
and his head more inspiring than a crown of gold
his hair a raven-black flame

a dove's eyes, clear
beside a soothing river
reflecting its depth, brimming

pools of tenderness—
indestructible jewels
set in whites of kindness

his gaze a penetrating shaft of light
so deft
it is milk—warm and familiar

his words are riverbanks, firm
lush spice beds
a lingering perfume

to remind you of his lips
which are roses
his beard a soft bed of grass

to lean against like a page of his words
bathed in transparent dew
flowing with myrrh

his arms form a vessel of gold
to hold me secure
as a voyager to Tarshish

his will is a sail
and his desires
are a steady wind

his belly is polished ivory—
and strong, clear as azure
is his skin—a cloudless sky

his legs are firm columns
fine as marble
and his feet like golden pedestals—

columns of a scroll, words of spun gold—
his appearance naturally noble as
Lebanon cedars swaying in the breeze

his breath a delicious breeze
words a golden nectar
sustenance and delight

he is altogether delightful—
this is my love
and this my true friend

who never abandons me
a love so pure
you will know it unmistakably

when you turn toward Jerusalem
nations of the world
and all your sons and daughters.

J O B

The poet who composed Job, *probably in the seventh century* BCE, *based it on an old legend. Embedded in the brief prose tale that frames the book, the legend tells what happens to a man in the grip of a terrible fate. Yet the poet of* Job *twists the legend beyond the pagan realm of "fate" and with much irony, so that when Job finally submits to his fate he's rewarded with a better life.*

A greater irony is that this is not a book about submission at all, since the poem that takes over the text refuses to submit—it rages against the indifference of fate. Job can't imagine that the Creator would be indifferent, and in his stubborn zeal for the truth, Job is made characteristically Jewish by the Hebrew poet, unconsciously venting the most unconventional blasphemies.

The poem is cast in the form of a dialogue between Job and his friends. They advise him to accept his fate, suggesting ways to rescue his dignity. Job will not resign. In the end, God becomes a character wrapped in a whirlwind, intimidating Job into resignation. Even in this scene, and in the framing scene where the Creator sits in his celestial court, Job is the truer character. The poet presents a caricature of God as a representation for conventional religion (itself the subject of caricature) in his day: Master of Nature, He lacks a human range of emotions. But one thing the character of God does not lack is a sense of irony; Job is the one who appears to be badly in need of it.

But Job's own words, as they reject irony—refusing to distance himself from pain—become an ironic triumph. How can we possibly live unless we hide some of our feelings? Job refuses the question; yet, in fact, he uses language and poetry gloriously—the very language that normally helps to sublimate feelings. In the character of Job, the Hebrew poet gives us a powerful portrait of a man divided against himself by language. And in this sense, he is echoed two thousand years later in English, in Shakespeare's Hamlet.

Both Job and Hamlet listen to themselves as they speak. The Hebrew poet lets the irony of Job's speeches comment on themselves, while Hamlet comments directly. And the framing comments of the Creator in Job and of Horatio, who represents the human memory of Hamlet's life, serve to draw further attention to the verbal gifts of the protagonists, Job and Hamlet.

I focused on Job's speeches, the heart of the book. The summation of contemporaneous thought in the friends' speeches suggests that the Hebrew poet enlarged his poem at different times in his life, making the complete Job his life's work.

Most acutely in the words of Job, the poet drew upon popular proverbial expressions for irony, and I've consciously used the occasional cliché and idiom of popular culture for similar counterpoint. Our airwaves are just as filled with contending superstition and folklore (disguised as commercials, propaganda or homily) as were the newsbearers of the ancient Middle East. Like many of the biblical poets and prophets, the poet of Job was a master of the satiric use of officialese.

In search of an English equivalent to the complex illusion of spokenness in Job's speeches, I found it suggested in American poetry's struggle with natural speech, especially as it absorbed the influences of jazz composition in the twentieth century. The shifts and changes in the flow of ordinary conversation, the often surreal collage of overheard imagery, heightens the sense of timing in the ear of William Carlos Williams—as it does for the jazz musician-poet, who composes as he performs. John Coltrane famously said, "You got to keep talking / to be real." I think the quotation is apt for the character of Job.

job

CHAPTER 3

Rip up the day I was born
and the night that furnished a bed
with people to make me

the pillow from every night I lived
smother that day   cover its light
so God can forget it

let death's shadow
hold the ether mask there
clouds obliterate it

a total eclipse
blackout
swallow it a tiny pill

and that sweat that night beginning me
black oil absorb it
a hole drilled deep in calendars

shrivel that night in the hand of history
let it soften in impotence
turn off its little shouts of pleasure

every science unsex it
genetic biology   advanced psychology
nuclear bomb

no next morning shine on it
through the afterglow
singeing the eyelids of dawn

because it didn't shut the door
of the womb on me
to hide my eyes from pain

why couldn't I have been
a lucky abortion
why were there two knees

waiting for me
two breasts to suck
without them I could have stayed asleep

I could have melted away
like spilled semen
in transparent air

wrapped up in quiet dust
with gods of power and influence
and the emptiness of their palaces

with rich families their money
paper houses
for plastic children

with criminals who can't break loose
there they rest with tired workers
no more hell from bosses or jailers

who all fall down
under one blanket
not the simplest machine to serve them

why should someone have to live
locked in a miserable spotlight
bitter inside

waiting for a death far off
they search for it restlessly
like the final person in a late-night bar

they can't wait to see the iron gate unlock
and the little grave plot
comforts them

why should someone have to walk around
blinded by the daylight
he can't wave off

that God throws on him
waiting at every exit
in front of me

a table of sighs to eat
and moaning
poured out like water

every horror I imagined
walks right up to me
no privacy no solitude

and my pain
with my mind
pushes rest aside.

CHAPTER 6

Weigh my anguish
heave my misery on that scale
heavier than a planet

a scale filled with sand
that's how words fail me
God's arrows spinning past me

poisoning my spirit
wearing me away
little petty arguments

would you like only egg whites
no salt to season
every meal

the soul blanches
dizzy at the sight
of my own white flesh

I hope God will change this prayer
white paper hope
to violence of reality

crush me
snip off my life
paper

what a relief
I'd leap with delight
that departing train of pain

knowing I broke no law
but where to get some strength to wait
cold patience

a head of stone
skin of metal
nerves frozen dead

no help from inside
I can't reach in there
anymore

sick spirit
my dear friends
disappearing frightened nurses

and snow falls
over mouths of pure water
hidden high in mountains

of themselves
sheer ice cliffs
face my simple thirst

spring comes
they dry up
fast as a mirage

caravans lost
looking for what they thought
new roads

new places
fresh faces
tricked

by nature's technology
human nature's
idiocy

and that's how you look at me friends
panicked
into your empty words

do I say give me
things or money
save me from enemy

pay my dues for me
so talk straight I listen
at my open mistake

honesty so easy to take
but not the "advice"
unsheathed metal

to pain me with words
and deaf to mine
the wind blows away

do you lecture disaster victims
high-pressure a friend
stab love full of arguments

now look at me
face into face
no place here to glibly hide

think again—your thinking stopped
as in a blind spot
you passed my integrity

my face wide open
as I speak
my tongue there true

not as if I couldn't taste
bitter fruit
my words in my mouth.

CHAPTER 7

We're all somebody's workers
in a big factory
grasping for breaks

reaching for paychecks and prizes
here I'm paid these empty months
heavy nights awarded

to lie down and wait
for getting up
dragged through toss and turnings

body dressed in a texture of scars
little white worms of skin
while days run on smoothly

through a tape recorder
to run out
beyond machine of hope

mouth making a little wind
eyes straining harder
to finally disappear

in front of others' eyes
as clouds breaking up
we fall beneath the ground

we don't go home again
house doesn't know me
so nothing holds me back here

listen to this mind in pain
this "educated" soul
in words it complains

am I some Frankenstein
to be guarded
can't go to sleep alone

find some dream waiting
to terrify me
break my neck

only to find it there again
why not a hand instead
to really choke me

shake hands with despair friends
I have all day
it's all one little breath

so leave me alone God
why think up a man
think so much of one

to open it for inspection
every morning
test it every breath

look over there
somewhere other
give me just one free moment

to swallow my spit
what did I do to hurt you
man watcher

what can you be making
what cosmic thought
I'm necessary for

you hold me here
insignificant comma
like a tie in a railroad track

why not forgive
forget
I'll just settle down in dust here

you won't have to think
to even look
for me.

CHAPTER 9

However true
we don't know how to win a case
against God

for every question we'd ask
there are a thousand
over our heads

however high and headstrong
who among us   heart of stone
is hard enough to resist him

he picks up a mountain
it doesn't even know it
and throws it down

when he's angry
he gives the earth a little kick
and it trembles

he brews up a storm
to hide the sun
erase the stars

he laid the universe out
on the blackboard of space
alone with himself

he paced up and down
thinking something
that charmed the primitive sea

his thoughts clear as stars
laid on the surface
of a calm sea

he passes by
and we don't see him
as our heads swell with impressions

each day
sometimes bitter
we'd say "wait, wait a minute,

what are you doing?"
but he has passed us
long ago

all the gods of human history
couldn't raise a whisper
to slow him down

so what could I say
to turn him
around

even if I'm right
even if he heard
a little murmur of human truth

it would only be irritating
stopping him for even a moment
he'd knock the breath out of me

as he brushed
a fleck of soot
or tear from his eyes

(he is the means
to make justice
his end)

I could be right
and my mouth
would say something wrong

totally innocent
and my words
wrap around me

in a cloak of pride
but I'm innocent
I don't care about myself

I don't know my life
as if it makes any difference
we're all destroyed together

guilty   not guilty
some disaster strikes
mixing innocence with despair

and someone is laughing at his experiment
the whole world is wrapped
in a cloak of pride

like a prize scientist
of pride   white and clean
it's all a desperate show

the faces of our judges are covered
with the gauze
for this human play

and he made it   you
who can prove
I'm a liar

my days print out
faster than a computer
they're gone like Western Union boys

fleeing from the horror
of "progress"
exploded bombs

if I say
I'll put on a happy face
grit my teeth grin and bear it

some inner torture takes over
every time   I can hardly believe it
you'll never let me go!

my life is a sentence
why should I struggle
in these chains of words

I could wash my mouth with soap
my hands in lye
and you'd drop me into some ditch

and I'd fall on my face
until I couldn't even laugh
or challenge his force

I'd hate myself
as if all my clothes
turned into prisoner's clothes

he isn't a man
with a hand to put a summons in
was I ever in a court

can my mind come up with a court
some kind of referee or witness
to step between us

let him put down that club
that terror of naked space
he holds over me

then I could find myself
put on consciousness openly
but he won't let me be.

CHAPTER 10

My soul is sick of life
pushes me to speak
to fill the air with wounds

don't leave me hanging God
let me see the case
against me   is there honor

just to cut me down
to think so little of the work
that flowed from your hands

that you sit back watching the mean
arrogantly misshapen
bask in the spotlight

and can you see through the tiny eyes of men
eyes of flesh
in the little prism of a day

are your years our years
that you make me suffer in
that you enter to turn upside down

though you only you know I'm guiltless
where could I escape
beneath your hand

hands that molded me alive
and now reach in to crush me—
remember the mud you cupped for me

it's only the same dust I can return to
the dust on the bottle of milk
you poured me out of

worked me up into something solid
like rich cheese
wrapped in a beautiful skin

and inside the dream architecture of bones
you filled me with breath and vision
a vision of reality a love

but you cloud these things in a mind
of your own
a sky I know the stars stretch back from

containing all time forever
you surround me with clouds
like a lens

to see if I will
with this little mirror of a mind
think I can escape

cloud myself in nerve
and if I do—God help me
and if I'm innocent I better not look up

drunk with shame
drenched in this misery
of myself

if I stand up you come to me
cold as a camera
your pictures are marvelous pictures

they multiply your anger toward me
frame after frame
an army of moments against me

why did you pull me through the womb
locked into the brutal focus of time
I could have died inside never breathed

no one come to look at me
a quick blur in the world
carried stillborn from womb to tomb

so few days this life
why not just leave me alone
let me smile a little while

before I go off never to return
into the deep shadow of death
utter darkness—the thing itself

stripped of the background darkness
into the flaming
sun of darkness.

CHAPTER 12

Of course you're all so cultured
when you die (what a loss)
wisdom dies with you

but I have a mind too
working just like yours
who doesn't anyway?

yet you come by almost laughing
at a man who called out God
and was answered

and in that innocence
I'm an idiot in a showcase
for all those comfortably hidden

in the things they've accumulated
a sideshow in a pit
for you thinking you're not trapped

looking down on me as if I'd slipped
out of weakness   out of love
for an immaterial illusion

a dreamy escape
while thieves pile up things in their houses   any man
sneers behind his mask at God

secure in his heartless estate
anything his hand can grab onto
is god enough for him

look at his dog or cat
and think where they came from
the pigeons flocking in the park will tell you

look at the ground and it will tell you
with the flowers on its blanket
covering over ages of living things

fish in the sea will speak to you
as you have to me bloated with words
you mouth as if you've learned

learned to mouth without feeling
we all everything swim from God's hand
everything we make with our hands

he put in front of us
and in time ahead of us
as we begin from little fish with tails

don't our mouths know what food is
and what tastes foreign
as our ears know what words

swim to the heart
does it matter how long we've lived
do we pile up wisdom in our nets

or do we dip them again every day in the river
because wisdom flows only from God
he feeds the mind

if he breaks a living thing apart
we can't rebuild it
if he shuts the door on a man

there is nothing there to open
no rain and the earth dries up
he lets the water loose we're immersed

he's the source of energy and reflection: wisdom
the power-mad and the slave
dissolve to the same source dissolve in the mirror

and if he wishes
the wise are stripped of their wisdom
judges go mad in their courtrooms

the belt of power slips from the wearer
clothes don't fit them
like poor men in mental wards

priests are stripped and led away
money slips through the hands of the rich
like water

those most full of confidence
lose their voices
men we trust lose their senses

heirs and those next in line
have contempt poured on their heads
mantles of power shrink out of shape

the muscles of strongmen are water—
death plots spawned in the dark
are totally exposed

like negatives to light
death's shadow is immersed
in light

he swells nations to greatness
then deflates them
a nation is swept off its feet

the minds of its leaders are blown away
scattered like old newspapers
blown through a cemetery

they grope for some kind of light switch
in an ancient tomb
they flail like men overboard

drunk on their own power
they stagger toward a caved-in door
in some ancient bar.

CHAPTER 13

My eye has seen it
my ear heard and grasped
the vision

I know what you know
nothing less
than you

so I'd speak to God
to the one
whose reason is all

you are all plasterers
you think you are doctors
but it's only broken walls before you

you smear them over
with a whiteness of lies
a color you take for truth itself

you should shut up before them
and your silence become
a road to wisdom

stop then on your way
here on these lips
is a little plea

you speak for God
and in that acting
you can only be false

you have a case amorphous as air
the court is only a conceit
behind your forehead

what can you say
when you catch him
in a lie or contradiction

will you make him squirm
can you make him speechless
in his witness?

his words will unmask you
your conceit crack and fade
like a painted smile of piety

you will crack in the sun
of his majesty and fall
to pieces before him

your heavy talk in the dust
of ashes
with the clean little homilies

the niceties broken like clay
lay there then in your dumbness
so I may speak

opening to whatever
becomes
of me

my flesh may become
the one last meal
in my mouth

my breath become
the one last drink
in my hand

though he slay me
yet these words stand
to speak up

to his face
they are my voice itself
no false witness

could find these words
you see I'm not cut off
stand back   listen

to the voice of poetry
that is making my case
and may be lasting justice itself!

who else is there
to argue with this song
cut the air out of my life

then I'd rest content with silence
death sentence
but still two things more

I ask of you
to allow me to open
myself in your eyes

remove the hand that falls
leaden on me
like a heavy depression

except that I move   falls
like silent terror
except that I speak

and lighten my fear
I want to walk out of the dark
to meet your fierce stare

call me and I'll be there
just as right now I'm speaking
for you to answer here

how many crimes and untold lies
am I unconscious of
how can I see them

with your face hidden
veiled in silence
what enemy is in me

that you squeeze in a vise
but at such distance
infinite space

am I a leaf spun away
in a burst of wind
impossible to see

what power in that leaf
blindly afloat
to feel terror

this numb piece of paper
you squeeze my feelings on
held in this painful air:

bitter words
you have written down
against me

a list I inherit
from the unspoken lies
of my past

my feet are also locked
as if you would hold me
ready for punishment

in that vise
some crime some slight
some monstrous pinprick

forced you to look
narrowly at me
narrowing my path

noting each unique footprint
brand of a slave
a voice singing out through the bars.

CHAPTER 14

Man swims out of a woman
for a few days of restless living
full of anxieties

a flower springing up
under the passing cut
of the share's thrust

a shadow fading out
of time
gone

disintegrating
like an old wineskin
an old coat

eaten away
by moths
drained

and this is the creature
you open your eyes on
take time to judge

as if pure earth can be extracted
out of lust-spattered hair
by a man himself

however young or innocent
he dies
in a dusty coat of experience

because our days are numbered
so we can count them ourselves!
approximate the whole

short story
you give us
with its "The End"

look the other way   turn your eyes away
why don't you
just let us be here

ignorant slaves
enjoying our work
enjoying our sleep

till we finish this simple story
and get a little rest . . .
even a tree cut down

has some hope
it can spring to life
old roots

start up tenderly
even if its body stump
dies in the dust

soon as it whiffs some water
it starts
growing like a new plant

but a man just disappears
one last breath
and where is he

lakes have completely evaporated
rivers shrunk away
and men laid down to rest

never to rise
or materialize
the sun can die

galaxy collapse
space evaporate
universe shrink to a ball

and we will not hear it
nothing will shake us
awake in our beds

if only you could hide me
beyond existence
outside of space and time

in a darkness
a secret
beyond the known

until your famous anger passes
and then you remember me
waiting for the book to close

waiting for an appointment!
    is it just possible
a man dies and lives again?

I'd bear any day   every day
        heavy as it is
            waiting

        for your call
    and I would answer
you want to hear me again

this creature you made with care
            to speak
            to you

but now you number each step I take
note so slight a false movement
        I can't even see it

    as if my guilt is sealed
under a coat of whitewash
faded from my eyes but there

        as a mountain
    that will finally fall
a rock that will be moved

a rain wearing away the stone
a storm a flood
washing the earth away

as you wash away
the hopes of a man
we are lost at sea

our faces go blank
unrecognizable
painted out forever

sunk out of your sight
we swam a little
and we drowned

our families rise in the world
we don't know them
or they fall

or they disgrace themselves
sink into despair
we don't think of them

we only feel our own flesh
rotting   only hear
the echo of our body:

the pains of its dying,
the mourning
of its self.

CHAPTER 16

I've heard these righteous clichés
over and over
thanks for the precious comfort

the heavy breathing
in a bag of wind
that just gets noisier

you want to drown me out
with monotonous whispering
platitudes?

I could do that if I were you
like putting any word in front of the next
while making faces at a baby

the tone is one of a sermon
you solemnly deliver
with just the right voice quiver

babble on
till the baby falls asleep
but when I really speak

my pain stays there
and if I hold myself back
I'm still alone with it

and him
his famous jealousy
wearing me down

like precious jewelry
over my entire body like skin
each minute becomes heavier

I'm distracted by myself
alienating all my company
who turn on me

like bribed witnesses—
the friends I counted on!—
lying into my face

friends who've disappeared
like flesh on my body
thinned by tension

wrinkled by despair
slim enough to be accused
as I'm barely standing

of paranoia or hunger
therefore craving bread
therefore a liar to myself

whose open face
hides these hot words
steaming in my mouth

but it's clear I'm consumed
on the flame of his anger
in the gnashing of teeth

in the eyes that flash
sirens across my face
the mouth that curls in a snarl

an arm reaches out a claw
slaps my face
my friends become a mob a beast

with the faceless energy called courage
of a bitten animal
raw violence

selfish masks
ripped away from the unconscious
faceless the way they really are

and I'm delivered
by my God
to this transparent world

of bitter losses vicious plots
covered with a veneer
of paper-thin consciousness

the masks of sincerity
dropped like hot coals
in God's rage against me

I was content
happy productive peace-loving
peace-making

until he grabbed me by the neck
spun me around
and shattered me

worried me to pieces
pulled me together a moment
to stand as a target

for friends and enemies
what's the difference
I could be them

blindly righteous
strangers to ourselves
we think our eyes are friends

confidently looking out for us
but they'd close in the instant
they saw the volcano within

the first volcano
and when we turn to look back at the world again
it's almost too dim to see

slowly we adjust to the light in the room
this is the world we're made for
but where is the human light

of justice coming from—through the crack
within   or from without
but space is all the same

and on both sides I'm a target
God's arrows spinning past me
his men surround me

and I'm hit
again and again
piercing my stomach my bowels

spilling my insides out
he clubs me down
leader of the riot

or the purge the pogrom
he is a policeman
and I am wearing rags

can't change my clothes
can't shave can't move
my life my plans paralyzed

till my head sinks into dust
heavy antlers
of a battered wild ram

humiliation
my face a red desert
from weeping

craters of depression
the dark eye shadow
of death

and not a drop or speck
of violence
from my own hands

not a bad wish
not a curse in the cleanness
of my daily creations

O earth, cover not over my blood!
don't be a tomb a museum
for my miserable poem

my cry against this sinking
leave my voice uncovered
a little scar on your face

face of the earth
open to the sky
the universe

where you can see
a justice waiting to be discovered
like an inner referee

the deep seat of conscience
where a creator sits
handing me these words themselves

these verses are my absolving witness
on this little home earth
from which they speed

out into the universe forever!
even as my tears
fall in the dust

before an angry God who hears and sees
my plea   words and tears
of a man

for the life of his brother or son
the love of another living man
who is also me

on the outside
and inside the listening unconscious
creator who is also he

as clear as the clearest dream
as the little ball of earth
seen in a photograph

whom I call with my breath
as if he were human
unlike these words living beyond me

for I know I'm sentenced to die
my little story of years
will soon be over

I'll be going down the road
to fall in the dust
just one time.

CHAPTER 17

My breath straining
my days fading
through a prism of pain

in my chest
thinning my voice my hair
getting me in shape

for the grave
surrounded by a chorus
of mockingbirds

who won't let me rest
my eyes wide open
on the hard bed

of their bitterness . . .
lay down something beside me
some collateral I can grasp

you yourself
granted me this speaking
no one else will back me

no one shakes this open hand
you've closed their minds
shrunk their hearts into a bird's breast

but you won't let them sing
over me   in the morning
because they're shut in their ignorant night

denying a friend
for some self-righteous flattery
precious blinders for their eyes

while their children's sight grows dim
who recognize my famous name
trademark for bad medicine

something to spit at the feet of
my eyes are also blurred
but by tears

my hands and feet
fading away
like shadows

if any man is really open
he'll stop in his tracks
at this trial

of standing up
on innocent feet
among brothers

and being covered with total abuse
still that man will walk on
through the heap of civilized refuse

the wasteland of clichés
spiritual materialism
and his legs will grow stronger

meanwhile the show goes on
men of the world
stone me

with the ready-made knowledge
any idiot can buy in the supermarket
my business totally collapsing

my days fading like an echo
of the shattering
of my ego   all my plans

my heartstrings
cut silently
in the night that switches to day

at the push of a button
like the unconscious habit
of false righteousness

taking the powers that be
for granted
and so I can't even sleep

you come to me with these rigid proverbs
these artificial lights
like "there's light at the end of the tunnel"

all I want to see is reality
of darkness   to make my bed
underground

grave you are my father!
worm my mother
and my sisters

so here I am in the dust
faithfully returned to
so this is the hope

I should bow down to?
where are we then
but in the fading light of the unconscious

turning dreams to lost memories
dreams of a decent life
who can see anyone else's   *but him*

the innocence of them
spontaneous trust
my spirit open to them

will they also go down with me and with
these dream mouths of friends
to the ancient bar of dust

the vast unconscious cellar
to become dry bones
all my dreams of a livable future.

CHAPTER 19

How long does this gale
of words go on
this wind

you turn on my spirit
choking me
each time you've opened your mouths

is an insult friends
a hot brand on me
cast-iron reproductions of advice

meant for sheep
it doesn't offend you
to goad me like one

let's say I did something wrong
it's none of your business
no example for your self-righteous

spiritual merchandise
the goods making you feel superior
as if this rag of skin is proof

of my poverty
open your ears your silk purses
a minute: it's God who's

done me wrong
this chain around my neck
is not my words or thoughts

if I cry help
I'm being strangled
no one can hear

where's the judge
to hear these groans
from a poor man

I'm locked in my own ghetto
the streets are dimmed
by walls of pain

my pride stripped away
my humble crown of faith
in my own work and spirit

knocked down
my body a truth horribly distorted
I'm nothing

torn down like an old building
gone before you know it
a vacant lot

paved over
not even the hope of a tree
my smallest hope makes him angry

kindling for his rage
I'm the enemy
surrounded by his troops

with your ironclad master plan
cut off the city
as if I were some Leningrad

but my brothers are far away
removed   remote
my friends totally aloof

relatives don't know me
my closest friends
don't remember who I am

guests in my house
never knew me
to neighbors I'm the worst kind of stranger

an immigrant a beggar a bum
in the eyes of women I supported
invisible to men who worked for me

even when I ask them humbly
as a poor dog
a few tender yelps

an intimate embrace a kiss
fills my wife with horror
just the smell of my breath

my whole family is disgusted
backing off
coughing in disgust

children on the street
hold their noses   spit
run from me

all my deepest friends turn away
can't stand the sight of me
all those I loved the best

my bones creak laughing at me
my skin loose around them
like toothless gums   leprous

my teeth disappearing
there's hardly one left or anything solid
holding me together

some pity friends a little pity
dear friends
I'm wounded   struck

by the hand of God
a serious blow you can see
why do you keep on hurting me

why is the pleasure of my flesh not enough
that you need to squeeze
the last breath from my spirit

Oh if only these words were written down
printed and reproduced
in a book

engraved carved
with an iron pen
into solid rock forever!

monumental inscription
filled with volcanic lead
hardened into my one solid witness!

but inside myself
I know my witness breathes
to answer me   God himself

giving birth to words
vision itself
my constant creator

an answering wind like out of my mouth
to turn my case around
in front of the world

my judge and referee
and I'll be there
even without my flesh

though cancer devours my skin
I'll stand up   behind this body
my spirit will somehow pull me up

even for a moment to see it
in the twinkling of an eye
through the open window

of my own eyes
still alive
my living heart feeling

the justice of his presence
beside me within me
before I die

as I almost did
when you joined the bandwagon
of my pain

waving at me to stop
as if it was all my fault
as if I started the engine

but you'll stop at a whistle friends
that blows you down
that blows your spiritual arrogance away

the sound of your own pain
opening your eyes
to a higher judgment.

Just listen to me
you're all sealed up
in the big consolation

of blind faith
that you offer me so generously
but if you'd just open a little hole

in your ears
I'd be happy enough being alive
speaking these words to living beings

then you can resume mocking
anyway it's not you not men
pushed me to voice my thinking

to have to speak my mind
total consciousness
to listen to my own self calling

to hear all and nothing
the answer in the call
more than one man can stand

so what good is patience
look at me head-on
and be amazed

as your hand jumps
to cover your mouth
gaping astonished

when I stop to think
myself
I'm paralyzed

my skin crawls
pure horror
here it is   hear it

why do totally corrupted men
go on living
grow old in style

grow richer every day
see their children grow
into their power and houses

in safety   insured
peace to them
and their brothers

God's arrows
don't reach them
no heavy justice for them

their bulls mount their cows
no sooner said than done
a calf without fail

they have a flock of children
frisky little lambs
they run out to play

and dance to the tambourine
and sing with the lyre
and absorb the melody of flutes

their lives close like a sunset
prosperous and peaceful
they head to the grave

go down softly under
and yet
they'd said to God

leave us alone
we don't want to know
of you

why do we need God
to be servants
and what's there to get

from meditating on it
what's the profit
in spending our time on him?

isn't their happiness
in their own hands
isn't this circle of corruption

outside God's orbit
as you think of the unscrupulous
do you see their lights

turned off
their careers in ruins
bodies struck by heavy hand

because God is mad at them?
how often
and do you see them turned

to rags
yesterday's newspaper
blowing in the wind

you say his children
will end up paying for it?
no—let his own nerves

strain for the price
his own eyes
see himself break down

a shattered mirror
blown apart
in a heavy wind

let him live and learn
and drink from the cup
that's thrown in his face

what does he know or care
how his house stands
like a man totally drunk

he's finished the bottle
of his life
died satisfied

is there something God should learn
from us
here

something about spiritual materialism
the debt he owes and forgot
to pay the corrupt and yes the self-righteous

because you yourselves
become his judge
when you write off the reality

of the world he made
set in front of you
just as it is

one man dies at a healthy age
drinking to the full
his milk pails were always full

marrow of his bones still sweet
body still attractive
to women   attracted by them

and another man dies shrunken
in a bitter spirit
not even a drop of happiness

and then they lie down together
in the same bed of dust
with worms to cover them up

and yes I know your thoughts
the wooden arguments
the corpses you're lining up

you want to ask your rigid questions
but where *is* Stalin's house now
or Franco's

not to mention countless
run-of-the mill criminals
never caught: Martin Bormann etc.

the loyal collaborators
the rich and privileged saluting
any flag that flies their way

reflected in the polished boots of chauffeurs
Mercedes-Benz
certain popes

and busy in the wings the faceless
you won't see them standing around
at any apocalypse

you ought to ask some tourists
who speak your language
open-mindedly

listen to some impartial camera clicks
look at the photographs
even postage stamps

you push me into irony
and out the other side
to common sense

the deeply corrupt disappear
in limousines and passports
flown to obscure small towns

or islands
relax or even return
after the dust settles

and newspapers have crumbled
no one stings him with pointed proverbs
under his beard

no one unmasks him face to face
he lives like a god
and dies on the shoulders

of the mass of dupes
who carry him to his grave
which becomes a protected museum

his mouth is fixed at peace
by the embalmer   the priest
throws no dirt on his reputation

he'll live in some history
while the masses supporting him
are barely a footnote

Hollywood extras
following the hearse
lining the curbs

why this empty comfort you point to
these empty nothings you argue
this empty room of thought

you goad and push me into
this dark and hostile consolation
this humorless nonsense of empty religion.

CHAPTER 23

Today again
my speech my poem
this hard-talking blues

this heavy hand
from the long deep writing
of my spirit

Oh if I could know
where to go
and there

find him
at home
in his seat of justice

I'd sit down there
to lay out my case
before him

my mouth would be full
like a river
of what my heart must say

my mind open
like a window
to hear his words

as easy to understand
as the sounds of people
on the street

I wouldn't be blown away
overpowered
by them

but my own voice would be steadied
like a tree outside
in a bracing March wind

wind between the wood
earthly music
stirring my spirit

in his house
where an upright open man
isn't afraid to confront him

to listen to respond
to contend   a human music
creating the air

for a higher justice
in which to hear
I'm set free

but now I look to the east
and he isn't there
west and a vast empty ocean

face north
like a true compass
see nothing

turn south
and he's still invisible
hidden from my ear

but he follows each step I take
even when I'm sitting doing nothing
and he puts me in the crucible

to have his gold
because I've walked all my life
toward his light

past the neon temptation
of unreal cities
surreal commercials for "normality"

my lips have opened
for his infinite word
in meditation

I've opened his book
in my heart
and read with open eyes

he is one
determined within himself
as end

and has an end
all changes all choices
rest in his mind

but how can I change his mind
his soul desires
and it's already been done

ancient history
past changing
beyond our time

here he hands me
part of a sentence
already out of his mouth

and there's more to say
just as the past fills
with more to discover

it makes me shiver
to think
I must face him

here on this earth
now in this life
present in the infinite

transfigured
as my inaccessible inner self
rises to his hand

I turn white
cold sweat of fear
washes across my face

I want to turn back
as if I'm walking in my sleep
out of a world I know

my own shadow
smiles back at me
a shadow in the night

the past is drunk with strangeness
and his presence
drowns my heart in naked space

because he brought me out here
into the darkness
where I must continue speaking

into the open
like a child holding tight
to the side of his trembling crib.

CHAPTER 24

The days of judgment
and everyone has one
are no dark secret

because God has finished his sentence
but men are mostly blind
and that's the way God made it

but why are his hearers
also deaf
to the coming of those days

while corrupted men
totally in the dark
cut through fences and honest agreements

and anyone in their way
knocking down the shepherd
stealing the sheep

they drive off
in the repossessed cars
of the poor

foreclose
on widows and orphans
lock up a workman's tools

shove the homeless
out of their way
terrorize old people

already cringing
in little groups
huddled in corners

and the masses
are exploited asses
donkeys up a mountain

or camels in the desert
they report for work
as they're told

as the sun rises until dark
carrying the water they can't take home
to their thirsty children

Job

they harvest healthy food
for corrupt masters
pick the ripe grapes

for the cynical toasts
of the power-hungry
spilling the precious wine of their sweat

to finally lie down
naked under cold stars
not a shirt on their back

to wear in the predawn
dew from the mountains
making them roll over in their sleep

and hug close
a rock
shelter from the storm

when it rains
while the privileged few
snore in their yachts

on the sea of the masses
on the sweat of their backs
on the milk of a mother's breast

from whose arms they'd wring
the brief soft luxury
that's all most men ever know

rip the child
from the widow's breast
as security

against some calculated debt
to keep the heads of the poor
under water

in a sea of desperation
naked of human rights
a mass of mesmerized slaves

walking through the rich waves
of grain
bringing in the sheaves

for a perversely ornate table
half-starved
the workers of the world

between stones
pressing oil for the ruling classes
only their sweat belongs to them

treading the winepress of the bosses
in life's oasis
dying of thirst in the desert

listen to those distant groans
far from the drowning hum
of the city

a wounded army of souls
gasping in their ancient tracks
but God doesn't hear that prayer

and in the cities
even among the elite
men get away with murder

darkness meets darkness
a blood pact
against his light

light of day
of reality
of the inspiration for making

electric light
and the continuing surprise
of every morning sunrise

there are men
who've lost the path
to daylight

rising at daybreak
to terrorize the caravans
of the huddled masses

murderers
and at night under their dark blanket
thieves

adultery: another broken commandment
under cover of darkness
and masks

any form of disguise
a man in woman's clothes
slipping into the harem

thinking under his veil
no one will see me
no one know but she

they break up houses
as criminals
break into them

into the ones at night
they marked that day
in an ignorant scrawl of a mind

blind
to the light
we are given

strangers in the morning
to their own shadow
floating on the surface of consciousness

they are submerged
in the nightmare unconscious
because they can't make anything

of the light of a star
focused like a conscience
in the eye of imagination

creating light
in the image of light
honest day light

I rise from a dream in
to discover the universe without
that was within

rising past superstition
idols and dumb images
having nothing to say in daylight

yes belief requires dreams
and every night
we go to sleep in this world

while those others are at home
talking and listening
to shadows

completely intimate
with the nightmare
of death's shadow

show me
this isn't true
reduce these words to nothing

to nonsense like a magician
and I'll show you as your new servant
my eyes were fixed on reality.

Since I'm so weak
and this poem so pitiful
so powerless

I'm lucky again today
to have such friends
such care for the feeble

how nobly you've lifted
this poor arm that writes
what a miracle

what strong donations
you've made to little minds
barely subsisting on the minimum wisdom

I can hardly know what I'm saying
except thanks to you
your fatherly advice spilling over me

but who filled you with it
and who are you speaking to
what possesses you

to form such a rigid piety
with a breath
caught in what flow of meaning

my poem has a way
to continue
even as I swear by God

who holds back my living right
to be free of bitterness
that damn it I'm speaking

my own mind as he allows
as these breaths come out of me
these shreds of phrases

my spirit revives and hangs on
to the wind God sends
through my nostrils

and the words that leap off my lips
fall true to the page
of my conscience

it's out of my hands
to let you get away
with your self-righteous platitudes

as solid as flotsam
but as long as I'm alive
I won't let go

of the stone rightness
my spiritual individuality
until I die

the page of my heart
opens to the wind
of his warming breath

let my enemy be as cold
as the heartless
my accuser suffer

the secret death chills
of the liar
perspire with the guilty

cold sweat flow
in his veins
dripping from a heart as stiff

as an icicle   a conscience
upright but hopeless
as he prays

for what help
meditates on what
burning sphere of thought

that may give him a push
through the world of things to accumulate
but what is there to get

when his body loses its grasp
on life   does God hear
the cry of this hypocrite

will he delight in his calling
man to God   a dialogue
or has this man's words been smothered

behind a mask
yes I know something about it
God's place

inside us
moving my hand
that lifts and calls

to him
it has nothing to conceal
my mind is an open book

for God's hand
take a look
you must have read there

so why have you become so proud
you blow your hot empty breath
your stream of words on me.

Who can turn me around
until I find myself
back in the old days

the good days
God watching over me
the sun shining

inside me
like inner light
to usher me past the nightmares

on the screen of giddy youth
my life was in focus
around me   it was autumn

wife and children growing
my walks were bathed in light
in cream

the heaviest rocks in my way
smoothed out
like oil

I was as if transported
wherever I went
on a stream of affection

when I went out the city gates
or when I came to my place
in the city square

the younger men quickly stepped
aside   like a wave disappearing
while the older men rose to their feet

celebrities stopped
in the middle of what they were saying
and almost covered their mouths

the voices of politicians trailed off
like old newspapers
blown in the wind

their tongues dried up
dusty leaves
swept to the back of their mouths

I mean men listened to me
you could hear a leaf drop
they wanted my opinion

when I finished I was allowed
the clarity of silence
my words fell gently on them

like spring rain
they were attentive as trees
opening their arms

stretching their hands out gladly
as if their minds were open
to the sky

and when I laughed or
made light of things
they were almost stunned

to be reminded I was human
their eyes would light up
blossoms the sun smiled on

I directed their thoughts
to the best way   a revelation
they followed like actors visibly

in the presence of a master
a man who'd paid more than his dues
inspiring confidence in the disillusioned

their ears would open
and mouths speak of me
graciously

anyone seeing me
became a witness
to my openness

I embraced a poor man
and an orphan
and a man with no one in the world

to turn to
a man dying gave me a blessing
a widow smiled with joy for me

I opened myself
and a cloak of pride
slid from my shoulders

I embraced a sense of justice
that wrapped itself around me
like a warm coat in winter

I was eyes to the blind
and feet
to the lame

a father to the homeless
a light in the midnight window
to the stranger far from home

I was a destroyer of nightmares
like a gentle counselor
in an orphanage

then I said to myself
I will die
in the open arms of a family

and my seed in that nest
outgrow the arithmetic of a lifetime
the calculations of a mind

or historical lineage
my spirit extends beyond time
like a phoenix rising

from ashes
an ancient poem
from the dust of pages

my roots reaching out
for water
each new coming spring

and the dew shall lie all night
on my branches
and I feel the sweetness of that weight

on me
that miraculous touch
of heaven

waking my heart
made light again
by the fire of love within

my pen returning to the page
like an arrow to the heart
a love as strong as death.

CHAPTER 30

But now it's all a joke
to the younger generation
I'm an outdated ape

too heavy to take seriously
for the puppies of men
who in my time I wouldn't

have insulted my dogs by going near!
dogs whose hearts were higher
among my flocks of sheep

men whose hearts burned out
in a destruction of spirit
shriveling their humanity into rags

they haunt the back alleys
of a civilized wasteland
like the "disgusting" gypsies

they stooped to revile
in false images
to make themselves feel superior

devastated Indians
of their own manufactured
nightmares

eating the weeds
they claw up greedily
like outcast witches

banished from the self-righteous society
that rightly hounds them
like fleeing common criminals

they huddle in unblanketed pits
in primitive dreams: caves
of obsolete railroad cars

wallowing in the mud
of self-pity
gnawing the worms of desire

their sons a gang of animals
monsters of inhuman pride
hands on their belts like horsewhips

and now I've become the bait of their humor
their theme song
their saddle their fetish

their figure of contempt
they are primitive giants of ice
aloof over me

I'm the floor
they spit on
because God has knocked me down

unstrung the bow of my back
unleashed the curs
of their tongues on me

these vile witnesses at my right hand
this vigilante lynch mob
has come down my road of ruin

there are no living heroes
to step out of nowhere
in their way

all my defenses broken down
inevitably as water
breaks through an abandoned dam

my nerves on edge
wild deer fleeing
from the cracks of a thunderstorm

terror faces me like a wall
or a wind blowing my strength away
my hope disappearing like a cloud

my soul emptied like a glass of water
and in my hand
are miserable tears

my very bones are sweating
at night my veins
restlessly throb

my clothes and skin
bleached beyond recognition
by the acid of my suffering

my collar shrinks tight
around my throat
the hand of God's wrath

which drags me down to the mud
my spirit itself is dressed
in dust and ashes

I speak to you
hard and true
over the heads of men

who look down at me
my voice goes out of me
a wounded bird

flying to you
in your sky   crying
its whole being is calling

to you and you
don't answer
I stand trembling before you

and you look at me
as if I'm not there
as if you don't know or care

what I want
you sit in your great high chair
and in your great satisfaction

toy with me cruelly
your hand bears down on me
heavy and hostile

I'm like crumpled paper
lifted in your wind
driven to the edge of existence

tossed in a tempest
my significance dissolved
in the heavy downpour

without the warmth of your care
even the word significance
bleeds dry

I know your arm is leading me
to my death
to the meeting house

where every living creature
lies down
before you

but did I ever lift
my arm
to strike or sweep away

a ruined heap of a man
whose tortured voice reached out
for help   to me

for a shred of sympathy
and could I not help but weep
with him

in his hour of despair
did my heart not stop
for this man

for the poor and wretched
of humanity
didn't I close my eyes

like a hurt child to feel
the boundless passion of inwardness
in every man opened by suffering

but when I opened my eyes
looking for something hopeful
desolation

I waited for some light
I hoped for light
but darkness came over me

and in the pit of my stomach
a cauldron boils
endlessly

days flow into days
like a miserable diarrhea
I wake in the morning

and there's no sun
no ray of friendship
I stand up crying

in the squares
in the bars
in the cafés

and I'm looked at as a brother
to dragons or lizards
crocodiles are my companions

owls and screeching ostriches
are the comrades of my
plaintive shriek of despair

my skin hangs on me
like a tanned wolfhide
my bones melt with fever

my lyre is stretched
to the pitch of wailing
my flute

is a voice turned
to a siren song
in a human holocaust.

CHAPTER 31

I came to a decision
behind my eyes
not to let them wander

over the innocent bodies
of young girls
I refocused their attention

what decision am I thus allowed
to see reaching into this world
from behind God's highest cloud

what sense of human
natural rightness
beyond the senses

is it really disaster
for the cold-hearted
hard-core manipulators

of sympathy and affection
devastating twisters
of all feeling in their paths

doesn't he see me
standing openly in the aisle
isn't that his light each step I take follows

if I walked beside high vanity
self-made lights of deception
and let my foot pull me dumbly

into the shadows of bitterness
then let my heart be weighed like stone
on an honest scale

in his hand of justice
and he'll know the lightness
my heart still clings to

if I let my legs
carry me away
in blind animal pride

or let my heart go
to the blood-lust of the world
before my naked eyes

or let my hands indulge themselves
in the mud and gravel of cement
for a wall between us

then let another mouth
eat all
I've worked and sweated for

and all the seeds I've planted
in the ground in my mind in the body
of my wife

be uprooted   totally
if I gave my heart away
        blindly

to the cold deception
of a heartless woman
        or the wife

left innocently alone
    in the sanctuary
of my neighbor's home

if I consciously even dreamed
        myself there
let my wife swallow every drop

of my lifeblood my honor
        in the seed
of every passing man

let them worship between her thighs
as greedily as men suddenly released
        from death sentences

then let her rise
to become their servant
to wash their sheets while I weep for her

while my eyes go blank with despair
before the total explosion
        of a life

I'd be guilty of a fire
swallowing up the air around me
destroying the spirit of others

as it's magnified in the mirror
of my silent rage within
gone blind with desperation

all my hopes dreams desires
utterly consumed
in the passionate proof

of my lifelong ignorance
boiling up within   temptation
for an untouchable woman

and forgetting that I'm a man
descended from men and women
who held their love humbly

as the free gift
of a baby in their arms
deserving adoration

if I coldly turned away
from the open heart or hand
of my humble servant

anyone I put
consciously or not
in a place to serve me

and who did so   freely or not
then where am I
when I'm in God's presence

how will I come to ask for
what no one can demand
the free gift of love

no longer mine to give
as I turned cold and heartless
in this body he gave me

that he made for us all equally
in the wombs of women
he alone   shaping us there

one creator
one hand moving
one conscious subject

if I refused
the needs of the poor
given to my spirit to bear

if I refused a woman   homeless
having lost her husband
and turned to me

a man in her eyes
growing dim with tears
someone other to look on

for help in the overpowering
needs one life faces
alone for the sake of others

if I swallowed my morsel of food
alone in the face of even one orphan
who had none

if I didn't raise that boy
as his father   that girl
as her true compass

if I've seen someone naked
hopelessly exposed
having lost the shirt off his back

or a poor man woman or saint
who barely ever had one
if that body was not a blessing

I was given to warmly embrace
with fleece from my flocks
if I lorded it

over anyone
because I had the cold advantage
of friends in high places

then let my arm be wrenched
out from its socket
my writing hand fall limp

the pen slip from my fingers
words dry up on my lips
because the turning of God

away from us   as we may turn away
is utter devastation
the dark side of the moon

I couldn't stand there
or breathe
unless he gave me some wisdom

to learn to shield myself
learning by facing terror
that love protects us

if I put my faith in gold
filled my sack of pride
with money

and talked to myself
as if I were precious metal
saying I hold my own security

if I stood up straight
held my head high
encased in rigid armor

the tin shield of fortune
I thought was self-made
forged with my own hand

if I stared into the sun   inwardly
mesmerized or blindly enlightened
struck by its shining riches

if I ever stood hypnotized
before the dreamlike beckoning
of the full moon rising   silver and gold

letting my heart be captured
by cults of sensuality
becoming a slave

to my own enlightenment
handed over to the power
of some physical light or master

some magical dazzling myth
obscuring the light of history on
the pages of human struggling

from generation to generation
to be free of idols and false images
and the hand holding the ax

at whose edge we tremble
dazzled by the glinting beauty
of secret fear or evil

as it slices through our thought
until we can't hold together
can't contain the reality

of opposing forces of energy
the physical struggle inside
of good and evil

if I fell
before idols
separating thought from feeling

if I kissed my own hand
to blow kisses
to some material body in the sky

then that is the height of superstition
the queen of lies
in the face of God

like incest
denying my nature
cutting off my human hand

if I secretly exulted
to learn my enemy
was cut down

struck down by his mean thought
like lightning
where he was hiding

if I let bitterness
slither through my lips
to poison his character

then let the men closest to me
pin me down
devour my flesh with passion

twisting my desire
to share with anyone hungry
my portion of meat

if I left a passing stranger
to sleep in the street
naked to darkness

and didn't open my door
to the open road
sharing my light and warmth

if I have hidden my sins
in a hole
in my heart

like the common herd
covering up the truth
with dirt and litter

because I was afraid to stand out
from the herd   afraid
of common gossip

and contemptuous eyes
of the self-righteous   boring in
with the cold severity of rock-drills

if I stood terrified at that thought
mute
crippled in the heart

afraid to open it or my mouth
to face my own weakness
the petty lies to myself

that I could not even walk
out my door
with my head on frontward

then I would not deserve the paper
I'm writing on
but here it is!

this is my voice
reaching out for the ear
open to hear it

where is the hearing   the time and place
to make my suffering real
an indictment a list of crimes

even if it were longer than a book
I'd carry it on my shoulders
with honor

I'd wrap it around me like a royal robe
bind it around my head
like a royal turban

I'd walk up to my judge
and lay out my heart like a map
before him

this incredible gift of a heart
feeling
my true thoughts

holding the history book of my life
open to his light
light is my defense!

as confident as a prince
I'd put my life on the line
in the words that are given me

in this court invisible to me
transparent as clean air
before the judge I live to hear

and if my land cried out against me
indicting me with the tears
that ran down in furrows

man made
on the face
of the earth

if I plucked the riches
its fruit   filling my mouth
and gave back nothing

not even a thought
expanding
in gratitude

if I have planted
any cause for anger
in the minds of its tillers

if one migrant worker cried out
because I forced the breath
of integrity out of him

then instead of wheat
let my hand reap
thorns

let it force to no end
this thistle
of a pen

let weeds grow
and cover this page
instead of words that grow wheat

and here for now is ended
the poem
Job speaks.

Trying to establish a date for Ecclesiastes helps reveal how later Hebrew poets collaborated with earlier ones. The book may have been written in its final form as late as the third century BCE, the poet having worked over material dating back to the seventh century BCE—and even further. The older strand itself was based on yet older, ancient scrolls, perhaps originating at King Solomon's court in the tenth century BCE. Our final author, however, is the "Qohelet" who imagined himself King Solomon in the third century BCE—a time when Greek modes were becoming influential in Judea.

This multilayered history is characteristic of the texts of Hebraic poets, just as it would be of the later, Talmudic writers and editors. A natural irony inheres in the reader's recognition of seemingly "quoted" older material; to reproduce the effect in English requires an emphasis on the psychological dimension. Unless a translator today creates a self-critical frame of reference, the old homilies and clichés that Qohelet is intentionally defrocking will come out sounding like the clichés themselves.

Ecclesiastes is a Jewish critique of the pagan genre known as wisdom literature, as well as a more subtle commentary on specifically Jewish conventions of wisdom literature. But the layers of embedded older works allow the poet to compose a moving poem, rather than a detached text. In its ceaseless ebb and flow, its unmasking of clichés and conventional wisdom, the poem depicts the process of awareness itself (as the prophets attempted in their own manner). No philosophy coheres throughout the poem, much less any theology; instead, we are left with a feeling of elation, just as we would be after an effectively dour sermon or elegiac symphony. The poet, wrapped in the trappings of his stubbornly Hebraic culture, finds a way to embrace a difficult world while seemingly rejecting it.

There is a residue of Babylonian cynicism, but it is transformed, along with Greek stoicism, into a Jewish version of earthiness. When the book recommends the benefits of going to a house of mourning over a house of mirth, it is also affirming the Jewish joy in an ethics of doing good works (while lightly bathing a pious sentiment in self-parody). However, when Ecclesiastes was translated into Western languages, it began to sound too much like the worldly material it assimilated and critiqued. Even today, conventional Bible interpreters mistakenly assume the book is full of corroding doubt.

No, the Hebraic poet was too wise for that. If not quite worldly wise like his Greek contemporaries, he was wiser in his judicious use and collage of a deeper Hebraic poetic tradition.

ecclesiastes

I

You can't take it with you
a breath
all we take in

in a life of action
and exhaustive playback
breath into breath

what progress
what dumb thing can we make
under the sun

out of human hands
greater than our sweat, glistening
in the brief flash of a human life

generations rise and fall
to the earth
that hardly changes

the sun also rises
and falls, gliding
beneath us

back to its starting place
like wind always returning
to us—from any direction

rushing past us
turning and returning
all rivers run

to a body, a sea
that hardly changes
like our deepest thoughts

contained in history
and the seabed of instinct
our words exhaust us

we are speechless
before this flowing
our eyes and ears

forever look and hear
and that's all they know
perfect little machines

everything that happens
happened
happens again

there is nothing new
to grow wild about
under the sun

including the man wildly shouting
"Look, this is new!"
he lived ages ago

in the beginning of time
before records
and even tomorrow

with its memory machines
is lost in space
by the men approaching the end.

11 (1:12)

I, the poet
was a king
in Jerusalem

I opened my mind
to explore to feel
everything

every reflection
under the sun:
an overpowering work

God gave a man
to make
with his life

I saw everything happening
under the sun
you can't take it with you

you breathe out
and a little wind shakes the world
alive around you

you can go with the wind
until you're exhausted
or against it and blue-faced

you can't save your breath
and you can't take
what isn't there

a tree bends to the sun
we can't straighten it
our mind can't overpower it

I said in my mind
I've grown rich
on experience

I'm the richest man
in Jerusalem
but what is this mind

and this desire
to abandon ourselves
in front of it

and I almost went mad
trying to add up
what I had

I grew nervous
I couldn't think straight
I was lost in the sun ...

it's painful to hold
everything you own
inside

we can't take it—
rooted
to the air.

III (2:1)

I said in my mind
I will abandon myself
take life as it comes

but that is another mirage
the laugh is on the escapee
as life passes him by

I made this experiment
drink and smoke a lot
embrace pleasure

but meanwhile: keep my purpose clear
and open to insight
think: what's best

for a brief little life,
thinking or feeling?
so I set to work

in the grand style
building an *oeuvre*
ten books in five years

works of love and despair
naked and shameless
I was married and divorced

I went to all the parties
the glittering eyes
and wit: passion-starved

a trail of blinding jewels
of experience behind me
more than any king in Jerusalem

I tried on every life-style
I pushed to the center
through many gaudy affairs

I was surrounded by stars
singers and dancers
and fresh young bodies

to choose among
at the slightest whim
I was high and I was courted

but I kept my sense of purpose
every imaginable distraction
surrounded me

I opened myself to sheer
luxury of feeling
my mind was out there

on the windy ledge
and this is what I learned:
we can take in *anything*

and we are still empty
on the shore of the life
our blood flows to.

IV (2:13)

Then I looked up
above my personal horizon
to see the sky

outstretching the sea
as wisdom
lightens a heavy body

a wise man's eyes
are in his head
while the absentminded

professor or egoist
disdains to wipe his glasses
while he sinks to the bottom of the sea

but wisdom as quickly evaporates
the moment a body dies
shipwrecked beneath its headstone

the most penetrating realist
hits rock bottom
six feet under

and the farthest seer
on the beachhead of life
gets his mouthful of sand

so even wisdom is a pocket
turned inside out
when it's time to pay the body's burden

the blind will lead the wise
beyond the furthest suburb of memory
into total obscurity

reentering the city of the future
as dust to be swept away
from the pages of the present

so where will I go
with this wisdom   this breath
in the sail of a fool

and so I turned again
blind as a hurricane
against the sea of life

where all works sink
like jettisoned cargo
under the lidless eyeball of the sun

the whole cargo of civilization
was a weight on my shoulders
my life's work dead weight

all life depressingly empty
hollow as cardboard dumbbells
in a bad circus

a bad dream
in which my fame honor wealth
all the earnings disappeared in a thought

in a dream circus where a clown waited
cocky in his painted face
of identity

to inherit all my works
and I am not to know
if there's a mind and heart of depth

beneath the greasepaint
or it really is the face
of life's unrelenting sideshow

in which my successor my reader
discounts my lifework
in a snobbish indifference

to the working man   common or
artist (and helmsman
of the direction life has dealt him

in working his will over it)
and my books my record
fade and crack in the sun

cast overboard like ballast
all that I've learned not even a shadow
cast in the desert

a little shade for integrity
my wealth empty as a mirage
of water

and so my heart sank
to the bottom
in the dry well of despair

empty of illusions
about the fine sweat we produce
under the sun

slave to a desire
for *whose* "one fine day"?
each day another sigh

accumulated
another groan for the harvest
of rich disappointment

each night
our hearts lie wide awake
lashed to the body's ship

ferrying that load of heartache
from day to day
with the constant of breathing

to fill the sail
and ripple the pages
of an empty book

the best thing for a man
is to eat drink and be
just be

satisfaction in the flow
of works and days
as it is all the work

of a creator
making me
aware of my body

and by its satisfaction
my need to be here
a pen in the hand of the Lord—

who will feel the pressure
of his will
if not I?

and if what I do is pleasing
in his eyes
I will see through my own

a work graced with beauty
a world open
to a fresh page of understanding

on which I create
my own happiness
an articulate self-knowledge

and if I project
only my own vision
with my tiny primitive hand-driven will

I will be the ancestral hunter
and gatherer   a slave
to the stalking of wealth and power

and the snobbish mask of nobility
the illusion of living
(in ignorance) forever

which at my death will be handed over
to another man   an open one
deep enough to hold his fortune within

fulfilling his creator
in the reality of commerce
between vision and self-awareness

adding a living dimension
to the flat mirror
of the future

the mirror in which puffed-up
self-centered lords
are drowning in vanity.

v (3:1)

There is time for everything to happen
under the sun   to lift anchor
in the flow of seasons

everything has its moment
under the uncounted stars
its season of desire

summer of being born
winter of dying
spring of seeding

fall of reaping
winter of killing
summer of healing

spring of uprooting
fall of rebuilding
fall of weeping

spring of laughing
winter of lamenting
summer of dancing

summer making love
winter of surviving
spring of embracing

fall of parting
spring of finding
fall of losing

winter keeping
summer discarding
summer of hot tears

winter of consoling
winter of silence
summer speaking out

spring in love
fall in anger
winter of war

and hating
summer of peace
and hugging

but what can a man add
to the interworking of things
of his own intrinsic value

is a man anything different
whether or not the sweat and thought
is wrung from his body like a rag

I have thought about the tatters
and felt the finest mindspun silk
these are clothes created for us

all men and women wear them
the work of their creator
who has dressed everything in space

each event in time
tailored to its place
and he puts a mannequin of desire

before the hearts and minds of men
so that we long to dress ourselves
create a vision of the future

in which our lives fit today
with a similar beauty of rightness
but the longing for a world of our own

defeats us   the world defeats us
like a mirror we may not look behind
though a taste of creation propels us forward

I have seen as with a long look
the best a man can make
is to create his own goodness

out of a clear image of himself
the satisfaction in simply being alive
the pleasure of his own eyes

seeing
as long as he can
as long as he lives

just to eat and drink
the fruits of your work
is a gift from your creator

the world is a gift that lasts
he gave
and nothing more can be added

no matter can be erased
the universe beyond us
came before us

and the wonder of our presence
is that we feel it all
in the awe before our own little creations

in the awe of our hearts moving
closer to their creator
as we ourselves become stiller

the grace to be still
in the flow of all creation
for a moment

and through the window of a moment
the opening of eyes within eyes
to see the ancient perspective of time

painted in a landscape with light
the future the eyelids opening
as of a prehistoric creature

under the ungraspable sky
that was
is

and will be: the airless height
of understanding   pure space we pursue
like fish the worms of conscience

and are drawn to
like a seed to air
in a new baby's wail

like a man to a woman
like a creature
to his maker

VI (3:16)

But when I looked further
under the sun I found
sitting in the seat of justice

beasts
and in the lap of wisdom
lizards

I heard myself thinking
the creator has made a road
from the heights of wisdom

to the conscience in every man
and each must find his way
meanwhile the court is abandoned

to the claws of influence
the school is abandoned
to the gnawing animal of despair

a season of disbelief
blows sand in the eyes
of the Lord's creatures

and I saw clearly
men are not higher than the camels
they must ride on

horse and rider
both arrive together
at the end of the journey

their skeletons come clear
like maps to nowhere
buried underground

their bones gallop into dust
together   they both run out
of breath

a breath is all
a creature takes in
in a lifetime of action

it joins the infinite grains of sand
on the shore of the life
its blood flowed to

who knows if the man's spirit
rises
while his faithful steed's falls

who has seen this parting of ways
in the midst of his own journey
fixed in life's precious saddle

and so I came to see
man is made to be happy
taking care and keeping clear

his own vision
embracing the world
with the arms of his work

along the road
of his conscience
who or what

manner of creature or act
could bring him far enough
out of himself

out of the sun's pull
to see the unbreathing future
beyond the living present

and beyond the little picture show
of stars and galaxies
cheapened by superstition.

VII (4:1)

Then I returned
to consider again
the oppression constant as daylight

returning under the sun
here are the cisterns of tears
of all men oppressed

by the ravenous animal
of injustice   no one human
enough to offer an arm

and shoulder of consolation
here are the fists of power
in sleeves of comforting armor

the dead are better off
having found some consolation
more than the living

still trembling inside
before a concealed weapon
death

and better off than all
the unborn   uncalled
to being witness

to the heavy work
of men holding down
men

drowning each other in air
absorbing the power and
dimming the light

in the bloodstream
under a sky
made of skin

human energy I noted again
comes from a heart's
envy of the world

it sees itself in mind's mirror
as a galley slave   its horror
gives birth to "free" enterprise

so, concealed beneath the surface of excellence
and talent and plain hard work
is a motor of fear

running against each man's neighbor
and the fuel
is suppressed desire

pressure to be free of the power
of others   and so
breathing itself becomes a mechanism

empty of spirit
men are busily at work
building models of this

the race is on
to the heart
of the human machine

and men are proud of this ladder of "progress"
of where they stand
in the eyes of status (their neighbor)

then there is the man who is
his own totem:
a brain made out of wood

hands glued together with indifference
to the rat race
thinned by idiocy instead of tension

so which do you prefer
a vain idiot or an idiot vanity
how about a breath of fresh air

instead of rigorous incense!
a handful of quietness
instead of both hands shaking at the grind wheel

and the heavy perfumes of oil and sweat . . .
then I looked away and saw
more futility masquerading under the sun

the man or woman determined to be alone
no one beside them
no family no children

so why are they working so hard
salting away money and power
piling up credit promiscuously

around the clock
no time to even think
just who am I sacrificing

my time my pleasure for
who am I and who will know me
when I'm gone

the apple of this one's eye
is gilded to conceal
a core of depression

but just as oppressive the clichés
like two heads are better than one
sure: they cover each other's failings

if one of them falls
the other can lift him up
yes there's brilliant logic in this!

for how foolish one looks when he sprawls
having fallen all alone
without the grace of even someone's worried look!

also two who are sleeping together
get some warmth on cold nights
one alone gets only cold   and looks ridiculous

and is exposed to attack
while two link together
and with another make a chain   to brandish

or a coat of mail
yes friend- and kinship
is a power that binds

like word to word an oath (however false)
to keep or hurl with confidence—
but one all alone is blown in the wind.

VIII (4:13)

They say it's better to be poor
when young—and wise
than a rich, old celebrity

a king   clamped
in the throne of his mind
unable to hear the clamoring streets

the youth can walk freely
out of a king's prison
to become a king himself

while the born leader
even become a dictator
can only topple over

in his heavy mental armor
reduced to his knees
like a wordless beggar

but then I thought about that youth
rising to take his place
how the mass of people were inspired

by him   by his success
as people embrace the rags-
to-riches morality play

the longing masses
eager to start over
to wipe the messy history slate clean

and suddenly the man as all men
is gone   and his son
slouches in his place

rain has fallen on the history books
and the sun bleached it dry
for the new generations

which are endless in number
as were the ones preceding him
and for both alike he is unknown

the living page of his time
bled white out of memory
another page lost in the sea of the present

where even the beautiful craft
of inspired imagination
have their sails reduced to tatters

and their vain hopes discolored
like old photos
by the vague tears of sentiment

the memory of that star
like any moment of triumph or despair
is cut loose from the mooring of its time

adrift like a lifeless raft
after an explosion
after the countless explosions of moments

and the photos a living mind has made
in fits of hope or doubt
forgotten utterly as the sounds

of shutters clicking open
spoken words
a wind has blown away.

IX (4:17)

Watch your step
when your feet automatically carry you
unconsciously   to the temple

it's better to see yourself
and feel
what you are doing

522

―――

PART III

―――

WRITING

―――

Ecclesiastes

than offer blind obedience
but go in
with your eyes open

and keep your heart open
to the right way
don't lead your heart blindly

into a marriage of convenience
don't be a fool   except for love
of the truth

and then you will know
what you love
and if you must suffer it

the pain will have some value
you'll know how to carry that weight
inside   your arms still open

to hold the life
you are given
as your own

those who watch their hearts
before they take a step
walk into sleeves of darkness

their hearts comfortably dressed
for the time they sacrifice to religion
walking down that narrow aisle

so richly upholstered   a tunnel
sealed against the life flowing
from the real temple's spirit

it is too dimly lit there
for them to know
what good or evil they are married to.

x (5:1)

But don't open your mouth
too quickly or spill out your heart
in an alphabet soup of prayers

his vision spreads across heaven
where a mouthful of words aren't needed
and you are on earth

where words can come cheaply
to someone so low to the ground
he can't foresee the next minute

the next second when suddenly
his mood changes
and he is denying what he just said

bad dreams daydreams fantasies
spread like blinding steam
from too much living in the moment

too many things to do
with no pause for real reflection
and hot air streams from the mouth

of someone who talks too much
if you've promised to do something
if you've sworn to God

do it
he has less time than you have
to sit in the steambath

and wish the world away
pay what you owe even as it pains
and your eyes will clear a path for you

better yet don't make promises
you can't keep
especially to yourself: it's your mouth

in your body
so don't let it betray
flesh of your flesh

and when you do
and when the messenger comes to collect on it
take your foot out of your mouth

don't pretend it was perfectly natural
to mistakenly be licking someone's foot
don't pretend your mouth is not in your head

but respect the work of your creator
who put it there   he is perfectly right
to be angry with your swollen voice

and to puncture the blister of things
you've accumulated around you
with the grasping hands

he also presented to you
along with the gift of language
you infect with mouths of stale air

from the disembodied chatter
of fantasies and dreams
false gods and persons

streaming from the unchecked mind
inflating the world with unreal messages—
wake up   and trust your maker.

XI (5:10)

A lover led by silver
will never embrace enough of her
his arms won't even reach behind her

and one in love with more
than he can hold
gets only more of the same: frustration

and another vain kiss the wind
blows away
like seed not firmly planted

in a body of earth
a measure equal
to a body's need

the more food the land produces
the more people grow up
to eat it

what satisfaction is this easy multiplication
to the stomach of its owner
who grows fat in the eyes

feasting on his own desire
to be bright and superior
in the social mirror

of shallow eyes
a surface flattened for respect
adding up to a fat reflection

while the undistracted worker
tired from sheer indivisible labor
melts into sleep

like a cube of sugar
in a glass of tea
regardless of what he's eaten

but the man bloated with possessions
living in a dream-stomach of selfhood
a pig of identity

this man digesting property
indiscriminately as a camel
in the garbage dumps on the outskirts

of Beersheba
this rich man with a full stomach
inside and outside

gulping the wine of self-imagery
and still this man just can't fall asleep
his peace sits at the bottom of his glass

a lump of stone
and the man who hides his wealth
like the man who lives alone

grows sick on the stale breath of himself
ends up in a daydream
where he tosses away his fortune

in an impulsive fit
and the hoard of his ego
falls to pieces within him

nothing to pass on
to his son   the milk soured in the heat
of a sudden passionate thought

his hand empty
the glass shattered on the floor
rock bottom   the pit

naked and wet
as when he came through
the womb where he was fashioned

and he will follow his mother
back again to a deeper
source in earth

the mother of us all
stripped to the dry skeleton
barest image of a human

falling back
into the hidden hand
of creation

his own hands slowly unforming
and all that they held
all the land and fruits

of labor   gone
another daydream gone sour
another life led down the path

into a falling darkness
another illusion for the instincts
naked he came naked returns

alone with his reality
a life struggling to grasp
something in the wind

to make something more
of his own breath
than the spirit his efforts obscure

the labor that eats away inside
like another hungry worker
toiling away in the darkness inside

this companion worker this utter
reality   born in frustration
in a fertile mind   bred in worry and anger

and this is what I learned
what's worth struggling to learn
is as beautiful as being

working to eat drink and be
satisfied in the flow
of works and days

like water shining under the sun
harnessed
to the energy burning within

the little sun of a lifetime
God has given   so
let's have a good time

in the simple space and time
of human vision
that I may hold

in my hands
like a telescope
the fact of memory

embracing the world
with the feeling of real arms
warm from their labor

and to those of us allowed
luxury and property and
grace to enjoy them

in this gift of a body
happy in the sun
on a smooth shore of a life

content by the glistening sea
of our own fine sweat
which brought us to a home we feel good in—

that home is a vessel
a gift of God
in which we travel awhile

a little journey equal to the breadth
of our vision
the depth of our memory

a present to us
buoyant on the waves
connecting past and future

the surges of wind and breath
keeping a mind clear
through dark passages of fear

that life is passing us by
blood washing over stone
making us rigid with fear   stone

but God makes a clearing in the heart
we gather our thoughts there   a labor
mirroring the work that reveals us to ourselves.

XII (6:1)

Another thing I see
weighing men down
in the invisible backpack

harnessed to every walker in the sun
or at the feet of one freely standing
is the load of injustice

a man or woman shining
in the eyes of their community
standing tall in mirrors of themselves

sure of their identity in the stylish dress
of God-given talents
confident on red carpets of success

rolled out from houses that hold
everything you could wish for
a happy family and nothing to wish for

a spirit filled to the brim
a table spread before him
but then—he can't eat:

he hasn't been allowed an heir
a visible future
as the present eats away inside him

someone else embodies his desire
his appetite materializes as another man
real or imagined

his fortune feeds that person
a stranger in the lap
of his reality

he stands before an empty mirror
staring into the abyss of vanity
unforeseen

(some other man will absently lounge
in the warmth and care
he skilled his hands to open)

and even if he were surrounded
with a hundred sons and daughters
and lived to a ripe old age

happiness could elude him a hundred ways
like echoes bouncing off stone
in a desert canyon

echoes from one unguarded shriek of recognition
terror-flash of the material world
black glimpse of an eternity

a nightmare instead of a miracle
a nuclear bomb
instead of a warming sun

all in a moment stripped bare by frustration
his soul stripped like a woman
in the midst of a crowded market that

was the world of his possessions
even if he were to live forever
that moment would gape behind him

like a freshly dug grave
the echo of violent recognition
and the vast explosive mirror-reality

of antimatter   blind to his reflection
in a soul   irreducible
shaping the universe within   heaven and earth

but he can only see the face of horror
the hot flash of recognition: only the material evidence
a momentary picture but haunting him everywhere

a stillborn child   even a fetus
aborted is better off
than someone in the midst of everything

life has to offer and still restless
in the desert of awareness   blunt exposure
to a sense of happiness somewhere lost

like the innocent whiteness of skin
under a desperate tan
worse off than that embryo of darkness

innocent of the self-made light
of inner desperation   who comes
in passionate night sighs

and leaves before dawn
no one seeing its face
its name its sex bundled in darkness

better off not having breathed
or seeing its image inflated
in its own eyes

for it never had to bitterly wish
for a comforting darkness
to be gratified in

even if the man lived a thousand years
two thousand
what good is the sum of his breaths of air

if he's satisfied with nothing but a wish
with which to pay for his journey
to the same dust as all that have beginnings

this person's work kept his mouth full
and still he gasps for air
on the shore

what difference does it make
if it's Siberia or the Riviera
to a fish out of water

what good will books and travel
do us   wise man and fool
flop in the net of their longing

following the wind
our breath longs to catch
as if we could be somewhere else

and the realist making his way
in caution and poverty
thinks he should have been born rich

this makes bitterness "real" instead of "imagined"?
it's better to hold a bull by the horns
than have two in the bush?

what you see is what you get:
more bull   the eyes never stop
walking down that narrow aisle

of the universal supermarket
which is another illusion
like theories of objectivity

like the posters of mild Hawaii
we make what we see
with the eyes of a double

longing to be merely here
in our shoes
learning how to speak walk and be

more than a spectator
with the watery baby-eyes of an old man
just to be somebody somewhere anywhere: fully alive

this too is deadly illusion
just wanting to be
where we are already

pursuing the wind
that blows through us
as if we could be another.

XIII (6:10)

Anything that has a beginning
everything
was a seed in the pot

planted before existence
and named by men
as it flowed into the world

man is also a kind of flower
whose growth is defined
and all that flows from his hands

and with our own little names
we can't argue with our creator
a name that's boundless

beyond identity
like death which takes back our names
and gives them to the living

the more words we use
the more bricks for the mausoleum
building castles in the air

that are ancient relics
the moment we exhale
passed on to ignorant children

when we die
they prefer sand castles
and when the tide comes in they will not cry

but watch   fascinated
no better or worse
than all preceding men

who knows
what the right thing to do is
with a life

that walks across a stage
of air
in a bathing costume of flesh

until night falls like a gown
over a beautiful woman
who sleeps alone

only our shadows remain
impotent watchmen
on the shore of the life

our blood flowed to
and suddenly they too are gone
as the sun again rises

piercing all wishes and dreams
and romances of the future
with the bones of light

we are stripped awake   leaving
a shadow on the shore
that had not seen its own body.

XIV (7:1)

They say it's better to keep your name clean
than your body   whether bathing
in baby oil holy oil or covering a stink

with expensive deodorant
no man stinks more than a dead man
but, if left behind is the inner perfume

of a good name—then his deathday is happy
so no more false happy birthdays
until a man is dead

then he can be famous
without having to grease a palm or wear
the painted mask of success . . .

they say it's better to be with a family
burying their dead
than one celebrating successful occasions

for all will pass beyond
these forgotten fêtes
your vision will serve to remind them

you aren't eating your heart away
in feasts of gratitude or envy
but opening it

to the face of loss
all must wear
and all will remember your presence

they say the face of grief
is better than the laughing
party masks of plastic

the raw skin of sadness
though bad for one's complexion
reddens the blood strengthens the heart

and improves the mind
a wise heart is anchored
in a natural seriousness   at home

even at death with its wall of silence
even in a house that wails
in tune with hearts exposed and beating

while, running away from itself
a foolish heart capsizes
in a sea of nervous giggles

and flails desperately
behind a happy face of plastic
swimming back to its place at the party

under a paper moon
calmed by the stereo dutifully playing
"it's only a paper moon"

they say better listen to stinging
criticism from someone knowing
what they're talking about

than lending your ear to "friends"
you turn on like a radio
to the muzak of approval

the best tunes become idiotic
when translated for the mouse-eared
masses   inertia

is playing even more softly
under a muzak of desire
to be somewhere else

to escape into a soft sculpture
of the world created
and played on by heavies

having no idea what to do
with themselves   an empty talent
bottling air   milking respect

from wide-eyed calves looking
vainly for approval: the hot breath
in the nostrils of a bull

is what you get if not despair
served in silver trophy cups
empty as the occasions they honor

but even humility in the wisest person
allowing him to say
exactly what he sees

resisting influence and flattery
hardens into a statue of identity
to grace the social scene

"words to the wise" spoken at a café
like the coffee itself turns to oil
greasing the social mechanism

and he is also a helpless victim
of naive hearts and eyes
he impresses his image upon

in his own naive sexuality
mistaking love for innocence
gratitude for understanding

they say it's better to listen
to what you think
you have to say   inner ear

and eye open to what happens
to the event
in speaking in becoming a mirror a judge

everyone is hungry for images
of themselves   better see through that
than start up new fantasies

keep your conscience a clear window
to see through
as your death approaches from a distance

better a happy deathday
unsurpassed
than happy birthdays increasingly desperate

let what's there be
to feel smell hear see
before you gulp down something

like a hungry dog or baby
better to see a thing come clear
in the emulsion of time

than lose your integrity
in the rush of pride
to impose an image on the movie

to expose a frame too quickly
outside the natural time
of creation

don't get mad and impatient
restrain yourself
when everyone seems to be getting ahead

it's a stampede of mice
a rat race   madness
quickening the mass of Disney hearts

don't look back in anger
at boats you think you missed
or whine about good old days

while you frown in the idiot's mirror
reading wrinkles as ancient ciphers of a dilemma
central to the origin of the big cartoon

in the past most people are living in
the vast expanding bubble of "progress"
that suddenly bursts

throwing water in the face
of the philosopher on the beach
dreaming of fountains of youth

what depths of disappointment spring
from fantastic wells of expectation
sunk in the false bottom of fantasy land

don't be so dumb as even to inquire
in the studied falsetto of a scholar
where has the past gone?

it will smack you in the face
for having turned your head
at every passing fancy

of knowledge shaped by the girdle of progress
then there are those who study it
accumulating knowledge as if it were money

better to marry it
better yet inherit it
so there's time to sit in the shade

after gazing into the sun
its reflection off the metal
of coin

to sit in the cool shadow
of the mind's reflection   safe
in the reality of sun

the difference is
(between accumulating and having)
the wise man has a life within

a harbor for his ship to come in
illuminated by an inner reality
feeling the sun's power as light

falling around a field or page
not to possess it from towers
but letting it be revealed

observe this working of God
light   in its own time
as it reveals the touch of its creator

a tree bends to the sun
we can't straighten it
our mind can't overpower it

when a good day
comes your way
embrace it

and when the bad one arrives   watch out
but patience   observe the contrast
light creates a room for shadow

one creator made each day
so we don't build up expectation
as a wall

but may see the stones fall
names and reputations
material ripped away to an open view

of the present around us
the dimension of depth
sweeping between light and shadow

between inside and outside
the dynamic of waves
sweeping away the tower

climbed by the one thinking he was master
of what he could survey: past and future
but it is drowned

along with elaborate constructions of myth
fortune-telling and other dark fortresses
built for a false security

each day is constructed anew
in the flow of time   perfect as the sea
bearing a ship to its destiny

that is *felt* to be there
and in that feeling we can find no fault
with the nights and days that surprise us

in our beds of doubt or certainty
we are made perfectly awake
to the fathomless depth of creation.

xv (7:15)

I've seen everything
in the rich days I've walked through
like a long hall

in a home I thought I owned
and from life's windows
I've seen it all

though inside I had nothing
but a little wind
to keep my eyes from closing

I saw those who breathe deeply
in the rare atmosphere
of righteousness

and I saw them dying in it
from lack of oxygen
while cynics whose mouths are full

of lies grow strong and healthy
and live long lives
in their sewers of deceit

so don't climb up high
after perfection
don't get carried away

in the altitude of lucidity
nobody remembers who you are
when you fall on your face identityless

like a bright leaf blown by a wind
as strong and true
as a will driven beyond the imperfect body

but don't bend to natural forces
too easily   don't hold on
to the rail when the ship is sinking

don't cling to yourself like a child
to its toy
don't be a baby

still wailing inwardly
for attention   ruthless
don't stoop so low

to wear the wound of need on your arm
to play on the innocence of others
to be selfish as stone inside

the idol of yourself
why swallow a stone
the stone of bitterness you cast

and die before you've opened
a door to human kindness—
locked in the arms of deceit

squeezing the life away
of you and your victims   don't suffocate
don't be too self-involved

or selfless—hold on
but keep your mind open
let God anchor your conscience

freeing you to be
neither ego's slave nor wisdom's fool
you swim beyond the wreck

of single-minded arrogance
first one arm then the other
and a sense of a higher, deeper order . . .

on the one hand intelligence
is a stronger defense than
a pantheon of pious figureheads

there isn't a righteous cause on earth
without its empty-headed champions
promoting their own hot air

not one perfect man or woman
who is always right   uncompromised
by the slightest distortion in the mirror

by which he knows himself
and forgets himself too: the flaw
in taking memory for granted

a distorting memory   reflected
through the glass of
a highly compressed fear

for it will explode as sure as a star
just as the present is always erupting
dispersing the precious crockery of the past

into the lap of dozing Justice
who has forgotten this appointment
with the bill collector of Time. . . .

Certainly it makes more sense to imagine that Ruth *was written by a woman than a man, although I have less literary evidence for it here than I do for Genesis, Jonah, Lamentations, and Judith. Written by one of the court poets in the century following Solomon's reign, it was still not unusual for an educated woman to practice the inspirational art of writing. In earlier times, Hebraic women were renowned for having been the great poets of legend, such as Deborah, Abigail, and Hulda.*

The subject of this poetic tale concerns a woman's position in both family and history. I'm persuaded that it was originally written as a poem when I hear the vestigial elements of poetic parallelism, together with a rhythm of key images and word patterns.

Ruth's vulnerability provides emotional drama throughout the book (scroll), especially in her relationship with Boaz. The drama is made explicit on the threshing floor, in the tension between restrained description and high risk. Perpetuation of a nation is metaphorically in the balance; and at the time of writing, both risk and restraint were uppermost in the nation's mind. The symbolic act of uncovering Boaz's legs (literally "feet," though that word does not convey the proper note of apprehension, since there is a Hebrew connotation of male genitals) until he wakes of his own accord is paralleled later in the ritual act of rejection by the closest kin-redeemer. That man takes off his sandal to symbolize his renunciation, rejecting the risk—or position of vulnerability.

Boaz takes the risk of winning the blessing: "this name will not disappear." And that name links up the line of descent down to David, confirming the right to live in the land. The union with the land is that of Boaz's union with Ruth, primordial native. Their child in Bethlehem, who will become the grandfather of David, is thereby a harvest of love. In the words of the vestigial chorus—the women of the city—"the Lord be blessed / whose kindness has not ceased / to this day, never leaving you / bereft of a redeemer." The word "redeem," here and elsewhere, weaves together the contractual ethics in all relationships, from property dealings to personal and family relations.

This contract, or covenant, requires a physical embrace, so that the men are equally in need of redemption in a woman's arms; after all, it was "Rachel and Leah / who built the house in Israel." In the same way, the reader is brought into the circle of witnesses represented by those at the "trial" and then the betrothal of Boaz and Ruth—"today, in this assembly / you are witnesses." The risk and the blessing reside in a union of equals, and they maintain it by their acceptance of vulnerability, or intimacy. As in Esther, that vulnerability is sometimes a curse, more often a blessing. It is in the intimacies of poetry, the author also implies, that we become witnesses, even as readers.

A probe into the authorship of Ruth was begun in my The Book of David (1997). Speculation is involved, of necessity if we want our Hebrew writers back, and especially since the ancient Hebraic culture has been buried under later agendas of tradition. A brief paragraph extracted from The Book of David suggests a relationship between writers as it would have existed in ancient Jerusalem, just as it does in other cultures. By fleshing out the characters of the writers, we can begin to look over their shoulders. Although the result may be imaginative, the text comes back to life in a way that conventional critics disallow. The convention requires a nod to tradition, even when modern interpreters can vary wildly about the characters within the text—King David, for example. But outside the text, the cultural context remains unexplored, as if the biblical texts had no original writers of consequence or an original audience.

Some recent scholarship claims the Book of Ruth was written anonymously after the fifth century BCE, disposing of responsibility for authorship altogether. No writer need be imagined when, in this view, the writing is reduced to its motivation or agenda: a satire on Ezra's new decree against mixed marriage. However, if it was written by a great writer such as J—as I suspect, along with other scholars who have judged it of Solomonic vintage—then the play between J and S, as discussed earlier in my introduction to 2nd Samuel, is poignantly deepened here. Naomi is transparently J (in the author S's eyes, for whom J served as tutor), and the redeemer she is blessed with is her young protégé himself, S: "she became like a nurse to him." His name? Oved, meaning "assistant," or "worker." And, "he was the father of Jesse / who was the father / of David." The "father of Jesse," for all intents and purposes, was S's invention—since it is S who provides this unknown father with a lineage in writing, just as he designates a line of descent from Ruth to David. None of this interaction between the writers, J and S, need be incongruous or subversive—any more than when Marlowe's The Jew of Malta is brought to mind for audiences of the time by Shakespeare's The Merchant of Venice.

r u t h

CHAPTER I

And it was back in the Days of Judges
when the law was not always lived
as the judges received it
and it was a time of famine
ravaging the land

There was a man, then
of Bethlehem, in Judah, who left
wandering to foreign soil, in Moab
with his wife and two sons—
this man was named Elimelech
and his wife, Naomi
and two sons, Mahlon and Kilyon
and they were Ephraimites, established Bethlehem Jews

They reached the fertile land in Moab
sojourning, then settling there
Elimelech, the man who had been husband

to Naomi, died, and she was left there
but stayed on, with her two sons

The sons settled down in Moab
each marrying a Moabite woman
one was named Orpah
and the second, Ruth
and for ten years they lived on there

But the two sons, Mahlon and Kilyon
also died, and Naomi was left there
without husband, without children

The woman, with her daughters-in-law
resolved to leave
to return from the fields of Moab—
it was there in Moab she had heard
how the Lord took care of his people again
and they had their share of bread

So she left that place
setting out with her two daughters-in-law
on the road that returns
to the land of Judah

Then Naomi stopped—
saying to them
you must go back, both of you
return to the house of your mother
may the Lord be kind to you

as you were kind to our dead
as you remained loving to me
and may the Lord take care of you
giving you a home of kindness
in the house of a loving husband

Naomi kissed them
and they broke out crying
protesting: no, we will return
with you, to your people

But she answered: return, my daughters
why go with me?
are there yet more sons in my womb
who would be husbands to you?

Return, my daughters, go your way
I am too old for husbands, because
if I said there is still hope
that even tonight I had a husband
that even now I was bearing sons
would you wait for them to grow up
would you stay home, waiting
shutting yourselves off
from husbands?

No, my daughters, it would be
even more bitter for me than you
knowing the Lord is against me
his hand already has shown my way

Yet they protested again, crying
and Orpah kissed her mother-in-law
in parting
but Ruth clung to her

Look, Naomi was saying, your sister-in-law returns
to her people, to her gods
return with her
but Ruth protested: don't push me away
or urge me to turn away
from you

Wherever you must go
I will go with you
wherever you must stay
I will stay with you
your people are my people
your God my God
wherever you must die
there too I will be buried

Let the Lord take me—if he must
no matter how hard it is
may nothing but that, death
separate us

Naomi could see Ruth's determination
to go with her
she stopped speaking, no longer
trying to dissuade her

the two of them walked on
together
until they reached Bethlehem

And in Bethlehem they found
the town struck with amazement
and interest in them, with the women saying
is this Naomi?
do not call me Naomi (pleasantness)
call me Mara (bitterness)
as it pleases Almighty God

I was full of life when I left
but I return empty-handed
on the bitter road the Lord provides me
why call me Naomi
you can see the Lord was hard
a stone in my pleasant way
Almighty God was pleased to point me away
from a good life, to futility

And so Naomi returned
and with her, Ruth the Moabite
her daughter-in-law
leaving the fields of Moab
arriving in Bethlehem at a time
of harvest—the barley harvest had begun.

CHAPTER 2

And Naomi had a relative there
an in-law
a man of character
from the established family of Elimelech
and his name was Boaz

Ruth, the woman of Moab, was saying
to Naomi: I am going
to the fields, so I may glean
the free grain that falls
behind, if one may
look on me kindly—
and she was reassured: go, my daughter

There, in the fields, gleaning
behind the harvesters, she found herself
by accident
in just that part of the fields
belonging to Boaz, from the family of Elimelech

And it happened Boaz came out
from the town, Bethlehem
greeting the harvesters: the Lord
be with you, and they greeted him
the Lord be kind to you

Boaz turned to his man
overseeing the harvesters

who is that young woman
and the young man replied
she is the Moabite woman, who returned

with Naomi from the fields of Moab
she made up her mind to glean
behind the harvesters, and there she's been
on her feet since morning
with hardly a moment's shade

And Boaz turned to Ruth
listen, my daughter
you will not have to glean
in other fields
you will not have to leave again
cling to us, stay here
with our young women

Your eyes will be on the harvest
along with the others—don't stand back
but go with them, I've asked
the young men not to treat you harshly
and when you're thirsty, walk over
to the canteens the young men have brought

She was overcome with gratitude
bowing her face to the earth
in a gesture of humility, then saying
why am I special in your eyes
why are you so kind

that I stand out as anything more
than a foreigner?

Because I learned more
Boaz was saying, for all to hear
how you cared for your mother-in-law
after your husband's death
and then left behind you
mother, father, and land
to come to a strange country
trusting in a people you didn't yet know

The Lord be a full guarantee
for your loving-kindness
the God of Israel reward you fully
with a rich life
as you have awarded us
your full trust
beneath his sheltering wing

May I live up to your kindness
Ruth was saying
and to the reassurance in your voice and eyes
my heart is stirred, as if
I were one of your workers
though I'm not worthy as one of them

When it was time for the meal
Boaz said to her: sit here
share our bread and wine

Ruth sat among the workers
and he filled her plate with roasted grain
and she ate her fill, with more left over

As she rose, returning to the gleaning
Boaz told his workers: allow her
to glean anywhere
even among the sheaves
do not embarrass her but
leave some fresh stalks already harvested
for her, let her glean among them
do not judge her harshly

And she worked in the field until evening
then beat out the grain
until she had a full bushel of barley
about an ephah
lifting it up to take to the city
to show her mother-in-law
who was surprised
at all she had gleaned, and then
Ruth showed her the extra grain as well
left over from the meal

And her mother-in-law was saying
where did you glean all this?
where did you work today?
where is there one so generous
to take kind notice of you—bless him
so she told her mother-in-law where

she had worked: the man's name
for whom I worked today is Boaz

And Naomi was saying to her daughter-in-law
may the Lord be kind to him
who has not forgotten loving-kindness
shown to the living, and with respect
for the dead—
that man, Naomi continued, is a relative
close enough to be within
our family sphere of redeemers

And Ruth the Moabite replied
he also said I should return
staying close to the young men and women
who work for him, saying: you will stay
until they have finished reaping
and the field is fully harvested

It is a good thing, Naomi was saying
to Ruth, her daughter-in-law, good
that you go with his young women
and not into other fields, where
you could find you are treated harshly

So Ruth stayed close to Boaz's young women
gleaning until the barley was fully harvested
and on through the harvest of wheat
returning afterward to the house
of her mother-in-law, the two
staying on alone.

CHAPTER 3

And Naomi her mother-in-law was saying
my daughter, it is up to me
to help find you sheltering—
a fulfillment, a rewarding security

I have been thinking of Boaz
our relative, whose young women
you worked beside—now listen to me
it is the night he will be winnowing the grain
at the threshing floor, you must
bathe, use perfume, dress
as an attractive woman
and go down there
to the threshing floor
outside the gate

Let it not be known you have come
until he is through
and finished his meal and drink as well

And when he lies down, then
notice the place—
you will go in and there
while he sleeps
uncover his legs and lie down

And then he will tell you
what you must do

Ruth answered: I will
do all that you say

She went down to the threshing floor
doing as her mother-in-law asked

Boaz ate and drank to his content
his heart full, the work fulfilled
and he went to lie down
at the far end, behind
the freshly piled grain

She went there, coming softly
she uncovered his legs
quietly, she lay down

And then in the middle of the night
the man shivered, turned in his sleep—
suddenly, groping about, he felt
a body laying next to him, a woman

Who are you, he was saying
I am Ruth, your handmaid
spread the wing of your robe
over me
as a marriage pledge
and shelter your handmaid

For you are a redeemer
to me

He answered: and you are a blessing
before the Lord, my daughter
you have made a fresh espousal
of loving-kindness, as you did at first
for Naomi—and this a greater pledge
as you stayed true to your journey
not turning, even to the young men
desirable whether rich or poor

Now, my daughter, you will not worry—
whatever you say I must do
will be done
everyone, those who come
to the gate of my people, knows
you are a woman of character

Now it is true, also
I can be kin-redeemer to you
but there is another, even closer
than I

Stay here for the night
when morning comes
we will see if he honors
his role as kin-redeemer
but if he turns from his right
I will stay true
redeeming you

—As true as the Lord
lives in our hearts—
and now lie down
until the morning

And she lay next to him until morning
rising before daybreak, before one could know
one person from another—
let it not be harshly judged
he had said, that the woman came
to the threshing floor

Take off the shawl around you
he was saying, give it to me

And she held it out
as he poured six measures of barley
then fixed it to her back

He went inside the city
as Ruth returned to her mother-in-law
who was waiting
what has become of you, my daughter?

She told her everything
the man had done to her
six measures of barley he gave me
saying: you must not return empty-handed
to your mother-in-law

Sit down, my daughter, until you know
how it will all turn out
the man will not rest one moment
until all is settled
this very day.

CHAPTER 4

And Boaz had gone up to the gate
where the people gather
and sat down in the square
just then the very kin-redeemer
he had spoken of
passed by: stop, you so-and-so
come over here and sit down
and he did

Then Boaz called ten of the city's elders
to come over and sit down
in the role of witnesses
and they did

He turned to the kin-redeemer:
the part of the field
that was like a brother's, Elimelech's
must properly be sold by Naomi
who has returned
from the fields of Moab
I pledged to make it known to you

it is your right: you may buy it
in the presence of our people's elders
in front of those seated here

If you will honor your role
as redeemer, do it
and if it is not to be redeemed
tell me and make it known
since there is no one else but you
to do it, and I after you
he answered: I will redeem

Boaz continued: on the day you buy
the field from Naomi, you buy as well
from Ruth, the Moabite
who is the widow, the role
of redeeming husband—
to renew the name of the dead
by her hand
and to raise children
establishing his inheritance
the kin-redeemer answered: I cannot redeem

Redeeming may harm my own inheritance—
why not take on the role yourself
the right is yours
I cannot redeem it

Now this is how it was done
in Israel in those days

in cases of transferring rights:
as a sign of validation
in all such things
the man took off his sandal
and gave it to the neighbor
and thus the thing was sealed

Buy it, said the kin-redeemer
to Boaz, and he took off
his sandal

Then Boaz, turning to the elders
and in the presence of his people
said: you are witnesses
that on this day
I am buying from Naomi's hand
what was Elimelech's
what was his sons', Kilyon's and Mahlon's

And foremost, I take on the right
to ask the hand of Ruth
the Moabite, widow of Mahlon
whom I will marry
renewing the name of the dead
establishing his inheritance—
this name will not disappear

And it will live in his family
and in the assembly of his people
at the gate of his city—

today, in this assembly
you are witnesses

Then the people standing at the gate
and the seated elders
said: we are witnesses
may the Lord make this woman
who comes into your house
fruitful as were Rachel and Leah
who built the House of Israel

May your character reflect on Ephraim
your name live on in Bethlehem
your house grow as that of Peretz:
as he was born to Tamar and Judah
may the Lord give to you
and this young woman
a seed that flourishes

So Boaz was pledged to Ruth
she became his wife
and he came into her

She conceived
and gave birth to a son
as the Lord gave to them
a love that was fruitful

Then the women of the city
were saying to Naomi
the Lord be blessed

whose kindness has not ceased
to this day, never leaving you
bereft of a redeemer

May his name live on
in Israel

He will renew your spirit
and nourish your old age
because he is born to the loving
daughter-in-law
who came beside you
and who has borne you more kindness
than seven sons

Then Naomi took the boy
held it to her breast
and she became
like a nurse to him—
the women of the neighborhood
gave it a name, exclaiming
a son is born to Naomi

The name they gave him was Oved
he was the father of Jesse
who was the father
of David

Now these are the generations
descending from Peretz
Peretz and his wife gave birth to Hetzron

he to Ram, he to Amminidab
he to Nahson, he to Salmah
he to Boaz, he to Oved

Oved and his wife gave birth to Jesse
and he to David.

PART III

WRITING

Ruth

The most misread poetical tale, the book of Esther *was probably composed in the second century* BCE, *following a new burst of biblical imagination. The poet used three older sources—one about Mordecai, another about Queen Vashti, and the last concerning Esther—each in a different genre, from satire to heroic tale. The surface of the book is deceptively primitive; its collage of scenes is dazzlingly cinematic, allowing a range of ironies from expressionistic to deadpan. Aside from the plot, the book itself is about* plotting.

I've chosen to translate portions of the poetry that suggest the terror of vulnerability, allowing for the giddy relief of satire that follows deliverance. The relationship between intimacy and vulnerability is represented in ways that echo Ruth *and* Judith. *The author is likely a contemporary of the poet of* Judith, *and her work may have been a model for his.*

The terrifying words of Haman and Ahasuerus (in their banality) permit the magnitude of deliverance to parallel the Exodus from Egypt. There is a striking contrast between slavery in Egypt and the vulnerability of assimilation in Persia (as there is between Egypt and a vulnerable Judean state, in Judith*). What do the Jews seem to want? Apparently, to maintain the sensibility of their vulnerability. Ahasuerus asks Esther (who has attained the pinnacle of power in Persia, as Joseph in Egypt and Daniel in Babylon had before her) what she would now have—up to half the kingdom. In the most poignant understatement, Esther replies (her opening words echoing the false humility of Haman): "and if your majesty pleases / grant me my life / it is my petition / and my people's life / it is my request— / we wish to live."*

The satire in the book fitted the Jewish festival of Purim; by late Talmudic times it was suggested that one be drunk enough on this occasion to listen to a reading of the Scroll of Esther *and be unable to distinguish between "bless Mordecai" and "curse Haman."*

esther

Ahasuerus ruled a Persian empire of 127 provinces. He made
a great festival for representatives from all of them, lasting half
a year. Then he threw open the palace for the common people
of the capital city, Shushan, for another seven days of feasting
and drinking. Drunk and enraged by an imagined slight from
Vashti, his queen, Ahasuerus heeds the suggestion of his coun-
cilors that she be deposed. The issuing of a decree, to be sent to
all the provinces, cites this action as an example to all males of
vigilant dominance. It is a rather comic decree, especially in its
bureaucratic formulation, but the process sets the precedent for
a later one, in which the prime minister, Haman, suggests the
Jews be murdered.

   A new queen must be chosen. Virgins from each of the provinces are brought to the capital. Esther, adopted daughter of
Mordecai, is among the chosen. Both are fourth-generation,
Diaspora Jews, dating from the Babylonian exile. Esther under-
goes a twelve-month beauty treatment, as required in the king's
harem, then is brought to the king and wins his favor. Mordecai, who remains close to her as an official in the palace government, has advised Esther not to reveal her Jewish origin.

Subsequently, she is made queen. During Esther's coronation feast, Mordecai learns of a court plot on the king's life, tells it to Queen Esther, and so he, too, wins favor when the plotters are caught. The stage is set for Haman.

CHAPTER 3

Not long after these things
King Ahasuerus appointed Haman
prime minister

so Haman, son of Hammedatha, the Amalekite
(remember the cruelty of Amalek)
was raised to the highest seat

among the high officials at court
and all the courtiers had to bow
right down to the ground for him

for this was the king's command
yet Mordecai didn't bow
let alone kneel to the ground

the officials at the King's Gate
asked Mordecai: how can you ignore
the king's commandment?

and this continued day after day
the courtiers reminding him
and he ignoring them

explaining that he was a Jew
words so striking and upright
these men exposed him to Haman

to see if Mordecai would stand
by his word
and be allowed to

and when Haman saw for himself
how he would not kneel
a rage swelled in him

that killing Mordecai could not satisfy
a deep contempt for this man's people
now that he was faced with them

until Haman could think only of how
to wipe out all Jews from his sight—
of whom Mordecai was one—

every last one
scattered across the vast kingdom
ruled by Ahasuerus

In the first month, Nisan
in the twelfth year of King Ahasuerus
they cast lots

or *purim*—as they were known
in the presence of Haman
who was looking for the day

of days, the month of months
which fell
in the twelfth month: Adar

There is a certain people
Haman was saying to Ahasuerus
scattered yet unassimilated

among the diverse nations of your empire
honoring different laws
from those of their hosts

refusing to honor
even the king's laws—
as long as they live

it demeans the king—
so if your majesty pleases
it would be in his best interest

and the state's
to issue a decree for their destruction
and expropriate all their assets

and I will raise several million in silver
for the king's treasury
to satisfy all involved

the king removed his ring
giving the royal signet
to Haman

son of Hammedatha
the Amalekite
the enemy of the Jews

the silver is yours to raise
the king was saying
and so the people are yours

if you please:
do what is right
in your eyes

Now in the first month, the thirteenth day—Passover eve
the king's scribes were assembled
and all that Haman ordered

was written down and addressed
to the king's ministers
to the governors of each province

and to the leaders of every people
each written in his own language
and each province in its own script

it was decreed in the name of King Ahasuerus
and it was sealed
with the king's ring

the letters were sent out
in the hands of couriers
to all the provinces, saying

the Jews must be destroyed
wiped out
you will round up the young with the old

little children with the women
and kill them
in one day of extermination

beginning on the thirteenth day
of the twelfth month
Adar

and everything they own
belongs to the executioner
loot it for yourselves

this document was to be published
as a decree—binding as law
in every single province

proclaimed in every tongue
so all would be ready
for the appointed day

the couriers left immediately
on this mission of state
even as the law was being posted

on the walls of the capital, Shushan
and Haman and the king
sat down to banquet

in the palace
but in the city of Shushan
tears and confusion reigned.

CHAPTER 4 (L-3)

When Mordecai learned of these things
he burst out in mourning
crying out, ceaselessly

dressed in black, in bitter grief
he walked out openly
in the midst of the city

in open protest
raising his voice inconsolably
a loud and bitter voice

a fierce protesting
right up to the King's Gate
a great mourning

as the Jews would make
in every province, loudly
throughout the entire empire.

Esther learns of the decree from Mordecai, who asks her to intercede with the king. But Esther, anxious and distraught, sends word to him that she can't do it without breaking court protocol and risking her life.

——

PART III

——

WRITING

——

Esther

CHAPTER 4 (12–14)

And when Mordecai heard Esther's plea
he did not hesitate to reply
returning her messenger immediately:

Esther, do not think for a moment
silently within yourself
that within the king's palace you are safer

than any other Jew
but if you persist in silence
in waiting

at a time so crucial as this
the Jews will still be delivered, yes
saved in another way, by another hand

but you and your family will pass away
like a moment of truth turned away from—
for you are only yourself for a reason

and who can know if you were not brought
splendidly into favor in the palace
for a moment like this—of action.

Esther acts, expressing her solidarity with Jews by fasting with them for three days. She risks her life, and it happens that her weakened state from fasting inspires the king's generosity, who grants Esther her petition. Before disclosing what it is, Esther sets the stage by throwing a banquet of her own, to which Haman is also invited.

Meanwhile, Haman has already built a gallows to hang Mordecai on. But before Haman can reveal Mordecai as a Jew, the king is reminded of Mordecai's favor in having saved his life and orders Haman to honor Mordecai by the same means that Haman had devised for his own honor. So Haman has a foretaste of his downfall—victimized by the quirks of chance in his own plotting—before he arrives at the queen's banquet.

CHAPTER 7 (L-8)

And the king
and Haman came
to drink with Esther the queen

the king again said to Esther—
while they were drinking wine
on this second day of banqueting—

your petition is granted, Queen Esther
even if it means half the kingdom
your request will be fulfilled

and this time Esther responded
if I am worthy in your eyes
of the king's favor

and if your majesty pleases
grant me my life
it is my petition

and my people's life
it is my request—
we wish to live

for we have been sold
I and my people
to be slaughtered

murdered and destroyed
yet I would not have spoken
had I been sold merely

for a servant girl
and my people for slaves
I would not have troubled the king

with news of a plotter
whose hatred outweighs
his concern for your honor

Who is it? the king exclaimed
and speaking to Esther he said
who would dare turn his heart to this

and lay a hand on you—where is he?
An enemy, a plotter! she was saying
no other than this bitter Haman

as he sits before us
and Haman was dumbstruck, confused
before the king and queen

and the king was so enraged
he stalked out from the banqueting
into the palace gardens

and Haman remained, trembling
but making a plea for himself
before Esther the queen

he had seen the king was convinced
and would make up his mind
to punish him

but suddenly the king returned
to the banquet hall
from the palace gardens—

Haman had fallen to his knees
and was now lying prostrate on the couch
where Esther sat

and the king was beside himself:
will he even violate the queen
rape her right here

while I am in the palace?
and the words were barely out
of the king's mouth

when it seemed the hood had already fallen
over Haman's face
like a man about to be hanged.

In the concluding three chapters, the process of Jewish deliverance is presented in the most earthly, striking terms. Haman's murderous contempt will be turned on himself and his family. The end of the story remains as stylized as the beginning: It's not revenge the Jews exact of their enemy, but the principle of la'amad al naphsham—the plotter doing himself in.

It's not just Haman's end that must be resolved, but the whole machinery of state and culture—which was set into motion, disseminating racial prejudice—that has to be halted and reversed. The real drama centers on the future of the Jews, not the fate of Haman.

One of the great narrative poems of Maccabean Hebrew literature,
Judith *was preserved in the Bible's Apocrypha. Composed in the sec-*
ond century BCE, *it typically incorporated earlier legendary material.*
This Hebrew scroll itself became a legend, after it was omitted from
the Hebrew Bible. It was read in the early synagogues to celebrate
the new festival of Hanukkah, but like the books of Maccabees,
Judith *only survived in Judeo-Greek translations (and like them,*
was reconstructed in Hebrew by Abraham Kahana in the twentieth
century).

   The Christian translations were popular, inspiring many poems
and paintings. John Ruskin, in Mornings in Florence, *character-*
ized Judith as "the mightiest, purest, brightest type of high passion in
severe womanhood offered to our human memory."

   However, one of the charges against Jews by early Christians was
that their "nationalism was an evil genius" (echoed in G.R.S. Mead's
popular twentieth-century account of Gnosticism, Fragments of a
Faith Forgotten). *In fact, the text of* Judith *makes it clear that the*
Jews do not look for victory but merely sweet survival: the victory
celebration in the book is a literary antidote to the enemy's cruel
intentions. It's as obvious a literary exaggeration as the victory over
Haman in Esther. *In similar manner, the popular imagery of war,*
heroism, and piety is stylized for effect.

   Characteristic of biblical poets, when vengeance is invoked it is as
an ironic mirror for the attacker's own self-destruction, a hope that
he will be trapped in his own destructive plan. Judith's beauty was
an instrument of truth allowing the inflated head of Holofernes to
fall of its own.

   Probably written as poetry, the book of Judith *loses much in a*
prose translation. Frequent use of biblical quotations and parallels
deepens the harmonics. In fact, the narrative is often secondary to

the immediate feelings these echoes arouse. Often, the poet plays with a deliberate anachronism, contrasting it with the revitalized Hebrew poetry of her time.

Just as the eleventh chapter of Daniel is probably a work of the Maccabean Age, even though it is set in an earlier age, Judith also portrays its own times in an older historical focus. There are several reasons for this convention. One is the obvious need to disguise contemporary political criticism: the King Nebuchadnezzar of Judith is probably the same Greek-Seleucid Antiochus as in Daniel. The customs of "prophetic history" were transparent to contemporary Jews, a source of both satire and inspiration. There is something heady about Judith carrying her cheeses into the pagan camp. True, the woman is keeping kosher, but the irony of the plan is that she will share these salty cheeses with Holofernes, heightening his thirst and hence his eventual drunken stupor. The poet has turned the ponderous nature of the dietary laws inside out. Likewise, the poignancy of the allusion to the rededication (the "Hanukkah") of the Temple in chapter four would not be lost on a Maccabean ear.

Judith's rage at Hellenic imperialism is sublimated into her beauty. A representation of Judaism herself ("Judith" means Jewess in Hebrew), she is religious yet acutely oriented to reality. Her physicality, rooted in domestic happiness and communal responsibility, contrasts with the inflated desire of the enemy. Judith's self-respect as a woman in the highest Jewish circles is played against the enemy's disregard for her except as a sexual object.

Jewish tradition preserved the story of Judith in later, less vital poems. The original poet was probably a highly educated woman, her work at variance with the representation of women in the Greek classics (which she no doubt knew well) as well as some Jewish religious stereotypes. The investigation into Judith's authorship has barely begun, but I would compare her poem to Aeschylus' Agamemnon (in the Robert Lowell translation of 1978). Clytemnestra, the queen, murders her husband—"I offer you Agamemnon, / dead, the work of this right hand"—an act motivated by vengeance. "Oh, deceiving and decoying Agamemnon to my trap / was work for a woman. I did the thinking." This representation of a woman's mind seems to me most likely a man's work, while the rich mixture of Judith's character—piety and physicality vying for respect—appears to betray a woman's hand. The two strands unite toward the end and focus upon the women of Israel: they are leading Judith in dance.

591

PART III

WRITING

Judith

Introduction

judith

In the twelfth year of Nebuchadnezzar's reign he began to plan
a war against the powerful nation of the Medes. When Nebu-
chadnezzar called on smaller nations to join him as allies, they
refused, unafraid, sensing his power was overplayed. He was
severely embarrassed, and when he later defeated the Medes
he planned retribution.

Holofernes, the Assyrian army's commander in chief, put
together a huge expeditionary force, with over a hundred and
twenty thousand foot soldiers alone, and marched out of Nineveh
toward Damascus, intent on destroying all resistance. After
devastating various nations, leveling towns across Mesopota-
mia and Arabia, "butchering all who resisted," the Assyrian
approaches Damascus.

And he surrounded the Arabs
burning their tents, looting their flocks
then came down into the plain of Damascus
it was during the wheat harvest and he set fire

to the crops, the fields were ablaze
herds destroyed, villages ransacked
and all the young men skewered on the sword

Panic gripped the coast
in Sidon, in Tyre
in Sur, Akko, Jamnia
Ashdod and Ashkelon lived in terror ·
they sent their highest messengers
begging peace: "We are here as servants
of the great Nebuchadnezzar, to lie at your feet
do with us what you like
the doors of our warehouses stand open
our flocks, our herds are under your command
every farm and field of wheat
lies at your feet
use them as you like
our cities and every citizen in them only wonder
what they can do for you, what's your pleasure"

These were their exact words to Holofernes
then he descended the coast and garrisoned the cities
where he made allies, chose conscripts
and received a hero's welcome
with garlands, tambourines, and dancing in celebration
meanwhile his army set fire to border villages
destroying claims to independent boundaries
he cut down all their groves of sacred trees
demolished all their pagan shrines
defiled every god they'd clung to
so it would be realistic for them to turn

to Nebuchadnezzar as a god
uniting nations under his worldly power
transcending all their local languages

Holofernes approached the plain of Jezreel near Dothan
where Judean mountains begin to be seen
he pitched camp between Geba and Beth Shean
staying there at least a month to regroup
and gather supplies for his army

By now the Jews in Judea had heard about Holofernes
commander in chief of the Assyrian army
under King Nebuchadnezzar, and how he dealt with nations
looting their sacred shrines, then leveling them
they were quite scared, near despair for Jerusalem
place of their one God's temple
they had hardly returned from exile
only recently had rededicated the devastated Temple
cleaning the altar, restoring the vessels
reunited in their land

Unlike the surrender pleas of their neighbors, the orders from Jerusalem were to occupy the mountaintops and passages, buying time for the protection of Jerusalem. The Jews were in no position to defend their country militarily, but they could hope to appear not worth the trouble of subduing.

When Holofernes heard that Jews had closed the passages to Jerusalem he was astonished. He asked his local allies what gave this people the nerve to resist, and he was told it was faith in their God, demonstrated by a long history of survival.

So Holofernes gave orders to wipe out this people. And the local allies advised a siege of the strategic city guarding the best route to Jerusalem. This way, the strategic mountain positions of the Jews were useless, and the Assyrians wouldn't lose a single soldier in battle.

After thirty-four days, Bethulia ran out of water. People were fainting in the streets. The town council accused the leaders of a grave error in not begging peace like other peoples. They would rather be alive as slaves than watch their children die. As a last resort, one leader appealed for holding out five more days; if nothing changed by then, he would advise surrender.

Judith, beautiful and devout, a widow still in mourning, visited the leaders and accused them differently. Who were they to set a time limit for God? They were actually negating their faith by setting conditions for miracles. But Judith declines to pray for rain when she is asked. When she does pray, in the psalm beginning chapter nine, it is for strength, in a plan of realistic action.

Then Judith kneeled
put her face in the dust
stripped to the sackcloth she wore underneath—
just at the moment the evening incense offering
wafted to the Temple ceiling in Jerusalem—
cupped her face in her hands
and spoke
her words rising outspoken
from her heart to the open sky
an offering, a prayer:

"Lord, God of my fathers
of Simon in whose hand you put a sword
to reward the strangers
who stripped off a young girl's dress to her shame
bared the innocence between her thighs
to her deep confusion
and forced into her womb
raped her in shock
to demean and disgrace her

For you have said in the Torah
this is an outrage
and you allowed these violators to be surprised
in their beds of deceit
the sheets stripped off them
their beds blushing with shame:
stained with their blood

For the lords among these strangers
you allowed equal treatment with their slaves:
slain on their thrones
their servants in their arms
their wives and daughters allowed to be spared:
captured and dispersed

Their possessions fell into the hands
of the sons you loved
for they listened to you
and were outraged
at the demeaning of a sister's blood

they called on you for help
and you listened

Lord, my Lord
now hear this widow's selfless words
you gave shape to the past
and beneath what is happening now
is your supportive hand
you have thought about the future
and those thoughts live as men and women

'Here we are!' they say
your thoughts are alive in the present
and you've cleared paths for them
into the future

Look, here we are, exposed to the Assyrians
parading their well-oiled muscle
preening in the mirrors of their polished shields
bullying the hills with their herds of infantry
vanity worn on their sleeves: tin armor
their spears thrusting forward
their trust in their legs and horses
their pride in the naked tips of their arrows
their hope in thoughts of total domination—
so locked in the embrace of themselves
they can't know you are Lord over all
fierce in your shattering of wars themselves
great armies of the past are dust in your presence
they were lords in their own eyes as they marched on

blindly
but there is only one 'Lord'

Lord, crush their violence
break their thoughts to bits in your anger
at their shameless threats of power

They want to force their way into your sanctuary
to cut off the ancient horn on your altar
to strip bare the ark
in which you are held holy
to demean your spirit with swords of tin and iron
to debase your name

Look at the arrogance of their thoughts
cut them off in outrage
bow their heads in shame
sweep a mental sword through their minds

Put your sword in the hand of a widow
give me the presence of mind
to overpower them with pointed speech
in the sheath of an alluring voice
to confuse them with an inner truth
shaping words of steel
to slay 'equally' masters with their slaves
servant and petty lord
while they are inflated by selfish desire
while they are charmed by feminine lips
while they are caught in their self-deception

shatter their pride
disperse their power
by a woman's hand

Your force is not visible in numbers and armor
does not stand at attention before men of war
your power is indivisible and disarms violence
and you are a Lord to the powerless
help to the oppressed
support to the weak, refuge to the humble
a sudden rescue, a saviour to the lost
warmth in the coldest despair
light in the most hopeless eyes

Please hear me, God of my father
Lord of Israel's heritage
Master of the universe, Creator of earth and sky
King of all creation
hear my psalm

Let my words be lies they cannot hear
sharpen my tongue with charm
my lips irresistible
mirroring their inner deceit
which stares back into their surprised faces
as my words cut deep
like a sudden knife
into those with cruel plans
against our heart, against your spirit
and the Temple of your spirit

the mountain of Zion
the house of your children
in Jerusalem, and let the whole nation
all nations
suddenly understand
that you are Lord and God and King
above all force and power

and Israel stands
by your shield."

⌖

Judith's prayer was over
she rose from the ground
called to her maid
and in the house removed the sackcloth
and widow's dress, then bathed
in creams and expensive perfumes
and did her hair
crowned with a subtle tiara
and put on her most attractive dress
not worn since her husband Manasseh died
and before that only on joyous occasions—
slender sandals adorned her feet
brightened by jeweled anklets
bracelets and rings on her arms and fingers
earrings and pins and other jewelry
making up such a beautiful picture
that any man or woman's head would turn—
she gave her maid flasks of oil and a skin of wine

fig cakes and dried fruit
a bag filled with barley cakes and roasted grains
cheeses
and loaves of sweetest challah
then carefully wrapped her own dishes
and koshered pottery
also for her maid to carry . . .

They kept walking straight across the valley
until sighted by Assyrian advance troops
who seized Judith, interrogated her
"Where do you come from?
What people do you belong to?
Where are you going?"
"I'm a daughter of Hebrews
but I'm escaping from them
because they are fodder for you
to be devoured as simply as grain in a bowl
I want to be taken to Holofernes your Lord
I can report the truth to him
I want to show him the simplest way
to take over the mountains and approaches
surrounding this country
without losing a single man
subduing it without so much as a bruise"

As these men listened to her well-chosen words
they saw the noble beauty in Judith's face
and (coupled with her directness) they were overwhelmed
by such physical elegance in a woman

"You have saved your life
not hesitating to come directly
into the presence of our lord
you will be taken straight to his tent
and we will announce you to him—
have no fear in your heart
when you are in his presence
because when you tell him what you told us
he will treat you with deep respect"
a detachment of a hundred men escorted the two women

So Judith and her maid came safely
to the tent of Holofernes—
but not without causing a stir in the whole camp
the news was buzzing from tent to tent
and while Judith waited outside the commander's tent
a crowd gathered around her
amazed at her beauty
this was the first they'd seen of an Israelite
and coupled with what they'd heard
they were amazed at the presence of this people
as their curiosity fed on her grace
"Who can despise a people with women like this?"
they were saying
"We'll have to wipe out this entire race
every last one of them
just as we were told to do
because any that survive will probably outwit
just about anyone in the world—
moved simply by the agony of loss

of such grace and beauty
to bring our world to its knees
as surely as a disarmed suitor"

Then Holofernes' personal guards came out
to escort Judith into the tent
where he was resting on his bed
under the fine gauze mosquito net
that was a precious, royal canopy
purple interwoven with fine strands of gold
studded with emeralds
and many other gems: as stunning as a crown

When Judith was announced he came out
silver lamps carried by servants leading the way
into the front part of the tent
and he saw her standing there and was amazed
at so beautiful a face
she bowed touching her face to the ground
in homage, but his servants quickly lifted her up
"Feel at ease, woman"
Holofernes was saying
"Have no fear in your heart
I've never hurt anyone who made the choice
to serve Nebuchadnezzar, king of this world
I didn't choose to raise a spear
against your people in the hills
they've brought me here themselves
insulting me by taking us lightly
now tell me why you've escaped from them

to join us—but first, be at ease
you have saved your life
take heart, you've found a new life here
free of fear
no one can threaten you tonight or any other night
you'll learn what it is to be at ease in your life
to be an equal and treated as well
as any servant of my Lord, King Nebuchadnezzar ..."

Judith's speech before Holofernes, like other untranslated passages in the following portion, is inferred.

Judith's words enchanted Holofernes
they were so well-measured
all his attendants were amazed at such wisdom
"There isn't a woman in the whole world
to match this fresh intelligence
lighting up the beauty of her face"
And above the buzzing Holofernes said to her
"God has done well
to bring you in advance of his people
into our hands, strengthening us
so we may bring a just destruction
to those so blind as to take us lightly
having insulted my lord by refusing to kneel—
your God will right their wrongs himself
if you do as you've said
for your words are well-chosen

and you are a beautiful woman
your God shall live and be treated as my god
as you will live in the palace
of King Nebuchadnezzar, so your fame
may spread through the whole world."

⊠

The fourth day after Judith arrived
Holofernes planned a private feast
bypassing the invitations most banquets require
to all the officers, and he called in Bagoas
his head eunuch who was taking charge of Judith
"Talk to the Hebrew woman
persuade her to join us for a feast
it's disgraceful not to know her better
everyone will laugh at us for not courting
such a beautiful woman while she's here"

When Bagoas came to Judith he was all flattery
"Have no fear, fair lady
of my lord, and he will be honored
if you will come into his presence
to drink wine and be his guest
at an intimate feast
and be a chosen daughter of Assyria
beginning to live today
like a daughter in the House of Nebuchadnezzar"
Judith was ready with an answer
"And who am I to refuse my lord?
I desire only to be of service

pleasing him will make me happy today
and will always be
something I will cherish until the day I die"

And so she began to dress
in the fine clothes she had brought
in the cosmetics, jewelry, and alluring perfume
and in gentle ceremony she sent her maid ahead
to lay the soft fleeces Bagoas lent to her
on the floor in Holofernes' tent
where she would eat and then lean back

When Judith came in and Holofernes saw her
leaning back on her fleeces
his heart was overwhelmed
and his mind filled with desire
lit by a wish to sleep with her
from the first time he saw her
in fact for these four days he'd been searching
for a way to seduce her
and so he was saying "Drink
relax and let yourself go with us"
"I'd love to, my lord
today I've found a reason to live
beyond anything I've dreamed of since I was born"

Facing him, Judith ate and drank
the food her maid had brought and prepared
and Holofernes having accepted her reason
for being true to her God's rituals

was disarmed at her acceptance of him
and so excited at the thought of having her
he drank to his heart's content
until he'd poured out more wine in one night
than he'd drank of anything in a day
since he was born

Now it was getting late and the staff
were leaving, tipsy, but quickly, as if they knew
Bagoas rolled down the outside tent flap
then dismissed the servants
(natural enough since they were exhausted)
and they went straight to sleep
leaving Judith alone with Holofernes
who had wound up sprawling on his bed
his head swimming in wine

Earlier, on the way to the feast
Judith asked her maid not to leave
if dismissed later, but to wait outside the bedroom
just as she did on previous mornings
since now everyone expected her early rising
and going out for ritual prayers
she had even reminded Bagoas and now
all had gone
not a soul important or unimportant
was left in the bedroom
Judith stood by Holofernes' bed
a silent prayer in her heart:

"Lord, my God, source of all power
have mercy on me for what my hands must do
for Jerusalem to be a living example
of trust in your covenant
now is the time to renew our heritage
give my plan life
to surprise the enemies
to bring them to their knees
who've risen up all around us
great herds coming to devour us"

Her hand reached up
for Holofernes' well-honed sword
hanging on the front bedpost
slung there in its jeweled scabbard
then, standing directly over him, swiftly
her left hand seized hold of his hair
"Make me steel, Lord, God of Israel—today"
as with all her strength she struck
at the nape of his neck, fiercely
and again—twice—and she pulled
his head from him
then rolled the severed body from the bed
and tore down the royal canopy
from the bedposts

A moment later she stepped out from the bedroom
and gave the head, wrapped in the canopy, to her maid
who put it in the sack she carried
with all of Judith's food and vessels

The two women walked out together
just as they usually did for prayer
they passed through the camp
walked straight across the valley
climbed the mountain to Bethulia
and approached the city gates.

(10:1-5, 11-23; 11:1-4, 20-23; 12:10-20; 13:1-10)

Chapter fourteen and the beginning of chapter fifteen describe Judith's reception in Bethulia, the rout of the Assyrians, and the victory celebration. A subplot is concluded, in which Achior, a neighbor who respected the Jews, identifies Holofernes' head, then asks to be circumcised and is "incorporated in the House of Israel forever." The book ends with the arrival in Jerusalem, and then a brief description of Judith's later life and death.

All the women of Israel come out to see her
on the way to Jerusalem
flushed with the victory they shared
of faith over power
grace and daring over brute force
some began a dance in celebration
Judith was carrying palm branches in her arms
passing them to the women around her
they were all garlanding themselves with olive
Judith at the head of the procession
to Jerusalem, leading the women who were dancing

and the men of Israel who were following
dressed in their armor and garlands
songs and psalms from their lips
lightening the feet of the dancers

Then Judith began this psalm of thanksgiving
and all the people joined her, repeating the lines
the psalm of a Jewess echoed by Israel:

Strike a beat for my God with tambourines
ringing cymbals lift a song to the Lord
a new psalm rise from a fresh page of history
inspired with his name
call on him for inspiration
My Lord is the God who crushes war
in the midst of the warmonger's camp

Jerusalem is pitched like a tent
in the camp of Israel
and here he has delivered me
from the grasping hands of my enemy

The Assyrian swarmed over the mountains in the north
with tens of thousands in armor
gleaming in purple and gold
hordes of infantry like rivers
flooding the valleys
an avalanche of horsemen
pouring down on the plains
my borders would be flames he said

my young men skewered on swords
infants flung to the ground
children seized for slaves
and my daughters for whores

But the Lord God has let them be outwitted
with a woman's hand
their hero fell
and not a young man's hand touched him
not the sons of warrior giants
neither a Goliath nor David
but Judith, daughter of Merari
stopped him in his tracks
paralyzed his brutal power
with the beauty of her face

And instead of fame for fleeting glamour
she is held in honor
because she didn't think of herself
but faced disaster head-on
firmly on the open path, God's way

She put aside her widow's dress
to save the honor of the living
those oppressed in Israel
she anointed her face with perfume
bound her hair beneath a delicate headband
and put on attractive linen to lure him
but only to his own undoing
her slender sandal imprisoning his eye

her beauty taking his heart captive
for the sword to cut through his neck

Persians shivered at her boldness
and Medes shuddered in terror

My humble people were suddenly raising their voices
my weak little nation was shouting with joy
while the enemy, shocked, ran off in fear
they panicked as my people danced in the streets
the sons of mere women pierced their lines
mama's boys chased them as they ran
willy-nilly they ran away like brave sons of eunuchs

Their battle lines were erased
like lines in the sand
under the pursuing boots of Israel

I will sing a new psalm to my God
Lord, you are great, you are our glory
your strength so marvelously deep, unconquerable
may all your creation recognize you
because you allowed everything here
to be
you said the word and we're here
and the breath behind it is our air
your spirit breathes the form of all things
it opens our ears
no one can resist your voice
the message of creation is always there

Mountains may fall into the sea
and seas crack open like a broken glass of water
rocks may melt like wax
but for those who live in awe of you
your presence is a steady candle
glowing warmth and a guide to safety
all the burning sacrifices are quickly mere fragrance
all the fat of sacrificial lambs a brief aroma
compared to one person in awe of you
whose strength is always there

All nations who come to destroy my people
beware of justice, you will disappear
your peoples will see a day of judgment
before God, My Lord
but all they will know is the fire in their hearts
sparked by inflated pride
a pain that will always burn there
as they are confined in the room of their minds:
their flesh will be consumed in it
and given to worms.

(15:12-14; 16:1-17)

Composed by several Maccabean poets in the second century BCE, the book of Daniel is based on sources existing in poems dating back to the Babylonian exile. They were presented as deliberately anachronistic and concealed provocative, contemporary references while transcending the political arena.

Chapter eleven describes the wars within the Greek empire, couched in stylized prophetic shorthand. Containing the awareness that the age of prophecy has passed, this genre will come to be called apocalyptic. In the hands of the Maccabean poets, however, the conscious irony permits parallels, impersonations, and a resonance of the prophetic books, particularly Ezekiel. The figure of Daniel echoes the Suffering Servant allegory in Isaiah, reflecting the transition from the older prophetic sense of a communal remnant of survivors to the later rabbinic sense of individual integrity, or saintliness.

A Hellenized Jew might take Daniel for an obscurely mystical work. The Maccabean imagination, on the other hand, would recognize its inspiration as supporting resistance to Hellenistic religion. A few hundred years of history are telescoped into a few stanzas, starting with King Xerxes of Persia during the time of the Babylonian exile and continuing up to Alexander the Great. It is a broad, dramatic literary convention to have the poem come from the mouth of an angel: no Maccabean reader was likely to believe that angels were prophesying history in Babylon. A suspension of disbelief is required, just as would have been necessary for Greek drama when gods and half-gods were speaking.

daniel

And now I will tell you
the truth as it unfolds
beyond the present page—

before the ink can flow from the pen
look: three more kings
succeed each other in Persia

and then a fourth, the richest yet
translating wealth to power
itching to challenge Greece

but there, in Greece, the strongest king
the world has ever seen
arises, doing as he pleases

and as he perches on his world empire
he dies, his kingdom falls
cracks apart

into four pieces like the four winds:
north, south, east, and west
none into the hands of his descendants

and none of his successors can put together
the strength that was his
for it is torn up by the roots

transplanted to yet more petty dynasties
by yet others than these
and mercilessly cultivated . . .

This passage describes the advent of Antiochus Epiphanes, who claims the throne of the Asian part of the Greek empire, the Seleucid kingdom. The "prince over people of the covenant" refers to the Jewish province of the Greek empire in Judea.

And then standing in his place
is the unrecognized—ignored
as if he'd been a harmless dolt

who then, when least suspected
scheming behind the scenes
seizes control

all opposition will be swept away
like water jars in a flood
and smashed—even the prince

over people of the covenant
is lost—
and even though his loyal party is small

anyone making peace with him
is drawn into a maelstrom
by a treacherous hand;

in placid, peaceful times
he will storm into the richest provinces
and succeed and be accepted

as if in a dream
all his detractors suddenly paralyzed
a fact his fathers wouldn't dare to dream

so unscrupulous the royal hand
that grabs like a thief
to reward just the loyal bullies

and with all this even he will dream
of conquering more fortress cities
and he will—but only for a while . . .

(11:21-24)

King Antiochus Epiphanes has consolidated his rule and has just fought a successful battle against a Ptolemy, the Egyptian representative of the Greek empire. Then he will again invade Egypt ("the South"), but this time he is turned back and vents his frustration on the Jews. Many of the Jews have become paganized according to his decrees, but others are strengthened in their resistance by the king's self-identification with the highest god of the world. (Coins of this time show Antiochus Epiphanes in the likeness of a Greek god.) This portion of Daniel offers comfort to the persecuted Jews by setting this king in a historical perspective that reduces him to mortal size. But he remains an archetypal figure, whether projected back into history as the Nebuchadnezzar in Judith, or projected forward into our own century as a dictator.

Then this king of the north
will turn back for home
followed by a long train of riches

now his mind has turned
to the people of the covenant
his heart set against its Temple

he will set his hand against it
as he passes through the land
before returning home

in a while he'll set out again
invading the South
but now the scene has changed

and in the background ships from Kittim: the west
Roman ships
he will be cowed and turn around

and with his mind sunk in rage
he will growl at the people
of the covenant, ravaging the Temple

rewarding the cowards who turn
against their own religion
then he will unleash his forces

to enter the Temple inner sanctuary
desecrate it
demolish the gates

beat and demean the pious there
defile the altar
set up idols

that make one fall to his knees
not in submission, not in humility
but in utter desolation

those who are eager to submit to power
to lick the feet of foreigners
will be soothed and flattered—for a time

they will slander their own heritage
but those who know a God in their hearts
have an inner strength to resist

and they are beacons of conscience
in the midst of flames some
will be burnt at the stake

or pierced or crucified
or thrown into slavery
tortured, maimed, robbed

but they will continue teaching
and be helped by some who are fighting
even those fighting blindly only for themselves

and those who resist with the openness in their hearts
even as they fall their teaching shines
like metal in the fire: refined

and purified and a healing
for the people to rise and continue
even as no end is yet in sight

the king appears to grow stronger
as if magnified in a mirror
free to strut in his own image

flattering himself above the gods
so arrogantly inflated
he sees himself as the highest god

speaking out of such swollen pride
as if his heart was engraved on iron
to last forever

and it will seem so until the wrath
like his life
is exhausted.

(11:28-36)

623

———

PART III

———

WRITING

———

Daniel

Ezra was a communal spokesman and pivotal poet-editor in the sixth or fifth century BCE, *one of the first to return to Judea from Persia. Perhaps a century later his works, and those of other poets associated with him, were collected under his name. Nehemiah was a close contemporary of Ezra's, and the book that bears his name contains chapters from Ezra—and vice versa. Scholars assume that both books were once part of a larger one.*

Nehemiah was a governor in Judea and no doubt established a circle of poets, some of whom would also have come from Ezra's circle. These were poets determined to revive older Hebraic sources, and they were probably responsible for editing Psalms, *as well as composing some of them.*

By the time Nehemiah returned to Judea, most Jews were speaking a Judeo-Aramaic dialect acquired in Babylon. The common people no longer understood the early Hebrew of the Pentateuch, and translations into Aramaic were commissioned. These interpretive translations, made by the Ezra and Nehemiah poets, were the first targumim. The poets themselves, or perhaps Levite interpreters, read them aloud in the earliest synagogues. The portion from the book of Nehemiah *depicts this process.*

Nehemiah pictures Ezra reading from the newly edited Torah scroll, or Pentateuch, or Five Books of Moses. It is a description of the festival of Sukkot, the most important days in ancient Israel, which were largely forgotten by the time of exile in the fifth century BCE. *It was unlikely that common people studied the Torah in ancient Israel, so that this passage from the book of* Nehemiah *describes the beginning of a process leading to the widespread study popularized by the Pharisees.*

The passage from Ezra *pictures a scene at the dedication of the new altar for the Second Temple. It has been only fifty years since the first Temple was destroyed. Joy was mixed with grief in a typically Jewish brew, capturing the essence of vulnerability.*

ezra/nehemiah

The workers had built up the foundation
of the Lord's Temple
the original outline was visible again

Cohens (priests) were there in their robes
they blew the trumpets of assembly
Levis were there with cymbals and lyres

as Asaph had been directed
by David, King of Israel
in his day

and they sang back and forth to each other
antiphonally
"Sing praises to the Lord in psalms

so good it is to be singing"
and the refrain:
"His mercy sings through us

to Israel
as it has
and always will"

Then all the people broke out in song
because the House of the Lord
was rising again

but many of the oldest Cohens and Levis
and heads of families
old men who had seen the first house

and who could see it still standing
fixed in their memories—
these men broke out weeping

loudly, openly
as they stood before this house
rising again in their living eyes

many others were shouting joyfully
a great noise was going up
people in the distance could hear it clearly

and they could not tell by their ears
the sound of weeping
from the sound of joy.

(3:10-13)

Raised up on a platform
in full view of everyone
Ezra opened the book

he was standing above them
as everyone rose
when he opened the Torah

and Ezra made a benediction
to the Lord, God above all
and everyone answered amen

amen—with hands stretched to the sky
in a feeling of deep reverence
then bowed their heads

kneeling, until their faces
touched the ground
their lips to dust

and Yeshua, Bani, Shereviah
Yamin, Akkuv, Shabbetai
Hodiah, Maaseiah, Kelitah

Azariah, Yozavad, Hanan
Pelayah, and the Levis
they were the interpreters

so all would understand the tongue
of the Torah, and the people stood
in their places, listening

as the book was read and translated
slowly, distinctly, from morning till noon
with the sense made plain

to be felt and understood
the Lord's Torah
by all the men and women

then I, Nehemiah, as governor
and Ezra the scribe-priest and reader
and the Levites, interpreters to the people

said to them all
this day is a day made holy
to the Lord our God—be at peace

we must not mourn, we must not weep
because everyone was weeping as they listened
to the sweet words of Torah

then Ezra continued: go, celebrate
with a sumptuous meal, a sweet wine
and send a portion to those

who have nothing ready for themselves
for this is a holy day to the Lord
and not for being involved with ourselves

we must not look so burdened with grief
today sadness is forbidden
it is our happiness in the Lord

that gives us our very strength—
and the Levis also were calming the people
saying: calm yourselves, be still

this is a holy day
and not for carrying personal grief
today no sadness is allowed

then the people went home to celebrate
to eat and drink and
distribute portions for everyone

to make a great festival
in the spirit of shared happiness
an unguarded joy

because all had heard and understood
the words openly read to them
and felt their sweetness within

and on the second day
all the heads of families
the priests (Cohens) and teachers (Levis)

gathered before Ezra the scribe
to look more deeply
into the words of the Torah

and there in the Torah they found
written before their eyes
by the hand of Moses—

inspired by the Lord—
that the family of Israel will dwell
in *sukkot* (booths) during the festival

of this month—the Sukkot festival
and when they heard this, together they made
a declaration, to be read in all their cities

not only Jerusalem, saying
go to the mountainside
gather branches of olive and myrtle

leafy palm and boughs of willow
from which to make *sukkot*
as it is written

so the people went out of their cities and towns
to gather them and make the booths
each family made one on their roof

or in their courtyard
or in the courtyard of the Lord's House
in Jerusalem

and in the avenue leading
to the Water Gate, and the avenue
leading to the Ephraim Gate

the whole community that had returned
from exile, returned
to make festival *sukkot* and dwell within

and since this had not been done so lovingly
from the wilderness days of Joshua
to this day (or so it seemed)

there was a great happiness
a deep joy
in living the words they were hearing

and Ezra continued reading from the book
day by day, each festival day
continuing in the Lord's Torah for seven days

and on the eighth day (Shemini Atzeret)
they held a solemn assembly
a closing celebration—as it is written.

(8:5-18)

HOW THE BIBLE CAME ABOUT

Telling, Seeing, Writing:

635

The Division in Three Parts of the Hebrew Bible

I.

While giving a lecture on the biblical writers of Abraham's life at Manhattan's 92nd Street Y a few years ago, I heard a typical question from the audience: "What do we have to lose by not knowing the authors?" This was intended as a "So what?" rhetorical question, followed by the suggestion that knowing them could even be a disadvantage: "Wouldn't it distract from the atmosphere of a sacred text?" What we lose, I answered, is ... To be honest, I can't recall my exact answer. I have many answers. If I had been a political candidate, I'd probably have begun my answer with "Great question!" It's the question that's been with me since childhood, when I was trying to make sense of the prayer books shelved in the synagogue pews.

A bit later, age ten and listening to parts of the Hebrew Bible being read in synagogue on Saturday mornings, I began an effort to follow along in English. I became the leader of the "junior congregation," but our understanding was limited to children's versions of the Bible and "condensed" translations that sounded to me like the Cub Scout Oath. In fact, I was a practicing Cub Scout in full uniform, but at least there we had a language heightened by a love of wild animals, a lingo of the "Den" and the "Wolfpack" to which I belonged.

As I grew older and used the English facing the Hebrew pages of the "Chumash"—the "Five Books" of the Torah and appended selections from other literary books of the Hebrew

Bible—I became frustrated. However formal the style and diction, I needed a living idiom within the translation, such as the English language I heard spoken. The religious and academic translators—whether they tried to be ancient or modern—dulled the senses. God, and all the situations in which he participated or was referenced, seemed to require portentous language. Ultimately, this led to a confusion of idioms, the modern mixed up with the medieval, until it was impossible for me in my youth to believe that the Bible was written to be electrifying, by and for enthusiastic, unconfused men and women.

Pursuing the question in adulthood, I came across an essay, "Wit and Mystery," by Walter J. Ong, an esteemed Catholic writer of our time. Ong was explaining the writing of St. Thomas Aquinas, for whom "Christian theology and poetry are indeed not the same thing, but lie at opposite poles of human knowledge. However, the very fact that they are opposite extremes gives them something of a common relation to that which lies between them: they both operate on the periphery of human intelligence. A poem dips below the range of the human process of understanding-by-reason as the subject of theology sweeps above it." These "opposite poles" of poetry and theology were, in fact, reconciled in the Hebrew Bible long ago.

And that is our great challenge in reading and translating the Bible today. It has only become possible for us because Hebraic culture and Hebrew writers are once again living in Israel. Whatever we make of them, we can now begin to reimagine the original living culture in which Hebraic authors wrote their books of history and law, poetry and story. Three thousand years ago, the culture of these writers already had something new to say, along with visions of its future and its past. It may even have started with Abraham, several centuries before Moses, who came from the culture that created cuneiform. Nevertheless, before the Hebraic writing began in Jerusalem, under Kings David and Solomon and their successors, there was already "telling" and "seeing."

The Hebrew Bible is all writing, but the first two parts, Torah and Prophets, establish the *need* for writing. The revelation of which they tell required interpretive and creative expression. It's the revelation that we all are created creatures and thus can only come from a higher authority: we're to be inspired by the consequences—historical and ethical—of living as a created creature. YHWH may be ultimately unknowable, but the higher authority of the Creator is something to aspire to and be inspired by—and writing is its embodiment.

How this creation of the Hebrew Bible unfolds is quickly grasped in a Hebrew acronym, by which the text is known. TaNaKh is made up of "T" for Torah, "N" for Neviim (Prophets), and "K" for Ketubim (Writings)—these are the three divisions of *Tanakh*, or Hebrew Bible. Torah for "Telling" (I would call it aspiring to revelation); Prophets for "Seeing" (I'd call it being inspired); and Writings for "Writing"—implying the necessity of a human audience of readers. This is also how the biblical books I have translated find their place in the three parts of *A Literary Bible*.

The Hebrew Bible is what scholars of all persuasions used to call the "Old Testament," but that Christian designation is falling away, since *Tanakh* has always been far more than a testament. It is a honed library of thirty-nine books written in the language of ancient Israel, Hebrew (with the tiny exception of a few late passages in Aramaic). Hebrew, both literary and spoken, went through many changes of idiom and style over several centuries, a creation of a living culture. Even when the *lingua franca* of the Jews in Israel was brought from exile, whether it was Aramaic or Greek, the Hebrew language continued to evolve and assimilate new influences. So, when referring to the Hebrew language of the Bible, we must locate it in a specific culture, the Hebraic, that includes everything a living culture requires, from artists to carpenters. It is precisely in order to avoid this necessity of reimagining the original writers that some academics have fabricated what they call biblical "tradition," consisting largely of redactors and scribes, prophets and priests—as if these professions existed outside the parameters of a living civilization.

Fortunately, it's not my job to pester you with explanations of why or how this happened (I address it in three of my recent books: *An Educated Man: A Dual Biography of Moses and Jesus*; *Abraham: The First Historical Biography*; and *The Book of David*). How the text got written is far more crucial knowledge to me than how it got edited and used. The latter may tell us something about the organized religion but not about culture. Still, we live in a time when the media is full of books and programs about the "origins and secrets of the Bible." These origins, however, are not about the writing of the Bible but rather its redaction and commentary, centuries later. These later "origins" are shadows of the original writing; they concern religion's use of the Bible, not the Bible's imaginative origins, divine or otherwise.

Why is our popular culture averse to the imaginative, to *creation*? I believe it comes down to our substitute religion of scientism, which is satisfied with an investigation into "facts"— when these facts are the traditional ones ascribed to the history of written commentary, rather than to the history of actual writing. The "origins of the Bible" studied today at Harvard and Yale, among other institutions, are actually the origins of its reading, at best. Traditions of reading and of religion make use of the Bible's creation stories, for instance, but tradition itself is unenthusiastic about the creative culture in which the Bible was written.

With the original writers we are closer to aspiration and inspiration, aspects of creation. I've drawn upon these words to suggest how Hebraic culture was enriched by requiring telling and seeing as its foundation for writing. "Telling" may have consisted partly of oral literature, but it also included the vast resources of written literature, going back two millennia from Solomonic Jerusalem, back through Moses and Abraham, to Sumer and Egypt. In the new Hebraic culture after 1000 BCE, some of this written literature needed translating. For the most part, however, it wanted retelling, and the early Hebraic writers made much of their sources, as we can see in the books that make up the Torah. There, retelling became a new Telling: our first telling of the origins and meaning of what would become Western civilization. Torah, in Hebrew, means telling.

"Seeing" may refer to the visions or dreams of prophets, but the prophetic books that make up the second part of the Hebrew Bible were written down or retold in various poetic genres by professional writers, just as was the Torah. And the third part of the Hebrew Bible, "Writings," absorbs the first two, engaging the truth-telling authority of the historical Torah as well as the personal authority of the Prophetic writers—in order to produce poetry and prose that complicates the boundary between the fictive and the truth.

A professional writer can begin with his or her own experience, but after that, how can he retell the history of the world, or see the meanings of present and future, without a vision of what is true—or, in modern terms, what is "relatively" true? The renowned sociologist of literature and the sacred, the late Philip Rieff, in an essay entitled "Is Not the Truth The Truth?" which appears in his posthumous volume, *The Jew of Culture* (2008), wrote:

> The order of the people to Aaron, brother of Moses, at least in Aaron's report—*Make us a God* (namely, the Golden Calf) suggests the complicity of truth and fiction that has emerged millennia after the fact of that making as the fictive truth.

Of course, Rieff is ironic; he is writing here about the Ten Commandments' higher standard of truth (as opposed to the Golden Calf) and the consequent sadness of the first Decalogue's loss—as if we today are represented only by the Aaron who "made a god" out of fear (or so he said to Moses) and the Moses who smashed the tablets to the ground. That was a disappointed Moses but nevertheless the equivalent of a great writer, like those few we've had in modern times—yet none of ours were optimistic about aspiring to an absolute truth, or being inspired by it. Although the best academic teachers of the Bible do attempt to bridge modern and biblical literature, their failures are instructive, as we are about to see. To start with, it may be helpful to know what this book, *A Literary Bible*, has actually contained and how it came together.

II.

While many of the books of the Hebrew Bible are composed of law and historical record, a majority of them, in whole or in part, are remarkable literary works. These books are usually translated in a uniform style, when in fact they were written by different authors, in diverse styles and periods, stretching over many centuries. When the Bible is taught as literature in schools and universities, it is mainly these literary works of the Hebrew Bible that are singled out. The translations in which they are read, however, are made not by literary writers but by clerics and academic scholars. The result is that the Bible—in modern translation especially—can sound ponderous; even the Books of Jonah or Ecclesiastes may sound inferior to the best of modern literature, although they are likely to be superior.

More than thirty years ago, I set out on a project to translate the literary works of the Bible as if they were written by poets and prose artists. I wanted to parallel the richness in language and imagery of the original authors—without distancing from them. This hadn't been done before; in fact, it only became possible in recent decades with the rebirth of a vibrant Modern Hebrew, whose supple idiom provides an echo of the dynamic lost culture that wrote in ancient Hebrew. While my Hebraic scholarship was focused upon revealing the sensibilities of the ancient authors, my practice as a poet was brought to bear on the English language: often I found myself as if remaking an ancient poem or sentence. Yet this is no different a position than many biblical authors found themselves in, working with and adapting much older sources.

When my translations began to appear as individual books in the late 1970s, they were greeted as new works in English, reviewed by scholars but also writers as various as Anthony Burgess and Donald Hall. Later, in collaboration with Harold Bloom, I began identifying some of the ancient authors in *The Book of J* (1990) and then on my own, in *A Poet's Bible* (1991) and *The Lost Book of Paradise* (1993). Now these and more recent translations have been brought together in one volume, opening student and general reader alike to a strikingly enlightened art veiled in the Bible. In regard to the New Testament, I've written of its Jewish authors in *An Educated Man: A Dual Biography of Moses and Jesus* (2010).

A crucial distinction from recent translations by academics is that the latter attempt to recreate the primitivism of the original, rather than approaching the authored text as if written by a living writer. The Hebraic writers are themselves overlooked and set on par with a religious notion of "Anonymous" that took root later. The original writers, however, were known as individuals in their day, and their poetry and prose deserve to be confronted. In *A Literary Bible*, eighteen books (including one from the Bible's Apocrypha, the book of Judith) have been condensed into accurate representations of their original literary form.

The Iliad, Odyssey, Divine Comedy, Beowulf—all these have inspired translations that have been absorbed into English literature as works in their own right. The same holds true for the King James Bible. But that was created in 1611, and in almost four hundred years there has not been an individual summation of the Bible as a work of art to contrast with it. *A Literary Bible* engages the new questions about cultural history asked of the Bible today and about the intention of its authors. As the questions are answered, we may be lifted out of the popular confusion about religious and scientific ideas that pass for biblical religion. One of the big clichés of our time is that religion and science are separate realms of knowledge; "They are separate kingdoms," wrote the late evolutionary biologist Stephen Jay Gould. However, conflict between religion and science continues because biblical language is distorted by both sides and by abstruse and homogenized translations. Not only is science discounted by literal-minded Bible readers, but religion is likewise dismissed by readers who are unaware of the radical psychological depth and dramatic nuances of the Hebrew Bible, in which the history of civilization is embedded.

The various Hebraic authors, male and female, can be breathtaking to discover. In addition to their surprising uniqueness, when taken together the original authors open up new vistas of commonality as well, as we hear them echoing one another over the centuries. "Rosenberg strives to capture the human voices at work in the Hebrew scriptures," wrote Kenneth C. Davis, in his popular *Don't Know Much About The Bible* (1998). Since he quotes me back to myself from thirty years ago, let me give him a bit more room: "Rosenberg discusses their human quality: 'One day, translating a psalm that I thought was written in anger and is usually presented as such, I suddenly realized it was not anger at all but an intense depression, a self-conscious awareness of failure. The psalmist was facing depression and not allowing himself to respond with anger. Instead, he overcomes despair with his song's ironic sense of never ending, echoing into eternity. And I felt the poet's utterly real presence.'"

The political or social agendas ascribed to the Hebrew Bible today need puncturing. For instance, King David is often described as "ruthless," an attribution that misses a deeper understanding of the Bible historian's purpose. David's underlying tenderness is used as counterpoint to his aggressive actions by his most substantial biblical author. The book of Jonah provides another example, when it is mistakenly said to deliver "a message of forgiveness" of one's enemies. Instead, it can reveal a deeper drama about human ambivalence when the perspective of the author is brought to light.

The biblical text does not neglect the basic human fear of annihilation. Nuclear and natural extinction are real issues today, and they are addressed when a literary translation reconciles the idioms of religious belief and secular self-knowledge. So in *A Literary Bible*, I hoped to recreate an ancient cosmic theater in which secular and religious interact without negating each other. For example, in the first verse from the famous Twenty-third Psalm, I've translated the relationship of shepherd and psalmist to give more psychological weight to the psalmist: he is not simply a sheep, as in other translations, but has human or secular concerns.

> The Lord is my shepherd
> And keeps me from wanting
> What I can't have

The words in Hebrew remain the same; the only thing changed is that awareness of the original audience comes back as the cosmic stage is brought into focus. Rather than a Lord who provides everything—as in the usual translation, "I shall not want"—the psalmist values his relationship to the Lord in itself: it keeps him from hungering after unnatural power. There is equivalence in the relationship between man and Creator, as the shepherd must also trust the sheep's intelligence.

Too many translations are off-putting to the general reader because they do not distinguish human from supernatural. When an angel is disguised as a man, for example, we need to know it. Natural and supernatural realms need boundaries so that they can interact without confusion. In the time of the biblical authors, supernatural faith and rational belief actually *tested* each other, and a productive culture arose from interaction between faith and skepticism. Many of the Bible translators of our day seem to have lost the spirit. We have a hard enough time just establishing the boundary between church and state—between secular culture and supernatural belief—yet that boundary was constantly probed by the ancient Hebraic civilization that wrote the Bible.

It wasn't so long ago that the biblical author's self-awareness was thought to be primitive, and even today scholars prefer to address the mind of a "scribe," assumed to be merely scholastic, or to address only a sophisticated "redacted" text in which the writers are submerged. In Hebraic culture, where authors focused upon the natural world of men and women, children and families, the biblical writer did not so much imagine the divine world as address it—as if in conversation with it, in narrative, and explicitly in psalms and prophecy. Or else divinity was backgrounded, as in chronicle and story. In other words, the writers were quite experienced in the various ways they probed the border of knowledge of the infinite. Their ancient, authentic erudition has defined my project. In many years of translating and interpreting the Bible, I've sought new ways to represent reason and religion bound together on a single stage. For example, consider the following scene in which natural man and divinity meet:

> Yahweh spoke further, "Descend, arise with Aaron. The priests and the people shall not come up, as boundaries destroyed will be their destruction . . ."
>
> Then Moses ascended, and with him Aaron. . . . They saw the God of Israel. Under his feet a pavement of sapphire was created, a likeness pure as the substance of the sky. He did not lay a hand on them, the noble pillars of Israel. They beheld God; they ate and drank.
>
> [Exodus]

Is this purely a religious scene? Not at all, since we are told that a boundary exists between God's presence and "the priests and the people." The art of the biblical author tells us what Moses and Aaron have seen—not what we, the people, might see. Maintaining the rational boundary between natural and supernatural is precisely what this passage from Genesis is about. "They ate and drank." And how do we know this? The character of Moses writes naturally (in the name of the biblical author) as if he were a detached observer. A *literary* Bible should make us conscious of the unnamed biblical authors as well as a cosmic theater stretching throughout the landscape:

It was the God of Jacob
And he is here
All around you

A sudden pool of water
From a desert rock
A fountain from wilderness stone—

Life from a heart of stone
And from bitter tears
Sweet-spoken land.
[Psalm 114]

The desert rock that is broken here is also the doubting heart; the tears are also life-affirming. No other translation has clarified this biblical stagecraft. We will come to see how the prime purpose of the Hebraic cosmic theater is to disentangle the supernatural myth from the experience of history. All our cards should be on the table, irrational feeling as well as a reasoned knowledge.

Unlike science, great art does not evolve in greatness—but our understanding of it may—as in a translation that allows the reader to experience the Bible as if, in some cases, it were written yesterday.

I'm tired of my groaning
My bed is flowing away
In the nights of tears

Depression like a moth
Eats from behind my face,
Tiny motors of pain push me. . . .

But my Lord is listening so high
My heavy burden of life floats up
As a song to him. . . .
[Psalm 6]

It has been over a hundred years since "The Bible as Literature" courses were introduced into schools and universities. Yet today, academic translations are used in the humanities to foster outdated theories of literary interpretation. The Hebrew Bible is said to contain the same literary elements as authorless, early European literature: saga, allegory, ballad, and epic. In other words, the Hebraic writers are thought to be on a par with a medieval "Anonymous." There is still no representative volume of translation to reflect the field of biblical authorship. Neither general reader nor college student has a book to turn toward that allows them to sense in contemporary terms how the Bible was read by its original audience. It was my intent to show, however, that the ancient audience resembled a modern one in this crucial aspect: it wanted to experience its own time set before the mirror of history.

Arthur Waley, a pioneering translator of ancient Chinese literature after the First World War, combined the role of scholar and poet but noted that it could only succeed "when scholarship is in a rather rudimentary state, as it was as regards Chinese when I started." In a striking parallel, the field of biblical authorship itself is still new today. Just as Waley provided the historical context—or literary archaeology—for his Chinese poems by exploring comparative cultural history, I've probed related fields, including Sumerian, Canaanite, and Egyptian studies, to enlarge the context for biblical authorship.

III.

"The Bible should be treated like this imaginary poetry book," writes M.Z. Brettler in *How to Read the Bible* (2005). "The criteria used for separating biblical sources are similar to those used to analyze poetry." And yet, the good professor also says emphatically: "We cannot read the prophetic texts as moderns—they would come across as too weird." That is an incongruous statement, and unfortunately Brettler has not read Allen Ginsberg or David Shapiro, Anne Waldman or Jorie Graham, among American poets today whose incantatory texts are considered quite normative. It may be too much to expect of biblical scholars that they be familiar with contemporary writers, just as most writers avoid biblical research. Still, Brettler's scholarly sources themselves are dishearteningly conventional, although they are what pass for insight in academic circles today.

It would be best if I apologize now to those readers new to the realm of biblical scholarship. Some of my criticisms in this field may sound severe; after all, shouldn't those immersed in the Bible have a generous attitude toward the failings of their fellow human beings? I assure you, however, that my comments will seem surprisingly mild when compared to the sharp elbows thrown by biblical scholars. As in most politics, when there is much at stake the arguments grow heated. And there is far more at stake in biblical studies than the Bible, as Philip Rieff has pointed out in his writings on contemporary literature and biblical authority. There is the issue of truth, and how to get at it. In modern philosophy and science, as well as art and literature, absolute truth remains an existential question: can we live without it, and can we live well? The original biblical writers expressed the depths of human experience by testing the existential question of truth's existence and meaning against a staggering range of history.

So it's surprising that Harvard's recent pillar of biblical studies, James Kugel, felt it necessary to write more about himself than the biblical authors in a book called, once again, *How to Read the Bible* (2007). In a chapter titled "The Rise of Modern Biblical Scholarship," a subheading reads "About the Author"—but it refers to Kugel, and the biblical authors are passed over. "As with Isaiah, scholars are not sure how much of the book of Jeremiah was written by Jeremiah. Many think it is a matter of poetry and prose," writes Kugel. As if being "not sure" is an excuse to avoid the subject—or worse yet, ascribe it to "poetry" written by authors who need not be imagined as individuals within their culture. Their entire Hebraic culture is swept under the rug and replaced with an overbearing plea for ancient religious commentary: "If we adopt the modern scholars' way of reading. . . . the divine inspiration of all of Scripture will be seen to be undermined." But the writers of the Hebrew Bible did not consider themselves divine. They wrote within a Hebraic culture that had its professional writers, artists, architects, and engineers like any other, albeit of a higher order when it comes to the writers. It is the gift of Hebraic culture that has been undermined.

A prominent literary critic like Robert Alter, for instance, may be so consumed by his own writing style that he ascribes lesser ambition to the biblical writers, to whom he grants the pretended wish of anonymity. It is one thing to admit that later generations had lost the original authors' names—writers who were no doubt esteemed in their lifetimes—but it's quite another thing to conclude that the writers themselves are not worth knowing. In *The Five Books of Moses* (2004), Alter writes that "a book in the biblical sphere was assumed to be a product of anonymous tradition," and then he goes on to bury the authors in that speculative tradition himself. When we lose even a consciousness of the original authors, it diminishes the liveliness of the original writing.

The late E. A. Speiser, however, was a literary-minded scholar to be trusted with the original biblical text. A rabbi who was also a professor of Assyriology at the University of Pennsylvania, Speiser's founding volume of the Anchor Bible, *Genesis* (1964), probes the original authors with panache. But then came an era of textual pedantry in academe. Even literary critics, swept up in structuralism and its aftermath, have pushed aside the creative trends in historical and cultural studies of the Bible. When foremost what is wanted is a sympathetic ear, they pound at the text with hammer and tongs. As most others do, Alter renovates history by recasting the phrase "Abraham of Ur of the Chaldees" as if the biblical author was blind to history and did not know that Abraham left his post-Sumerian city of Ur long before the Chaldean empire arose. There are plenty of clues that both original author and original audience knew that Abraham came from an Ur that was a historical cultural center of Sumer, so why "of the *Chaldees?*"

Most likely the biblical writer wanted to be geographically precise, citing the city as it was known at the time of writing—and here we glimpse the author's natural regard for his contemporary audience. He knew about the cultural renown of Sumerian Ur, having already referred to Sumer in Hebrew, *Shinar*. But the author wanted Abraham's journey (he was then known by his Sumerian name, Avram) to have a heightened realism for his audience, so he gave Ur its contemporaneous name, as it was now called, many centuries after Abraham. A small detail, perhaps, but it illustrates how crucial it can be to keep the author in mind.

Imagine I was to write, "Julius Caesar returned from Antipolis in France," when there was no France yet, just Gaul—my ignorance would be showing. But many American readers might not know where Antipolis was; placing it in France adds immediacy. I might also use its current name, Antibes, though it did not exist in Caesar's day. To imagine the human impulse of the biblical author when he wrote "Ur of the Chaldees" is to leap beyond what biblical scholars may merely see as an opposition between "source criticism" and "literary criticism." In effect, it is to hear the biblical source more clearly, with a literary ear for authorship. It is no different on a much larger scale. The designation of Ur may seem a small thing, but it's no different when it comes to the momentous near-sacrifice of Isaac. Without an ear for the author and his culture in northern Israel, literary critics miss how it is written as a dream, a nightmare.

In *The Jewish Bible* (2008), several contributors attempt a bird's-eye view of academic textual studies today. Published by the Jewish Publication Society, where I was once editor, I well understand the book's desire to simplify the field for the uninformed. But if the field itself is overgrown and confused, can it be simplified? For instance, we read: "A great deal of repetition occurs in biblical stories, but we should not consider the writer who uses repetition as careless. The writer purposely triggers our attention through repetition." As with most academic textual engagement, we are in the realm of explaining-as-knowledge— pop cultural knowledge, however rarified. The disarming of such "knowledge" is what we are most in need of; the closer we get to fleshing out the historical writers, the more we may experience a soulful Bible.

This issue of pop knowledge brings us to a divine point: "Biblical law receives its validity from being a divine pronouncement," explains *The Jewish Bible.* "In Mesopotamia, on the other hand, it was the king who composed the laws . . . The human authorship of Mesopotamian law clarifies many of the differences." In other words, delving into the human authorship of the Bible could cause embarrassment about the Creator's role, a challenge to the text's "validity," although human authorship in other cultures, such as those of Mesopotamia, is taken for granted—even if their kings were "divinely inspired." The biblical authors, although sometimes given lip service, are brushed over in the blink of an eye. Too many scholars are quick to designate as "lost" the fecundity of Hebraic culture and authorship, apart from religion.

By obscuring the history of Hebraic culture, we also lose the writers' knowledge of the world, their resources. In the biblical studies I've mentioned above, little trace is to be found of the Egyptian sources behind the writing of Moses' books and the Sumerian sources used by the J writer of Genesis. Archaeology and history are cited but rarely contended with. Instead, we're confronted with explanations of differences between the Hebrew Bible and the Old Testament; but when it comes to the actual reading, these differences are minor. What is hugely absent, especially in most new translations, is a concern for the biblical writers.

In *The Psalms* (2008), as translated by Robert Alter, we find lines such as these from Psalm 18:

> And the torrents of perdition dismayed me,
> The cords of Sheol encircled me,
> The traps of death sprung upon me.
> In my strait I called to the LORD . . .

Consider the effect of these lines on a sensitive, English-speaking reader, one who would be unlikely to use words like "perdition" or "dismay" very often—and even less, "the torrents of perdition." Further, "the cords of Sheol" are one thing, but to have them "encircle me" is to brook the abstruse. "The traps of death"— okay, I can imagine a mousetrap, but if I were caught in one would I describe the predicament as "in my *strait?*" And would I not more likely be shouting than calling? There are many English words and phrases that can just as accurately reflect the Hebrew, but here we confront evidence of a scholarly grandiosity that comes from too much explaining and not enough hearing.

When the biblical authors are discounted, the Bible remains its old anonymous self, just one among many books that influence Western tradition. In a recent survey of modern Yiddish literature, for example, it's not surprising that even Harold Bloom neglects the Bible's influence, and along with it the New York poet, Yehoash (Solomon Blumgarten), who translated the Bible into a supple, stunning Yiddish. For Yehoash, as for the Yiddish Nobel novelist Isaac Bashevis Singer, the convention of a Bible "unauthored" yields a divinely ironized author-Creator, central to the work of many Yiddish poets and novelists. The same holds for modern Hebrew poets, including distinguished ironic agnostics like Amichai and Yeshurun, as well as the ironic believers, Schimmel, Pincus, Govrin, and Zelda.

IV.

At twenty, while a student at the University of Michigan, my manuscript of poems won the Hopwood Award, enabling me to buy a car and visit my girlfriend off-campus. Such transport supplied motivation. I did have some stories and essays as well, so it was a gamble to concentrate on the poetry. The ruling power of genre was as entrenched then as it is now—it remains improbable to be simply a "writer," regardless of genre. Yet the best biblical writers managed many genres; I doubt they were divided by them, as poets are from novelists today, or historians are from psychologists.

During almost forty years of Hebrew Bible translation, I've aimed to recreate lines pointing back to the rock-solid literary monument of the Bible itself. The underpinning of all modernisms, collage, has remained my ear's slide rule, and although collage bears resemblance to the Bible's poetics of parallelism, my focus differs from a purely literary one. The Hebrew Bible's great concern is character—the possibilities of depth in an individual and the culture that sustains him. The characters in the Bible are strong enough to be imagined as the writers themselves: Moses, David, Solomon, Isaiah, et al., down to Jesus and his note-taking disciples.

So instead of reading a sacred book, our experience of reading becomes devotional if we can share it with the original audience for whom the words were written—a similar experience to reading Shakespeare's tragic play *Hamlet* as if we were in a seventeenth-century London audience, rather than imagining it in contemporary fashion to be a neurotic's holiday. We can do the same—keeping in mind their original readers—with modern works that have already become classics like Lawrence's *Lady Chatterley's Lover*, which might otherwise seem comical today, or Kafka's *The Metamorphosis*, which contemporary readers might mistake for comic irony rather than a less funny kind of moral tragedy, uncannily written.

When I began publishing my translations, sometimes as original poems, it was a time of lost memory; I had the Anchor Bible at my disposal but the "Bible as Literature" courses had disappeared. Jewish Studies departments were in their infancy, spurred by a realization of how much Jewish literature had been forgotten and was not taught there. One of the successful textbooks of the 1980s was entitled *Back to the Sources*, as if they had been left behind somewhere. Yet because the Hebrew Bible was at the basis of the synagogue prayer books, nobody thought of it as lost as well. Besides, it had always been taught in religion departments, appended to the New Testament—until 1964, that is, when Speiser's Anchor Bible *Genesis* burst upon the scene.

Speiser's concern with the historicity of the writers influenced budding New Testament studies in the historical Jesus and in the Gospels' original writers. With Speiser's sudden bestseller status, the Hebrew Bible became a hot topic in archaeology and cultural studies, for a while. And then an avalanche of textual disciplines, from structuralism onward, buried the biblical authors again, along with inconvenient questions about the sources they assimilated from other cultures, their level of irony, and even their sexuality. The writers of the Bible became lost writers once again, just as they had been to the Christian scholars of the nineteenth century who labeled them J, E, P, D, and others in a "Documentary Hypothesis," but who shrank from imagining them as flesh and blood Jewish writers, of whose culture they wanted no part.

In a recent review of one of the few contemporary writers to whom the term "great" is applied, the late Chilean Roberto Bolaño, American novelist Jonathan Lethem says that "writers are omnipresent in Bolaño's world, striding the stage as romantic heroes...yet they're also persistently marginal, slipping between the cracks of time and geography...vanished, erased." Although it may be hard to imagine the Bible's writers having doubts about their works' chances in the game of posterity—as Lethem speculates about Bolaño—their culture itself was under existential threat. Doubts, however, were turned inside out. Their attitude to the unknowable was that it needed a name; they were devoted to dramatizing their relation to it. I've called it a "cosmic theater," in which YHWH and angels share the stage with humans.

Since we are in the audience of the cosmic theater, we at least have the grace of being a witness. The Creator's name is the most uncanny one we know—"I am that I am"—but YHWH is a name nonetheless. The biblical authors had given name to the unnamable—no less than Bolaño did "for an instant at least," according to Lethem. And that is perhaps the difference between the modern writer and the biblical one, who fuses the "instants" into a cosmic theater of the eternal and the historical.

Even in the theater of daily life, where we go here or there, think this or that, the biblical writers thought that a cosmic theater is necessary—without it, without the authority of a creator, all the strength mustered by an author-Creator is pretense: a pretense of creaturehood. True, we have our stand-in great moments, summoning a "superhuman" strength to write from one heroic or anti-heroic instant to the next on an imitation cosmic stage. That is how Bolaño could believe in our modern substitute religion of art, philosophy, and literature. I can't deny it myself, although I don't intend *A Literary Bible* as a substitute Bible. I would hope it to be a reflection—for the moment—of the Bible's staying power.

So here's what I would say: Conscious of our modern "lost generations," we can still go on seeking Jerusalem's original writers. Will their rediscovery redeem us? The late Jewish philosopher Emil Fackenheim wrote that because Israel's God is one of world history (including natural history), history is transparent and through it we can sense redemption. This belief is embedded in the works translated in *A Literary Bible*. It's been my experience that purely reading over the biblical writers' shoulders renders the text uncanny, if not history transparent.

I had only one uncanny mentor in the Bible, the late Philip Rieff, sociologist, student of Jewish history, and historian of Freud. Get down from your chair and onto the floor, he suggested, where you're closer to the dead; listen to their voices yourself, don't let the academics herd you. I was already knee-deep in biblical scholarship, and one summer together in Jerusalem, Rieff and I explored the unconscious taboos against conceiving of the genius in ancient Hebraic literary culture. In contrast, it was acceptable, at least in universities, to refer to the Jewish "genius" for religion, since it could be more easily understood as "superseded" by later religions.

One day during that summer in the early 1990s, after a conference of Ethiopian-born Torah scholars in Jerusalem, some of them still in the tunics they wore in Ethiopia, Rieff said to me, "Maybe the Bible's writers in Jerusalem looked more like them than like rabbis." I concurred; these scholars of Amharic and Hebrew also looked more like writers who could fit in in a Jerusalem coffeehouse, either today or three thousand years ago.

V.

After thirty years of translating from eighteen books of the Hebrew Bible, I'm still asked by my writer friends: Isn't that enough? Why go on proving the same point over and over, namely that the original writer's hand is not only often ignored but needs rejuvenating? Taken in by the vogue of theory, my colleagues and I sometimes think of literature as "texts" that can be engaged apart from their authors—as artistic, cultural, social, or political artifacts, for example. Indeed, I was drawn closer to biblical scholarship in the somewhat pretentious hope of finding a poetic structure in ancient Hebraic texts that would render them as cultured as Proust and Kafka. If I could read a Proustian text unencumbered by its author's provenance, then I could read just as freshly a biblical text. Under this banner of liberation, literary critics of the twentieth century wished to tackle the Bible and yet avoid digging into the historical culture that produced it. But as I began to recognize the disdain for the original Hebraic writers, I jumped off this scholastic bandwagon.

Fortunately, the state of Israel was once again in existence, and it took only a few months of living there to make it apparent that a Hebraic culture, ancient or contemporary, breeds poets and prose artists who are fiercely distinctive. At bottom, they need to establish freshly minted names in order to gain authority and make a living. It was just as true in ancient days for the original biblical authors: their names were lost within a century after their passing, yet enough traces survive to indicate they were esteemed in their day. It hardly matters how they were supported by their culture; even the writing rabbis of the first century CE, in the Roman provinces of Israel, had their names affixed to their biblical comments. The reputations they developed sustained them. And even when these rabbis did not write down their sermons, lectures, or discussions, their students did it for them.

Further back, in the early days of the Kingdoms of Israel, the culture of writing and reading was a bit more exclusive but no less complex, involving scripts and languages that were classical at the time, such as Akkadian and Sumerian. It was already a Hebrew renaissance—after years of oral and proto-Hebraic writings—that produced the early Bible. Such a cultural renaissance requires powerful writers as well as scholars, translators, and historians. But most of all, it requires an audience that is passionately curious about itself and the world. That was how I found modern Israel in the 1970s, and that also ended my academic infatuation with literary theory. Talking with Israeli writers, it was clear that their best modern poems and stories, drawing upon ancient Hebrew echoes, could not have been sparked by fashionable theory. So when I returned to my own translations of the Bible, I vowed to feel my way toward the ancient individual writers suppressed behind their texts.

HOW THIS BOOK CAME ABOUT

Getting Through to the Writer

The conventional thought is that it's the writer's task to get through to the reader, and it's the critic's task to elucidate how it happens. But in such a complex work as the Bible, where the writers are largely lost, it becomes our work today to reclaim the ancient writers and the culture that informed their words. This great task is parallel to a contemporary one: How does one become a serious writer within a culture that is lost in time such as ours, uncertain of a cosmic destiny, anchored in space on a ball of reason that may or may not be unmoored?

The better part of my own life as an author of books and texts has been a journey toward discovering a lost writer. Whether that writer was an ancient one or myself, the road was rarely marked. It seems that the best writing of our era has been about unmasking ourselves—about becoming aware of an existential fork in the road and which, if any, way may save us. Will art and literature suffice, as it did to serve and produce the Bible? Have we a comparably compelling vision of past and future?

And if our times are strange to us, which made for my generation's comedy, satiric melodrama, and high-minded language-play (overriding the despair of an earlier generation and the cynicism that followed), then we must ask the writer today to stop, figurative pen in midair. To get through to the writer, we must ask from where his words come. We expect neither a direct answer nor a Jacques Derrida-like interrogation, but rather a rephrasing of the question: What is the source of creation? No more desperate making light of it, or of our own dances of avoidance. If this, then, were the writer's and reader's task today, shared equally, I would have to go back to the Hebrew Bible and confront the original authors, lost in time, only their faint traces exhumed by modern scholarship.

Consider a cultural parallel. A popular trope of the day, "What would Jesus do?", began profoundly, but it led to "What would Jesus say?", "What would He drive?", and "Where would He vacation?"—*ad infinitum.* The precursor to this conceit was the philosophical, theological, and uncanny "If Jesus returned among us, who would recognize him?" More to the point, would He stand in danger of being crucified, at least intellectually? With that question we are thrown back upon an original Jewish ambivalence toward all prophets, many centuries before the birth of Jesus. The notion of the prophet-poet unheard in his own country, without honor, without stature, runs through many of the Hebrew Bible's Prophetic books.

One day in my twenties, I woke up to the prospect of a career as such a postmodern poet at the margins, appreciated only by a coterie. Even a poet's unstated virtue of living near the poverty line would turn into a shibboleth of lifestyle, lost among the more successful lifestyles. So why should I not consider fully inhabiting the role of a lost poet? And what writer in the history of Judeo-Christian civilization is more lost to consciousness than the original biblical writer? Even today, nobody speaks of him, nobody is interested in him—only redactors and sages are spoken of. The question finally returns: If one of the great biblical poets of the Hebrew Bible were to walk and write among us today, would anyone notice? Would anyone care to read or listen? Would office doors open in our hallowed halls of learning?

Imperfectly for sure, I could not avoid enacting that poet imaginatively. My first collection of psalm translations, *Some Psalms* (1973), was published with a small press on New York's Lower East Side; two hundred copies were run off on a mimeograph machine in the "Poetry Project" office of St. Mark's

Church. The publisher, of considerable avant-garde cachet in those days, was suitably named Angel Hair Books. My next volume of psalms a year later, *Blues of the Sky*, also published by Angel Hair, became the first mimeo book to receive a full-column review in *The New York Times Book Review*. So thirty-five years ago, my embodiment of a biblical poet appeared sustainable, but in order to keep it from overwhelming me with conceit, I had to inhabit the disguise of a poet-scholar (and as so often happens, the disguise became me). It started a few months after the review was published and I'd been recruited by B'nai B'rith to lecture around the country.

A few weeks later I found myself in Dallas before an audience of hundreds at an esteemed black Baptist church. I was surrounded afterward, poked and prodded, smothered with adoration. The same thing happened the next night, crosstown at the Jewish Temple. The levity required to sustain such a level of sanctity was beyond me. Not that there was any profit in it; in fact, some hosts seemed to think I would be embarrassed to be paid. But the crisis came a week or two later, after a lecture-reading at Harvard. The night before, I had received a typical standing-room only reception at the prestigious Jewish temple in nearby Roxbury, but at Harvard I came face to face with an audience of approximately ten, all academics from either the English department or the Divinity School. I turned off the redundant microphone and they listened in stony silence (they had clapped after every psalm in Roxbury!).

Then came the questions, each one prefaced with a disquisition on some literary theorist or biblical scholar in fashion. Which structuralists had I read or studied with? Which theorists of linguistics or translation? Gershom Scholem, who had recently delivered lectures there, was quoted back to me. After that, what else but to become a poet-scholar who would leave the country and go live and study in a foreign land for a few years—Israel. Nobody paid much attention there, and I was free to develop the blueprint for a poet's life in the Bible. Its guiding principle: to resist and survive the ongoing carnival of academic theorizing ("academic" not to be confused with "intellectual") and biblical studies sanctimony. Of course, to resist it required knowing it well.

Later, back in New York, I could sustain a living and pursue the role of poet-scholar by writing books on the Jewish festivals, the Kabbalah, and eventually, the lost writers of the Bible itself. That proverbial ancient biblical poet who arrives in present-day New York was now someone I could address intimately. Occasionally, the mask would fall and I'd incur the opprobrium of some colleague or professor who seemed to represent the dour minyan of the Harvard crowd I had encountered at Cambridge in the mid-seventies. Mostly, though, it was not criticism but indifference that was proffered—as in the question, "How do you know anything about the life of biblical writers?" Well, I might answer, if I were a biblical poet, I'd drive a white Susita. Susita, which means little horse in Hebrew, was the first car manufactured in Israel, available only in white, and its unreliable components could make its owner a laughingstock. In 1977, I was a passenger in the 1950s Susita driven by esteemed Israeli poet David Avidan. Its putt-putt got us around midtown Tel Aviv, but alas, Avidan's reputation as a prophet was nil.

Some of this afterword that follows was originally drafted in 1991. At the time, unavoidable misunderstandings arose between my former collaborator, English professor Harold Bloom, and me having to do with mundane matters for a poet and a literary critic, although they may appear grandiose to others. For several years, we had been at unspoken odds over what constituted living poetry, what sacred meant, the necessity of culture for a poet (and not simply companion poets), the influence of the modern Hebrew language revival, translation as a literary art, poetry as a form of living, prose as poetry, the necessity of deadpan humor and humility—but all these came to a head when our respective literary agents began fighting over the viability of our next collaboration.

If that situation seems ironic, it is nevertheless necessary to describe the affectation that reigned in academe and publishing at that time. As a poet, it was assumed that I would be more comfortable with impoverishment. After all, by insisting on the ancient Hebraic passion for poetry (over the genius for religion), I was consciously deflating the marketability of my efforts. It was a predicament made even more poignant by my insistence that a poet was foremost a *writer*, so that ambivalence toward genre, whether poetry or prose, was essential. This position could not even help me on the poetry scene, which covets a territory, however marginal, all to its own. At the time I was beginning this afterword, the academic poetry establishment was hatching its plans for the national salvation of poetry, which would culminate in National Poetry Month. What better lifeline for it than the Bible, I may have naively thought.

When I turned again to the Bible as a poet-scholar, I rediscovered a category of poetry that not a single prize is awarded to, anywhere, unless one takes a job as an academic. In the same antithetical manner, my insistence on the underlying poetry of so much of the Hebrew Bible may have injured the pride of biblical scholarship, which had become obsessed with pigeonholing a whole coop of ancient genres, few of them resembling what we mean by poetry.

Finally, the suspicion that I might be undermining the gravity of the Bible convinced me to write this afterword in defense of authenticity. Yet apart from preserving my love for the Bible, what was my purpose? The experience of reading the Bible must be a cosmic one—*that* was my aim for the secular reader—but how could it be conveyed? I began by insisting on poetry, ancient and modern, as the proper intensity of reading, but with marginal success. Eventually, I developed a conception of cosmic theater as the meeting-ground for what we can know and for all that is unknowable to our species. It led to a diptych of investigation: *Abraham: The First Historical Biography* (2006) and *An Educated Man: A Dual Biography of Moses and Jesus* (2009). But even in 1991, when I began this afterword, I understood that such a cosmic theater needs unconventional writers. I turned to the most acute point of conflict: the decidedly *non*-cosmic atmosphere of the university classroom.

Let me rephrase the case. The Bible, arguably the most important work of art in the Western literary canon, is an uneasy subject in the classroom. Why are our great poetic stories taught in the dullest of ways? I believe the fault can be traced to a failure of imagination in academic life. Imagination can be guided or stifled by dogma, but it also can be flattened by theories that handle merely the skeletons of texts. The Bible is a luminous guidebook to our past yet it is put out of reach by colorless professors. At the same time, the broad range of poets who gave voice to the original words has been rendered voiceless by pedantic translations. Reading in a spiritual community may lift a graceless translation, but once, the poets lent us what one critic has called, in the context of soul music, the "spiritual magnitude of the individual voice." Is it unthinkable to rediscover that original text?

Many brilliant men and women wrote the Hebrew Bible and Apocrypha during a period of ten centuries, building upon the example of the original J writer. Modern scholarship and archaeology allow us insights into ancient life, and by comparing the cultures and languages of other kingdoms of the period we can conceive of the Bible's authors as professional writers from the educated classes, schooled in languages and world literature—and not predominantly religious in outlook. Even the biblical text reminds us they were esteemed individuals in their own day; some of their names survive in the verses, like Asaph, Baruch, and the pseudonym Qohelet. To restore their human dimension, we need to rediscover them as vital, sexual human beings like ourselves. Among the women writers (who inherited a tradition of creative women dating back to Deborah, Abigail, and Hulda), some may have been widows and orphans, as well as sisters, wives, and daughters of the elite classes—even during times when custom circumscribed the sexes in the general population.

Few of us were inspired to discover these original writers in Bible classes. In effect, the authorship of the Bible continues to be suppressed. Why does it seem to be so difficult for religion to discover the humanity of a great classical culture? I believe the answer is weak imagination. The powerful Hebraic culture in which religion found a way to speak has been locked in the basement—as if the intelligence of the original writers was an embarrassment. But can we imagine a rabbi, priest, or professor of religion having authored such subtle and ironic poetic texts as Jonah or Ruth? Do we know of any religious writers who could equal the poetry in Psalms or Isaiah? As we flesh out the traces of these writers, a new vision of the origins of Western culture emerges to refresh the spirit—and revise our ideas of how we may learn from the past.

The Hebraic poets of the Bible are more like our writers today, in ambition and talent, than the conventional religious stereotypes. The representations of the Creator among biblical writers varied as it still does among modern writers, and several books—from Ecclesiastes to Esther to Judith—are sublimely ambivalent toward the Creator. These books and parts of many others make up an imaginative literature greater than the Hebrew Bible itself, including the Apocrypha and other noncanonical works. Psalms, Isaiah, the books of the other prophets, and Job and Jonah are among those abundant with differing visions of a nevertheless uniquely singular God. The poets who wrote these books constitute only a fraction of a great culture of writers—poets of primarily literary texts, even when unfolding prophetic dreams—and many of whose works have been lost along with their names.

To discover the living traces of the biblical writers—three thousand years old, in some cases—I needed to reimagine myself as a writer determined and bound by culture, grappling for freedom from convention. The mandates of conventional religion exist in any age; for the earliest and latest biblical poets, the impinging religion might have been pagan; today, it is just as likely to be secularism. The biblical prophets are only the most famous examples of poets who could resist many of the prevailing conventions.

Most of the Bible's writers question the habits of their audience in quietly provocative ways. Just as yesterday's cutting edge can today be pedestrian—and yesterday's convention can already be no longer habitual—I want to keep in mind what a Hebraic writer was up against. Readers would have been moved only by the power of their own sentiments, and not by the writer's vision, if the writer merely followed custom. Instead, he stays one step ahead of the reader: where a cliché is expected, it is broken, and where grandiosity is expected, something familiar and simple pops up. And even an archaic cliché, when unexpected, can come back to life.

To imagine any biblical writer as human—to make him or her personal—I have to consider what conventions he is called to struggle against. To do this, I myself have to break with scholarly convention and judge the limitations of my own personal history, particularly because the Bible permeates so many levels of our culture. Some kind of faith is necessary for a poet—it's his calling, basic to the bond between reader and writer. It's a reaching, for sure—a need to reach out. There is certainly helplessness in it, and grandiosity as well; the mixture may differ in writers and in ages, but the formula remains the same.

Both religion and art encourage a step out of time. Once I'd decided to test this relationship by translating the Bible, my childhood religious experience became crucial. My life opened for inspection in a manner I'd only imitated before, influenced by my college instructor, poet Robert Lowell. The effect of my early encounters with two cultures outside the mainstream—the Jewish one and the African-American—came home to me, stronger than any religious practice. Many cultures have migrated to America but these two retain their energy. Another, the Puritan culture of New England, nourished Lowell, and although he never said so, I thought of him as coming from an immigrant culture—based upon the older England from which the Puritans sailed.

My parents and grandparents were European immigrants. My maternal grandparents lived out their lives in our home in Detroit, yet stayed within a Yiddish-speaking and Hebrew-reading culture into which I was initiated. By the time I reached first grade at the Yeshiva Beth Yehuda in Detroit, I was dressed in the ageless role of a scholar: tzitzes (fringed garment) hanging out of my pants, my soft forelocks resembling the silky beards of my teachers—just as their pale, baby-like skin resembled mine. Instead of playground time, we had milk-and-cookies time, and the toothless old men ate and drank along with us.

After my grandfather's death, I found myself in public school among a majority of African-American students. Aretha Franklin is one Brady classmate I remember: her father was a celebrity, host of Detroit's gospel music hour on the radio; I listened, entranced. Later, I would value African American culture—its ironic, untamed diction, its music steeped in gospel, the inflections of blues lyrics—aware of how it mirrored my earliest Jewish culture. The senior citizens in both cultures lived close to the youngsters. In black culture, old people danced and jived like the children, so that it made the children seem old beyond their years.

In my kindergarten Yeshiva, the old Jewish men seemed childlike in their femininity: soft, shy, determined, easily moved, withdrawn. We children were taught the same virtues. Most of all we learned to chant, and that is how I remember my first teachers, always chanting. Often from the Bible, of course. And then, I would pass the Christian Pentecostal storefront churches in my neighborhood in the evenings and hear the chant-like surge of song. For some reason it was mostly women who attended—or else they sang the loudest. It was all I knew of any religious culture outside Judaism, but unlike the latter it was already sounding more familiar to me, the foundation for the larger culture of soul music forming in Detroit.

At my inner-city bar mitzvah I was a divided boy, baseball pants beneath my suit so I could dash from synagogue to Little League (on my Negro league team's roster of twenty, I was the only white boy). The test of manhood was managing the division of cultures. Later still, in the contemporary world of art, I would try to engage American culture with a sensibility of an immigrant—pretending we can all remember how we came from the old world, as much in despair as in hope.

When I was memorizing Longfellow's "The Song of Hiawatha" in the fourth grade, public school represented an anachronistic culture: no grown-ups I encountered would be caught reading this lengthy mock-epic, much less memorizing it. (Jewish grown-ups, on the other hand, would study the same Talmud as the kids; black kids might prize the same jazz and soul as the adults.) This irony would not be lost on poet Longfellow were he still alive—but irony was something I would only learn to absorb later in life, when Longfellow's High Indian idiom, like T.S. Eliot's High Church idiom, would earn their proper resonance.

I'd been educated to think the Bible was half the story of Western cultural origins; classical Greek and Latin was the other half. Yet I found a familiarity with ancient Greek in the Hebrew Bible itself, as I was translating Ecclesiastes. This author, known as Qohelet in Hebrew, had absorbed a great deal of Greek literature, and I started to think of his manner of appropriation as more modern than I'd expected.

I began to also find in the greatest psalms and elsewhere an awareness of the larger world and a cultivated irony in assimilating other literatures. The author of Ecclesiastes seemed to me one who put on the mask and speaking voice of King Solomon with a modern tonality in the third or fourth century BCE. I only follow in his footsteps when I make Solomon's voice my own.

Qohelet pictured Solomon as a poet and builder, a renaissance man who embellished his literary career with gardens and vineyards; I modernized this portrayal by giving Solomon a more prominent writing career and returning to him all his attributed books. Solomon's feasts became contemporary parties, his passions my own. I imagined nothing that the original author had not imagined in his own way, but I made the Bible's music more personal—just as Qohelet impersonated the old king in his own image, six centuries later:

So I set to work // in the grand style / building an
oeuvre / ten books in five years // works of love and
despair / naked and shameless / I was married and
divorced // I went to all the parties / the glittering eyes
/ and wit: passion-starved // a trail of blinding jewels /
of experience behind me / more than any king in Jerusalem // I tried on every lifestyle / I pushed to the center /
through many gaudy affairs // I was surrounded by
stars / singers and dancers / and fresh young bodies //
to choose among / at the slightest whim / I was high
and I was courted // but I kept my sense of purpose.

In addition, the ancient Hebraic writers, who probably knew several languages, played with current usage by setting it against the echoes of foreign words and officialese. You can sense this more in some books than others: Job, for one, plays heavily with Aramaic; Judith, perhaps, with Judeo-Greek.

My apprenticeship in reclaiming biblical authors began, at nineteen, when I was Robert Lowell's student in New York,

Pound in one hand, Rimbaud in the other. Lowell was in the midst of translating from several languages, in a mode he called "imitations." When I began my translations of psalms ten years later, Lowell was again my colleague at the University of Essex, in England. He was working on Aeschylus' plays, and I saw that my command of Hebrew could match his Greek—his ambition spurred my own.

One day another decade later, I was sitting in a barebones Jerusalem café with the Israeli poet Harold Schimmel. Over glasses of *botz* ("mud coffee") he was telling me of an earlier visit by Lowell. "He wanted to hear about the Hebrew Bible and how it sounded to us," Schimmel mused. "He was entranced to learn how modern Hebrew poets handled it intimately." As I listened, I could imagine Lowell in Jerusalem, toying with the idea of "imitating" some of the biblical poets, and I was confirmed in my guiding passion of imagining the original authors. Instead of imitation, I thought of my work as "personal" translation—I was straining for a dialogue among writers, biblical and contemporary.

Although I knew that great modern writers like Singer or Kafka had Jewish antecedents, it was not until I read the modern Hebrew poets that I imagined the biblical authors as living men and women. Modern translations exchange poetic irony for terse sentiment. But the original biblical irony appears to be an urge for personal encounter (rather than ironic distance), giving the Bible a sophisticated quality of spokenness. Many of the authors imagined the reader hearing their words as if the text were not there. This ancient irony echoes the modern literary convention of verisimilitude, lending psychological as well as social reality to fiction and poetry.

In the same way, I imagine ancient prayer—in terms of the book of Psalms, but also psalms that are rephrased in other books—as idealized speaking on a cosmic stage, out into the realm of eternity. It requires a literary trade-off for poets: you don't write letters home to your parents in verse, yet in this instance—verse as prayer—you speak as if to a spiritual parent. If the literary practitioners at King Solomon's court included even one great writer (and I presume there were several) it would be no surprise if he or she was revered because she would not compromise her art for rigid devotion. Even now we're assured by Freud, in *Totem and Taboo*, that "in only a single field of our civilization has the omnipotence of thoughts been retained, and that is in the field of art."

For readers wishing to compare my translation of the Bible with others, a list of corresponding chapter and verse follows.

Under the page numbers given in *A Literary Bible* below for GENESIS, EXODUS, and NUMBERS, the list of the chapter/verse citations (standard in most translations of the Hebrew Bible, or Old Testament) correspond to the J or E narrative I have translated. Each chapter/verse citation refers to each succeeding section within the given range of pages in *A Literary Bible*.

The same numbering applies to the 2nd BOOK OF SAMUEL.

GENESIS

pages 9–18	4:25–26
2:4b–7	6:1–2
2:8–9	6:3
2:10–17	6:4
2:18–25	6:5–8
3:1–7	7:1–5, 7
3:8–12	7:10, 12, 16b
3:13–15	7:17–23
3:16–19	8:2b–3a, 6, 8–12
3:20–21	
3:22–24	*pages 19–28*
4:1–2	8:13b, 20–22
4:3–7	9:18–19
4:8–9	9:20–27
4:10–16	11:1–9
4:17–18	12:1–4a
4:19–24	12:6–17

675

———

INDEX

EXODUS

ADDITIONAL BIBLICAL BOOKS

Chapter/verse citations for other biblical books in *A Literary Bible* are found within the text.

For permission when needed, my thanks below to the publishers, where portions of the text, in different form, once appeared.

To my editors at Counterpoint: Jack Shoemaker, who was listening, long ago and up-to-the-minute, and Laura Mazer, who heard every word carefully; and to Counterpoint cohorts Sharon Donovan, Kristy Bohnet, and Tiffany Lee; also to steady John Oakes, editor, while he and I were briefly at Atlas and Co. And to the editors and publishers who were listening over the years: Lewis Warsh of Angel Hair; Clayton Carlson, Marie Cantlon, and John Loudon of Harper; Randall Greene of Doubleday; Seymour Barofsky of Schocken; Aaron Asher and Joy Johannesen of Grove; Andrew Motion of Faber; Robert Miller of Hyperion; Shaye Areheart of Harmony; Elizabeth Maguire of Basic; Hayden Carruth of *Harper's Magazine*; Frederick Morgan of *Hudson Review*; Martin Peretz of *New Republic*; Grace Schulman of *The Nation*; Michael Andre and Erika Rothenberg of *Unmuzzled Ox*; Barry Callaghan of *Exile*; Joachim Neugroschel of *Extensions*; Arthur Vogelsang of *American Poetry Review*; Peter Cole of *Tikkun*; Jonathan Rosen of *The Forward*; Nessa Rapoport of *Conservative Judaism*; Richard Flantz and Nili Cohen of *Modern Hebrew Literature*; David Avidan and Gabriel Moked of *Achshav*; Jonathan Omer-man and Adin Steinsaltz of *Shefa Quarterly*; D.M. Dooling of *Parabola*; Marie Syrkin and Joel Carmichael of *Midstream*; Zev Shanken of *Response*; Arthur Waskow of *Menorah*; Philip Slomovitz of *Detroit Jewish News*; Bill Zavatsky of *Sun*; and Harold Schimmel of Talpiot.

To my daring agent, Howard Morhaim, guiding me through the lion's den of shrinking literary publishers and into the creative confines of Counterpoint. And to my biblical-minded agents of former days: Heide Lange, Lynn Nesbit, and Lew Grimes.

To my coterie of stalwarts: Grace Schulman, Walter Brown, Joyce Davidson, Rochelle Broach, Sanford Rosenberg, and my late, loving mothers, Shifra and Wanda.

To my coauthor, Rhonda. Because "there is nothing new under the sun" (*Ecclesiastes*)—all this, again.

Poet-scholar David Rosenberg is coauthor of *The New York Times* bestseller *The Book of J* (with Harold Bloom) and the former editor-in-chief of the Jewish Publication Society. A poet of Toronto Coach House, New York School, and Jerusalem Cricket lineage, he has published several volumes of poetry.

Rosenberg is a survivor of the writing programs at The New School (with Kenneth Koch and Robert Lowell), University of Michigan (with Donald Hall), Syracuse University (with Delmore Schwartz), and University of Essex, England, where he pursued doctoral studies. He taught for several years at York University (Toronto), City University of New York, and as a Master Poet for the New York State and Connecticut Arts Councils.

At the age of thirty, Rosenberg retired from teaching. For two decades, while working as a literary editor and translator, he studied the origins of ancient Hebrew literature and the Bible, in New York and Israel (with Robert Gordis, Harry Orlinsky, and Chaim Rabin), while his work appeared prominently in *Harper's, The New Republic, Hudson Review, Paris Review* and elsewhere around the globe (most recently in *Chicago Review, Jacket* in Australia, and *Open Letter* in Canada). *A Poet's Bible* won the PEN / Book-of-the-Month Club Prize, the first major literary award given to a biblical translation in the U.S.

Rosenberg is the author and editor of more than twenty books, including volumes of contemporary writers on the Bible that first raised the question of how Judeo-Christian culture can be newly reinterpreted. During the past decade he has studied the context for ancient biography, leading to a diptych: *Abraham: The First Historical Biography* and *An Educated Man: A Dual Biography of Moses and Jesus.* He continues to publish critical essays on poetry, as well as his long poem, *The Lost Book of Paradise* and a literary version of Kabbalah, *Dreams of Being Eaten Alive.*